DICKENS' INFERNO

The Moral World of Charles Dickens

SUSAN JHIRAD

This book is dedicated to all those who keep alive the passion for social justice.

Contents

Introduction

"Abandon all hope, ye who enter here." Who would ever connect Dante's grim warning at the entrance to his Inferno with Charles Dickens' cheery conclusion to *A Christmas Carol*, "God bless us every one!"? And yet in Dickens' works there are characters as irrevocably damned as in Dante's imaginary world created five centuries before in Catholic Italy. This book drags Dickens' villains out of their natural settings in 19th (and 18th century) England and drops them unceremoniously into their appropriate circles of Dante's *Inferno*, emphasizing the moral and Christian aspects of Dickens' novels. At the same time, it is in complete accord with those who have treated Dickens primarily as a social critic and reformer, including Karl Marx and George Bernard Shaw. For Dickens, political and spiritual issues were always intimately connected; child labor, indifference to starvation and cruelty towards the poor and outcast were not merely unjust, they were "sins." In his understanding of the Bible, our role as human beings is to help others and "love thy neighbor as thyself," a gospel of the needy and against the greedy. Ultimately, it is as impossible to separate Dickens' political concerns from his religious ones as it is to separate Mahatma Gandhi's or Rev. Martin Luther King's social activism from their spiritual beliefs.

Still, why compare a Catholic writer of the Middle Ages (1265-1321) rooted in the traditional theology of his era, with a liberal Anglican turned Unitarian of the mid-19th century? In fact, the similarities are striking, although literary scholar G.K. Chesterton once explicitly contrasted the two authors:

> The fierce poet of the Middle Ages (Dante) wrote 'Abandon hope all ye who enter here' over the gates of the lower world...But if we are to understand the story which follows, (Dickens' works) we must erase

that apocalyptic writing...unlearn that sinister learning that you think so clear...Abandon hopelessness, all ye who enter here.[1]

Naturally, Chesterton is unfair to Dante, whose larger vision, including Hell, Purgatory and Paradise, is far from "hopeless." Dante called his great work The *Commedia* (the "divine" was added later by Boccaccio) precisely because it has, at least for some, "a happy ending." It's true that Dickens' version of Christianity is different from Dante's. However, the two authors have far more in common than first appears. Both delve deeply into human nature and its struggles with good and evil. Each creates an entire moral system with gradations of "sins," and situates them in specific characters: in Dante's work, mythological and real people from his era and earlier, in Dickens', the creations of his vivid imagination, some based on individuals from his life and times. Both are omniscient "God-like" authors. Both were Christians with a sincere belief in God, sin and redemption, punishment, and an afterlife.

On the surface, the literary forms they choose, the allegorical poem and the novel, may also seem very different. However, Dorothy Sayers, Medieval scholar, translator of Dante and noted mystery novelist, advised us to "...forget about the distinction between "prose" and "poetry" and to approach the *Comedy* as if it were a serious and intelligent novel—which in fact it is. For in the fourteenth century, the allegorical poem was precisely what the novel is today—the dominant literary form, into which a writer could pour, without incongruity, everything he had to say about life and the universe."[2] Both Dante and Dickens were critics of their respective epochs: the corruption, violent conflicts and schisms of 13th century Florence, and the greed, graft and social inequality of Industrial Revolution England.

While there is no concrete evidence that Dickens was directly influenced by Dante, English translations of *The Divine Comedy* were popular in England by Dickens' time, and Dickens frequently traveled to Italy, living there for a year and even teaching himself Italian prior to his first trip. In the early 19th century Romantic poets and artists like Coleridge and Blake were fascinated with Dante, and public interest in his work was widespread. William Blake's paintings of *The Divine Comedy* stand among the greatest illustrations of the work, despite Blake's own theological differences with Dante.

In his travel work *Pictures from Italy* written in 1846, Dickens makes one brief, but significant reference to Dante while visiting Florence:

> And here, a small un-trodden square in the pavement is 'The Stone of Dante' where (so runs the story) he was used to bring his stool, and sit in contemplation. I wonder was he ever, in his bitter exile, withheld from cursing the very stones in the streets of Florence the ungrateful, by any kind remembrance of this old musing-place and its association with gentle thoughts of *little* (italics mine) Beatrice?[3]

Is there perhaps an unconscious link in Dickens' mind between Dante's beloved Beatrice and his own little Dorrit and "little" Nell?

At least two articles have directly compared Dante and Dickens. Stephen Bertman ("Dante's role in the Genesis of *A Christmas Carol*") points to important similarities in form and theme between *A Christmas Carol* and the *Inferno*. He has also researched possible conscious influences of Dante on Dickens' work (although his evidence is largely circumstantial). He notes Dickens' friend Thomas Carlyle's enthusiasm for Dante, Dickens' own respectful references, and the fact that Dickens' library included, if not *The Divine Comedy* itself, a book of illustrations of the work. Meanwhile, Susan Colon ("Dickens' *Hard Times* and Dante's *Inferno*") analyzes the fourth circle of hell, specifically its depiction of the sin of "sullenness" or repressed anger, as seen in the character of Louisa Grandgrind. Both writers discuss Dickens' insistence on the theme of redemption, as his characters are saved from psychological "hell" often through the intervention of saintly characters or guides. This echoes Dante's trip through the Inferno, guided by "his master" Virgil and watched over by the celestial spirit of Beatrice, who will later become his guide in the *Paradiso*.

Bertman and Colon limit their comparisons with Dante to single works, but in fact all Dickens' major novels contain parallels to the circles of Hell created by Dante, and his descriptive passages often evoke visions of the Inferno. Fire, smoke, water, cold, and pollution in 19th century London resemble Dante's infernal landscapes, while for both authors setting is symbolic of the moral condition of society, as well as deeper mythical themes. The law court of Chancery in *Bleak House* might well bear the infamous sign "Abandon all Hope, ye who enter here," while the factories depicted in *Hard Times* are just as William Blake suggests, "those dark Satanic mills." ("Jerusalem")

Bodies of water also play an important symbolic role for both authors. The river Thames becomes strikingly Stygian in novels like *Our Mutual Friend*, where the damned characters will be drowned, and the "saved" ultimately reborn and brought to safe shores. In *David Copperfield* and *Great Expectations*, dramatic ocean scenes prove critical to the plot and deeper meaning.

Dickens' Religion

There is some disagreement over Dickens' religious beliefs. Certain authors emphasize the criticisms of organized religion represented by pious frauds like Rev. Chadband (*Bleak House*), Rev. Honeythunder (*The Mystery of Edwin Drood*) or Mrs. Clennham (*Little Dorrit*). Sir Humphrey House and W.H. Auden used Dickens' sharp attacks on such representatives of organized religion and his temporary turn towards Unitarianism to argue that he was a secularist and not a "real" Christian. Others, like Gary Colledge on the unpublished text Dickens wrote for his children, *The Life of Our Lord*, maintain that Dickens was more of a mainstream Anglican than many suppose. The following quote from Dickens, in a letter to Rev. D. Macrae, speaks for itself: "All my strongest illustrations are derived from the New Testament; all my social abuses are shown as departures from its spirit…" [4] Tolstoy and Dostoevsky evidently agreed when calling him "that great Christian writer." [5]

In an insightful discussion of Dickens' beliefs, Dennis Walder develops the implicit and explicit Christian themes woven through all of Dickens' novels, from the comic *Pickwick Papers* to his dark last work, the unfinished *The Mystery of Edwin Drood*. At the same time, Walder maintains that "Dickens was not a religious novelist," in that his novels were not overtly teaching theological lessons like many popular (and lesser) novels of his day. [6]

Of course, good fiction is never mere propaganda for religious or political causes. Even the great Tolstoy is arguably at his weakest when he preaches too overtly, as in his late novel *Resurrection*. George Orwell ("Charles Dickens") contends that Dickens is, at least subliminally, teaching a lesson: "He is always preaching a sermon, and that is the final seat of his inventiveness."[7] However he points out that Dickens' lessons emerge naturally through his artistic telling of the story itself, not through direct moral pronouncements.

Dickens has been hailed for his social conscience by many on the left, as well as criticized for not advocating a full scale revolution, although his works helped bring about reforms of child labor, prisons and the treatment of prostitutes, among many causes. He has also been praised by Anglicans for his faith, while reproached for his lack of religious orthodoxy. However, even Orwell, whose standpoint is largely political, acknowledges that Dickens is essentially "a moralist," and suggests that his artistic greatness actually derives from his profound moral concerns, conceding, "Roughly speaking, his morality is the Christian morality..."[8]

Dickens was indeed a life-long Christian, with a firm belief in God and the afterlife, as well as sin and redemption, although he despised hypocrisy, sectarian strife, and all forms of human cruelty committed in the name of religion. His hatred of religious war is best expressed in his historic novel on the anti-Catholic riots of 1780, *Barnaby Rudge*. Although he disliked the formalisms of the Catholic Church and opposed the establishment of Catholic dioceses in England, Dickens forcefully attacks anti-Catholic prejudice in this novel whose sympathetic Catholic characters are sharply contrasted with a violent group of Protestant fanatics.

Dickens' treatment of Jews has been more controversial. There is obvious anti-Semitism in his stereotypical characterization of Fagin in *Oliver Twist*, who is referred to *ad nauseam* as "the Jew." Yet one could argue that Fagin (based on a real criminal named Ikey Solomons) is merely one "bad apple" amidst bushels of rotten Christian "apples" in his novels, and that references to "the Jew" are merely reflections of the language that would have been used in his time. Dickens' personal views evolved, from passive acceptance of the anti-Semitic assumptions of his day, to his later years, when he developed a close friendship with a Jewish couple, the Davies. In her letters to Dickens, Eliza Davies reproached him bitterly for his portrayal of Fagin. In fact, Dickens makes amends for Fagin in his last completed novel *Our Mutual Friend*, where the Jew Riah is an unusually saintly character, explicitly portrayed as the victim of cruel anti-Semitic prejudice. Davies later thanked Dickens for admitting the harm his Fagin caricature may have caused the Jewish people, and apologizing for it directly in a letter.[9]

Dante expresses similar ambivalence towards Jews in his *Divine Comedy*. In accordance with Catholic belief, Jews cannot be "saved" before Christ appears on the scene, and there is at least one unfortunate allusion the then-official view of Jews as "killers of Christ," (*Canto XXIII*) as well as a deep section of Hell named "*Judecca*" (critics debate whether this refers to Judas who is placed there, or to a section of Florence where Jews lived in Dante's time). On the other hand, Dante gives Jewish heroes of the Old Testament a special dispensation in Paradise. His beloved Beatrice will ultimately be seated on a celestial throne next to the biblical Rachel. Indeed, half of those placed within the celestial "rose" of his *Paradiso* are Jewish. Apparently Dante himself was not personally anti-Semitic and had at least one close Jewish friend and mentor, the poet Imanuel of Rome.

Theological distinctions were naturally less important to Dickens, for whom actions always spoke louder than words or specific theology. His turn to Unitarianism after a visit to the United States in 1840 was based on his view that the Unitarians actually put their beliefs into practice. In a letter to his American Unitarian friend Cornelius Felton, he wrote,

> "I have carried into effect an old idea of mine and joined the Unitarians, who would do something for human improvement if they could; and practice charity and toleration."[10]

His sympathetic characters—Catholic, Protestant, Jewish and non-believer alike—all show genuine charity and kindness to their fellows in the true spirit of the Gospels; his pious villains preach morality, while demonstrating hard-heartedness, especially towards children and the poor. In this Dickens resembles his Romantic predecessor William Blake, who ironically chastises "the wise guardians of the poor" ("Holy Thursday") that preach piety while supporting socially oppressive institutions. Mr. Bumble, the beadle in *Oliver Twist*'s hideous workhouse, takes pleasure in beating its starving inmates and even jokes about the small size of the children's coffins.

Dickens sharply criticized the repressive "Poor Laws" of his time that broke up families and destroyed children, yet were fully sanctioned by official religion. This is clearly demonstrated in *Oliver Twist* as well as in *Our Mutual Friend*, where the poor but proud Betty Higden would rather die of starvation out in a field than fall into the hands of the state's "welfare" system.

In *Our Mutual Friend*, his last completed novel, he depicts the dying Higden dreaming herself at the foot of Christ's cross:

> "I am safe here," was her last benumbed thought. "When I am found dead at the foot of the Cross, it will be by some of my own sort; some of the working people who work among the lights yonder."

Perhaps when he was writing this novel, as its postscript suggests, Dickens was sensing his own imminent death and contemplating not merely the moral world in which he lived, but the possibility of one beyond. Dickens' experience of a frightening train crash where passengers literally died in his arms as he strove to help them, as well as his own illness, exhaustion and depression seemed to bring on "intimations of mortality."

There is ample evidence in his letters, conversations and fiction that Dickens believed in an afterlife, supporting Colledge's claim that "in order to vindicate the destitute and the oppressed, or those who have been victims of heinous crimes, an eschatological judgment and punishment of some kind was necessary for those *hardened individuals* who through indifference, malevolence, self-interest and greed defaced God's image in their fellow creatures."[11]

Dickens' vision of the afterlife remains somewhat vague, certainly when compared to Dante's. Yet there is a fundamental sense that the good will be rewarded, the evil punished, and repentant gradually "purged" through a process of suffering and remorse. A perfect expression of this belief is found in the last, heartfelt plea of Barnaby Rudge's loyal wife to her husband, as he sits in prison, condemned to be hung for murder:

"Husband, dear husband, if you will but implore the forgiveness of Heaven and those whom you have wronged on earth; if you will dismiss these vain uneasy thoughts which can never be realized (that he will escape) and will rely on Penitence and on the Truth, I promise you, in the great name of the Creator, whose image you have defaced, that He will comfort and console you."

Deaf to his wife's pleadings, Barnaby Sr. will certainly wind up in Hell—or for this book, in one of the circles of Dante's *Inferno* reserved for the most depraved sinners.

Dickens directly refers to an afterlife in the novel *Bleak House*, where Richard Carstone has slowly been killed by his greedy addiction to the endless, futile lawsuit, Jarndyce vs. Jarndyce. As he lies dying, he begs his faithful wife Ada to forgive him:

"You will forgive me all this, Ada, before I begin the world?"

The fictional narrator Esther Summerson then comments:

A smile irradiated his face as she bent to kiss him. He slowly laid down upon her bosom…and with one parting sob began the world. Not this world, oh, not this! The world that sets this one right.

Dante's View of Punishment, Redemption and the "Contrapasso"

Like Dickens, and most Christians, Dante believed in the fundamental notion of forgiveness for those who show genuine contrition. The inhabitants of his *Inferno* are there not merely because they have sinned against God, nature or their fellow man, but because they have never truly repented. As both writer and character in his *Divine Comedy*, Dante sometimes shows sympathy for those he sees trapped eternally in Hell (weeping for them, addressing them kindly), yet through the guidance of his mentor Virgil, he ultimately adopts the official church stance of condemning and punishing their sins. Of course Dante's *Divine Com-*

edy, while based on Catholic beliefs of its time, is no religious tract; it is a work of imagination and in fact, never received the imprimatur of the Catholic Church itself. The work is peopled with characters out of classical mythology about whom the medieval church had nothing to say. Pagans like Virgil receive a special dispensation. Although he can never enter heaven with Dante, Virgil becomes the moral center of the *Inferno,* wisely advising Dante when his faith and spirits falter.

Dante's *Inferno* is based in part on the concept of "retributive justice" as found in the Old Testament. Going still further, Dante uses the *"contrapasso,"* where the form of the punishment graphically fits the crime. The adulterous lovers Paolo and Francesca are caught up in a whirlwind, spinning through eternity, just as they let their passions carry them away in life (*Canto IV*). The soothsayers, who falsely claim to predict the future, are tortured with their heads twisted back from their bodies, eternally doomed to look backwards (*Canto XX*).

There are numerous examples in Dickens' work of *contrapasso,* such as Steerforth's stormy fate at sea in *David Copperfield,* although his unrepentant villains are punished mainly in this life, as their fate in the afterlife can only be imagined.

Most critics and biographers agree that Dickens was essentially a liberal Protestant. He disliked an overemphasis on retribution, adopting the more forgiving stance of Jesus in the gospels, the "turn the other cheek" notion expressed in his Sermon on the Mount. In fact, one critic has dubbed him, rather dismissively, "A Sermon on the Mount Christian" (Philip Collins). [12] Dickens strongly criticized the Calvinist view of the essential sinfulness of man, and like the religious reformers, Unitarians and Transcendentalists of his time, stressed humanity's capacity for good and redemption. His "good" characters are in general rewarded, while his "bad" are invariably punished. However, for those characters who sincerely repent—and they are many—there is hope.

Dickens' penitent characters might well belong on a corresponding terrace of the *Purgatorio* (Dante's version of Purgatory is a mountain divided into "ledges" or terraces where they are punished, then gradually cleansed of the last stains of sin before moving upwards to Paradise.) To acknowledge this, one chapter will be devoted to Dickens' characters that might be found in Purgatory.

On the other hand, Dickens clearly has his unremorseful sinners, those whom he dubs "thoroughly bad," like Bill Sikes (*Oliver Twist*), or those guilty of more than one sin, like Bradley Headstone (*Our Mutual Friend*) whose sins include envy, sexual obsession, murder and finally suicide. These characters will be placed in their appropriate circles of Hell based on their worst crime, or as theologians would call it, "their besetting sin."* This generally follows Dante's system, as many of his characters are also multiple sinners. For Dante, the lowest depths of Hell are reserved for frauds, the treacherous and the creators of discord, while the suicides and the lustful are in higher, less punitive circles.

While emphasizing love and goodness, which generally win out in the end, Dickens clearly understood the darker side of human nature, and as his novels evolve they become even more pessimistic.

In the end, while no direct influence of Dante on Dickens can be proven, they are both profoundly moral Christian writers, depicting the spiritual pilgrimage from sin (darkness) to redemption (light). They infuse their great works with their own personal struggles. Dante's midlife "dark wood" finds its counterpart in the "middle" of Dickens' life—particularly after the death of Mary Hogarth—and at its end, cut short at age 57 by overwork, guilt over his broken marriage, and illness. They each create worlds of characters in varying states of sinfulness and were outspoken critics of their respective societies, deploring not merely individual, but institutional evils. Their explorations of the vast terrain of human morality in all its forms run along parallel tracks. Among great writers, none present a comprehensive, Christian-based moral system like Dante and Dickens. Whether or not one can prove a direct influence, a comparison between the two authors can, I believe, illuminate the works of both. At the same time, both Dante and Dickens still compel us to confront most of the same social injustices we face today.

---

* I make exceptions for a few characters, like Headstone whose dominant sins may be different from their "besetting sin." *Mea culpa.*

I

Dickens' Characters: The Good, The Bad and The Saved

Volumes have been written about the long list of Charles Dickens' memorable characters. Some critics dismiss them as "types" without psychological depth; most praise their variety and vibrancy. They leap off the page, and while never quite like "real" people, can never be forgotten. From Pecksniff to Podsnap, from Murdstone to Silas Wegg, from Pegotty to Mrs. Boffin, from "little" Nell to *Little Dorrit*—his characters have made millions of readers laugh, weep and gnash their teeth for over a century and a half. As T.S. Eliot put it, "Dickens excelled in character; in the creation of characters of greater intensity than human beings." [1] According to one Dickens biographer, "It is the real, unconquerable rush and energy in a character which was the supreme and quite indescribable greatness of Dickens." [2] Through the workings of Dickens' powerful imagination, some of his characters attain a kind of mythic or symbolic status. Their carefully chosen names: "Vholes," "Honeythunder," "Pecksniff," "Murdstone," "Cheeryble," as well as their various tics and physical traits, all represent distinct moral and emotional qualities.

Those who dismiss these characters as "types," which of course, many of them are, miss the point. Each of Dickens' characters stands rooted firmly in a finely graded moral universe. At the same time, although not always realistic in the modern sense, they are often based on real figures in Dickens' life—albeit writ large and sometimes caricatured. It is well known that the feckless Mr. Micawber is based on Dickens' father and the narcissistic Mrs. Nickleby upon his mother. As some critics have pointed out, many of his characters are "morally complex," if not always psychologically so.[3] Yet they can be capable of internal struggle and change. The emotionally blighted Louisa Grandgrind (*Hard Times*) is a nuanced female character who undergoes a definite shift in consciousness in the course of the novel. The resentful yet compassionate Edith Dombey (*Dombey and Sons*) shows real emotional transformation, like Dombey himself. Both David Copperfield and Pip, the protagonist of *Great Expectations*, evolve in subtle and significant ways throughout their respective novels.

Dickens directly rebuts those who criticize some of his characters as "exaggerated" in a late Preface to the novel *Martin Chuzzlewit*. Here he is speaking of the murderous Jonas Chuzzlewit:

> I conceive that the sordid coarseness and brutality of Jonas would be unnatural, if there had been nothing in his early education, and in the precept and example always before him, to engender and develop the vices that make him odious. But so born and so bred, admired for that which made him hateful and justified from his cradle in cunning, treachery and avarice; I claim him as the legitimate issue of the father upon whom those vices seem to recoil.

In short, do people as bad as Jonas really exist? Based on a glance at the daily newspaper or television news, apparently they do.

There is no question that Dickens has his perfectly good characters or "angels," and they are, as for Dante, mostly female, like Nell, little Dorrit, Florence Dombey, Agnes Wickfield and Lizzie Hexam. Often, they serve as guides and protectors for their morally flawed parents or lovers. Dickens' view of young women as "saviors" has been analyzed psychologically, in terms of his relationship to his own flawed parents and his idealized sister-in-law Mary Hogarth, who died young in his arms, but this is not the project of this book. It is worth noting, however, that while in Italy Dickens had a dream of Mary Hogarth appearing to him in the form of the Virgin Mary, and in this dream at least, he fleetingly contemplated converting to Roman Catholicism.[4]

Feminist critics like Kate Millett (*Sexual Politics*) understandably scoff at Dickens' "insipid goodies" who bind themselves in suffering to unworthy males, particularly Nell in *The Old Curiosity Shop.*[5] In truth, it can be infuriating for a modern woman to witness little Nell's self-sacrifice for her infinitely selfish grandfather, even to the point of her own death. However, if Nell's life is an example of "the Imitation of Christ," her actions make a certain sense.[6] Nell is one of Dickens' many innocent "child-women," unsullied by the ugliness and materialism that surrounds her and willing to sacrifice herself for those she loves. Despite fervent pleas from his readers to spare little Nell, Dickens understood that she had to die at the end of the novel, just as for Christians, Jesus had to die to save a sinful humanity.

Dante's Beatrice is a similarly angelic "child-woman." He first encountered and fell in love with her when they were both nine, and as shown in his lovely pre-*Commedia* work *La Vita Nuova*, his idealized view of her remains with him even after her death. In *The Divine Comedy* she will be his guide in Paradise, and makes guest appearances (from a safe distance) in the *Inferno* and *Purgatorio*.

At times, Dickens resembles Blake and other Romantic precursors in his belief in the natural purity of children and women who are both childlike and maternal. Many characters become parents to their own weak parents, like Jenny Wren, the "doll's dressmaker," in *Our Mutual Friend* who actually refers to her alcoholic father as "my child" or little Dorrit who mothers her own father. Similarly, in Dante's *Paradiso* Beatrice frequently addresses Dante as a mother would a child.

There are also similarities between Dante's return to the courtly love tradition of a previous era, which merges the love for a woman-object with love for God, and Dickens' debt to the earlier Romantic tradition, in his depiction of a perfect woman's love as a form of redemption.

At the same time, Dickens diverges from more optimistic Romantic predecessors in painting portraits of evil that can rival or exceed Dante's. Contemporary novelist Jane Smiley states it bluntly: "It seems that Charles Dickens, the most influential English author of the 19th century, was genuinely drawn to criminals and psychopaths."[7] Juliette John attributes this to the influence of Victorian melodrama which Dickens adored from childhood.[8] However, Dickens himself contrasted the overly glamourized image of melodramatic villains with his own more realistically sordid characters (see his introduction to *Oliver Twist*).

Dickens probes his villains' psychology far too deeply to accuse him of mere melodrama. In fact, many suggest that they represent a troubled part of the author himself. In her recent biography of Dickens, Claire Tomalin offers a striking quote from Dostoevsky, purportedly quoting from a conversation he once had with Dickens, whom he profoundly admired:

> He told me that all the good simple people in his novels, Little Nell, even the holy simpletons like Barnaby Rudge, are what he wanted to have been and his villains were what he was (or what he found in himself); his cruelty, his attacks of causeless enmity towards those who were helpless and looked to him for comfort, his shrinking from those whom he ought to love, being used up in what he wrote. There were two people in him, he told me: one who feels as he ought to feel and one who feels the opposite. From the one who feels the opposite I make my evil characters, from the one who feels as a man ought to feel I try to live my life. [9]

While fascinating and somewhat revealing, this quote should be taken with some skepticism. First, it is a paraphrase by Dostoevsky, a writer who dwelt far more than Dickens on the darker side of human emotion, and obviously identified with his characters like the murderer Raskolnikov (*Crime and Punishment*). Dostoevsky's bias shows in his reference to Barnaby Rudge as "a holy simpleton." While he is certainly simple, there is nothing particularly "holy" about Rudge, unlike Mishkin, Dostoevsky's own Christ-like hero of *The Idiot*.

Also, this conversation supposedly took place in 1862 towards the end of Dickens' life, a period filled with illness, guilt and some depression, when he had left his wife for a young mistress—to the condemnation of many close friends and family members. This was undoubtedly the period of his life when he felt worst about himself.

At the same time, the darker feelings Dickens experienced within himself cannot be dismissed, nor his life-long struggle to act as a moral human being while battling internal demons. When writing his novels, he often acted out his characters' roles, speaking their lines aloud in front of a mirror. This, of course, includes his most heinous villains, and occurred long before he performed their scenes so impressively before the general public. Clearly, he is able to enter into their thoughts in a way that would be impossible if he did not understand their worst impulses. His close friend John Forster admits in his biography, written soon after Dickens' death, that Dickens identified with both his heroes and his villains, confiding during the writing of *Barnaby Rudge*, "I have let all the prisoners out of Newgate, burnt down Lord Mansfield's, and played the very devil."[10]

Of course as much might be said of any human being. From either a religious or a psychological standpoint, it is clear that we each have some capacity for evil. Dante himself understood this very well; in his own life he was apparently no saint. Perhaps this is why he is no mere "observer" of the Inferno. He must make a personal pilgrimage into Hell, and experience its sufferings and sins directly.

Like Dante, Dickens also has at least one villain in each novel that he considers beyond redemption. Some like Bill Sikes, are murderers; others like Sir John Chester in *Barnaby Rudge* are "sowers of discord" while still others like Mr. Merdle in *Little Dorrit*, are financial scoundrels. In his last completed novel *Our Mutual Friend*, he presents his darkest view of humanity, with a host of damned villains, such as Roger Riderhouse, Silas Wegg, "Fascination" Fledgeby, and the pathetic, hideous Bradley Headstone. His final, unfinished *The Mystery of Edwin Drood* presents us with John Jasper, a villain who appears to be both sexually obsessive and psychopathic, and indeed has been the subject of much psychoanalytical speculation. For Dickens' purposes, Jasper's sins are those of lust, treachery and murder.

The fact that some of Dickens' villains are as humorous as they are evil, like Montague Tigg (alias Tigg Montague) in *Martin Chuzzlewit*, Alfred Jingle in *The Pickwick Papers* or even the demonic dwarf Daniel Quilp in *The Old Curiosity Shop*, doesn't diminish their moral significance. In Dante's *Inferno*, as we shall see, there are characters simultaneously devilish and humorous (*Canto XX*).

This book will not attempt to list and categorize Dickens' hundreds of characters. This has already been done by George Newlin in his thorough multi-volume taxonomy *Everyone in Dickens*. Nor will it attempt to encompass all his numerous villains. Instead, it offers some of the most salient examples of each type of "sinner," similar to Dante's method, as Dante gives the reader only a few dramatic examples of a specific sin in each of his nine circles. Like Dante, Dickens also puts greater emphasis on certain sins, since they are more prevalent in his (or any) society. It's obvious, for example, that there are far more greedy people in this world than soothsayers.

We can trace Dickens' moral values through a classification of his most notable villains, situating them in their appropriate circles of Hell, in the same categories where Dante himself placed his representatives of flawed humanity. While there are extreme (perhaps too extreme) examples of saintliness, like Nell as well as villains like Bill Sikes, the majority of Dickens' characters lie somewhere in between. They may not immediately seem endowed with the psychological complexity of characters in modern novels, but they can be multi-dimensional, capable of change, and of understanding their own weaknesses.

Smiley notes that as Dickens' novels progress, they actually show more psychological insight into his villains: "What is important, technically, is that with each new novel, his way of portraying his perpetrators becomes less dramatic and more internal." [11] In *The Mystery of Edwin Drood*, we actually enter the novel from inside John Jasper's opium-addled brain. Still, our emphasis here is less on Dickens' psychological credibility, than on his life-long obsession with the problem of good and evil.

As in Dante's system in *The Divine Comedy*, characters who show genuine contrition might well find themselves in the *Purgatorio* rather than the *Inferno*. Eugene Wrayburn in *Our Mutual Friend*, for example, is initially selfish and heedless, but ultimately redeemed by true love and suffering. Even Dickens' protagonists like Pip in *Great Expectations*, David Copperfield, or the young Martin Chuzzlewit, while the focus of our attention and sympathy, fall victim to the sins of pride and selfishness.

The most obvious example of a deeply flawed character who is eventually redeemed is, of course, the famous miser Ebenezer Scrooge.

For Dickens, unlike traditional Catholics, redemption is not necessarily accessed through faith in God or formal religious ritual, but through the capacity to love other human beings, the sincerity of one's repentance, and purgation through suffering. Of course, Dante himself deviates from Catholic doctrine by having a pagan Virgil lead his fictional self into the Inferno. Dante is finally brought up to heaven, not by a priest, but through the offices of his celestial loved one, the dead Beatrice. Even at the entrance to the Inferno we find him approached by three angelic female figures: Beatrice, St. Lucy (light) and the biblical Rachel. How far is this from Dickens' various redemptive female "angels," from Nell to Lizzie Hexam? Dickens also gives us a redemptive female character named Rachel in his novel *Hard Times*.

If Dickens' heaven is mainly to be found on earth, in the form of earthly human love and happy endings, so is his hell to be found in the moral torments of conscience that belatedly attack villains like Bill Sikes, Ralph Nickleby and Bradley Headstone, who some believe to be a darker version of Dickens himself. At the same time, these villains are primarily concerned with their own safety or feelings of anger and revenge, rather than genuine remorse for their actions, and as impenitent in the true Christian sense, will presumably descend into the same Inferno prescribed by Dante, where they are trapped for all eternity.

II

Dante's System of Hell

Before gaining admission to Dickens' "Hell," a brief introduction and "road map" to Dante's *Divine Comedy* (or *Commedia*) and more specifically to the *Inferno* is necessary.[1]

Dante undertakes his masterwork in the middle of his life, (*"nel mezzo del cammin di nostra vita"*) at age thirty-five—considered the biblical mid-point of human existence—in a profound state of personal crisis. It is 1302, although for religiously symbolic reasons, Dante sets the events of the work in 1300, on Good Friday. He is in a deep depression, caused by the recent death of his beloved Beatrice (Bice Portinari) and his own permanent exile from Florence for a crime he apparently did not commit, "barratry," or corruption of public office. He was a member of the "white Guelphs" who were in conflict with both the "black Guelphs" and the Ghibellines. The struggles between these groups, based primarily on theological disputes over the importance of the Papacy vs. the Holy Roman Empire, also involved personal and political divisions between various Florentine leaders and families and even allegiances to foreign powers. In the course of these struggles, wars were fought, hundreds of innocent people killed or exiled, and Florence itself virtually destroyed. Little wonder that "sowers of discord" who incite internecine hatred are relegated to one of the deepest circles of the *Inferno*.

The work involves a spiritual journey down through the nine circles of Hell to its darkest depths, guided by the Roman poet Virgil, then up through the ledges of Purgatory (also with the guidance of Virgil) and finally into Paradise where Virgil disappears and Dante is finally reunited with his beloved Beatrice. This idealized, unconsummated love is more fully described in Dante's *La Vita Nuova*. Although they met periodically during their lifetimes, Dante and Beatrice were both married to others. However, she remains for Dante his perfect woman and becomes a central character in his *Paradiso*.

In his pilgrimage, Dante describes the gruesome punishments of the damned souls, who include contemporaries, recent historical predecessors, as well as characters from mythology and literature like Odysseus (considered more villain than hero in the Roman versions of the epic known to Dante). What makes the work so poignant and even personal is Dante's confrontation of his own sins and weaknesses, like the pride or violent anger that spontaneously erupt during his journey into Hell. Dante is not merely the narrator, who describes, judges and explains, but a character in the work, which is told in the first person and the *"dolce stile nuova,"* the spoken Italian of his time, instead of the Latin typically used in literature.

In the course of his mentally and physically perilous journey, Dante expresses a range of emotions: fear, despair, shame and finally joy as he is cleansed of his own sins and reunited with his beloved and with God. The allegory operates on four levels: "the historical, the moral, the literal and the anagogical (spiritual)."[2]

The *Inferno* is rich in references to history, theology and other literary works: classics like *The Aeneid*, Greek and Roman theology, and particularly the works of Aristotle. Religious sources like St. Thomas Aquinas, and of course the Bible, are critical points of reference.

In simple terms, Dante's sins are divided into two main categories, with subdivisions among them. These categories are first, sins of incontinence, or weakness, and second, sins of malice, involving those deliberate sins whose explicit goal is to do harm. This is Dante's own construction, and not the official doctrine of the Catholic Church, which distinguishes only between "venial" and "mortal" sins. However, Dante's system is based on church writings of his era, particularly those of Aristotle and St. Thomas Aquinas. Moreover, the "seven capital vices" (popularly known as "the seven deadly sins") represented in the *Purgatorio* were part of Catholic theology at the time, although the specific form of Purgatory as a mountain with "ledges" was Dante's own imaginative creation. As Dante descends into the depths of Hell, moving from the circles of incontinence to those of malice, the corresponding punishments become significantly harsher.

Similar distinctions can be found in Dickens. For example, a lazy, self-indulgent parasite like Harold Skimpole in *Little Dorrit*, while repulsive to the reader, is considered far less evil than the malicious Sir John Chester in *Barnaby Rudge*. Skimpole's punishment will be banishment from the "heavenly" home of John Jarndyce and not the torments of jail or death faced by Chester and other darker villains.

Dante's system for the classification of sins has been subject to some debate. It is impossible to treat these theological discussions in detail here. However, questions arise, such as why murder, for example, is in a less deep part of Hell than fiscal corruption, or why the sins in Purgatory don't actually correspond to those in Hell, when repentant sinners are, in principle, able to move from one place to the other.[3] W.H. Reade suggests that two issues are at work in Dante's assessment of sin. The first is the goal of the sin: is it malice, the conscious desire to do harm, or rather the result of extreme sensuality or weakness? According to Reade at least, sins of malice do not and cannot appear in Purgatory, unlike sins of incontinence.

Another thorny issue is that of "internal" sin or sinful intention, as opposed to sinful action. For example, if a character attempts to carry out a failed murder, is that character as evil as one who succeeds? The Catholic Church would say yes, and both Dante and Dickens would likely agree. Unlike civil society, which only judges those crimes actually committed, the spirit and intention of moral action is central to Christianity. This point is made clear in the Sermon on the Mount itself, where Jesus states that "lusting in the heart" is as bad as actually committing adultery (a bit tough, but there you are!) In this light, we may consider Bradley Headstone, whose elaborately plotted attempt to murder Eugene Wrayburn only fails by accident. But let us take up these questions in more detail, as we enter the circles of Dante's *Inferno* itself, and descend, with him, into its darker regions.

Apart from theological considerations, there is clearly a personal element in his work. Dante repeatedly expresses his loathing for Boniface, the corrupt Pope responsible for his exile, and his Florentine contemporaries who took part in it. By the same token, Dickens' novels relentlessly attack adults who neglect and abuse their children, deriving at least in part, from his sense of abandonment by his own parents to work in a blacking factory at age twelve. This was apparently the single most traumatic experience of his life, and one from which he never entirely recovered.[4]

The Entrance to Hell

Before Dante enters Hell itself, he finds himself on the shores of the river Acheron that bears souls to the place where they will be judged by the mythical character Minos (in reality, God) to be placed in their proper part of Hell. Here, he encounters the "neutrals," (sometimes translated as "the indifferents") those cowardly people who have done nothing for good or ill, and are clearly objects of Dante's contempt. Wasps and hornets sting their eyes (blind to God?) and blood streams down to their feet, mingling with tears and crawling with loathsome worms.

Gathered in this circle are those destined for Hell, wretchedly bemoaning their fates. They will be ferried into Hell by Charon, the mythological boatman. Upon entering Hell, they must pass through the gate bearing the dreaded quote, "Abandon all hope, ye who enter here."

Limbo, the First Circle (Canto IV)

The above mentioned sufferers are not yet in the first circle of Hell proper, Limbo, home to the "virtuous heathens." The souls Dante meets in Limbo were generally not privileged to live in the time of Jesus, yet are respected by Dante, in some cases as precursors to Christ, in others as wise and moral teachers. Virgil, of course, is the most important of these. Among others noted here are ancient philosophers like Socrates, Plato and Cicero, great scholars like Galen and even the Muslim philosopher Averroes. All this reflects Dante's profound reverence for art and knowledge. Poets like Homer and Virgil are—naturally—treated especially well.

The fact that the people in this circle are dealt with more kindly than the indifferent "neutrals" is understandable; someone who lived in a time where Christian redemption was available, yet who failed to seek it, is more to be condemned by Dante than someone who had no access to salvation. When we come to Dickens, we will find characters that might be placed in Limbo, because they have not had the benefit of a true Christian education, although of course we cannot find any who lived before the advent of Christ.

The next four circles include the various sins of incontinence, those moral weaknesses which are more animalistic and instinctual than deliberately malicious.

Circle 2: The Lustful (Cantos V and VI)

Circle 2, one of the most famous and beautifully described circles of the *Inferno*, is home to those who have been swept up in the emotion of love to the point of adultery, violating the laws of God and man. Here we meet the famous Italian lovers Paolo and Francesca, as well as mythical characters like Semiramis and Helen, whose "lust" supposedly caused the devastating Trojan War. As one might expect from an author influenced by the traditions of courtly love (Lancelot is also mentioned here) Dante treats adulterous love with more sympathy than many other sins in the *Inferno*. As for Dickens, a product of the Victorian era who eventually succumbed to a secret adultery, what he makes of romantic passion will be discussed in later chapters. In Dante, their punishment or *contrapasso* is to be tossed continuously by violent winds, just as in life they allowed their emotions to carry them away.

Circle 3: The Gluttonous (Canto VI)

Far less appealing are the gluttons, embodied by Cerberus "the raven-ous worm" and represented here by a Florentine known to Dante named Ciacco (the hog). The sin represented here is animalistic, succumbing to the lowest form of craving. The gluttons are punished by being subjected to driving rains, groveling in the mire (like animals?), and a hideous smell pervades their circle—perhaps the smells of rotting food?

A modern reader might wonder why relatively harmless gluttons would be found in Hell at all. But in the Middle Ages, major Catholic theologians like Thomas Aquinas believed that "gluttony" was Adam's primary sin, connecting gluttony to over-attachment to the body and the neglect of the immortal soul.

Circle 4: The Avaricious and the Prodigal (Canto VII)

This is the circle for "those who hoard and those who squander," doomed to torment each other for opposite sides of the same vice. Dante tells us, "Here I saw far more people than elsewhere," suggesting that there are many more people guilty of these sins than those of lust or glut-tony. This would certainly fit well with Dickens' world. The "avaricious-prodigals" are forced to roll weights back and forth against each other's chests "with great howls," as they shout and taunt each other. Dante implies that an obsession with worldly wealth causes intense conflict, as we moderns can assuredly attest. Among the avaricious and prodigal in Dante's *Inferno* are monks, yet they cannot be specifically identified be-cause their own "lack of discernment" is part of their punishment. Some of the avaricious sinners "rise from the grave with closed fist," symbol-izing their grasping tendencies.

Dante and Virgil descend into the "muddy bog that is the Styx," where they find an even more miserable group of sinners, the wrathful.

Circle 5: The Wrathful (Canto VIII)

In this circle, we find those who allowed themselves to be over-whelmed by anger, guarded by the spirit of the furious monster Phlegyas, who ferries their souls across a marsh. He even attacks Dante, mistakenly assuming him to be a resident of the Inferno. There are two types of wrathful, those whose anger is expressed openly, as they attack each other on the surface of the marsh, and those "sullen" wrathful, who are buried in the mud, "gurgling underneath the slime." Among the openly wrathful we find Fillipo Argenti, a Florentine known for his pride and ungovernable temper. It is interesting that in this *canto*, Dante has his own outburst of rage at Argenti. Whether this is Dante's own uncontrolled anger at a political adversary, or, as some have suggested, "the beginning of a spiritual development in the right direction" is open to interpretation.[5]

At this point, Dante and Virgil are leaving the circles of Incontinence and are about to enter *Dis* (the realm of Plutus), a dark enclosed city of pain and severe suffering. The next circle they encounter, the Heretics, is perplexing to some scholars, as it is not entirely clear whether its sin belongs to the world of incontinence or that of malice. The issue in brief, is how much heresy is a voluntary sin, and how much involuntary. In any case, it is much more a sin of "the intellect" gone wrong, rather than the unbridled emotions. Sinclair calls *Dis* (or Satan) a part of "lower hell," home to the "willful" sinners.[6]

Circle 6: The Heretics (Cantos IX and X)

The walls of *Dis* enclose an ever more terrifying landscape. The "archheretics" are found here, and their punishment is particularly horrible. They are locked into open tombs, burning alive and screaming in pain. Here we see one of Dante's relatively rare references to a fiery Hell. This is a somewhat mystifying circle. Just who are these heretics and what exactly are their crimes? Dante first mentions the ancient philosopher Epicurus, who "believes the soul dies with the body," an obvious theological error. After that we encounter Farinata, a Ghibelline of the generation preceding Dante's, whose main crime seems to have been religious factionalism, yet who is depicted with a certain dignity and respect by Dante. After that he meets the Guelph Cavalcante, father of the poet Guido Cavalcante who was in fact a poet-friend of Dante's. In this case, the exact nature of Cavalcante's "heresy" is unclear. It also seems to be connected with the sin of "epicureanism," or the belief in the death of the soul.

Both these men display a measure of pride which, although not the specific sin depicted here, suggests some connection between pride and heresy. We may be able to see some connection between these two sins later in considering Dickens, in particular his "false prophet" Mrs. Clennam (*Little Dorrit*).

In *Canto XI* Dante (through Virgil) introduces the "three lesser circles" they are about to encounter, all relating to violence or "*forza,*" and divided into: violence against others, violence against self, and violence against God. These all form part of Circle 7. It also looks ahead to the even more serious and larger Circle 8 that encompasses all types of fraud or "*frode.*" Dante actually explains here why, in his moral system at least, fraud is worse and lower in Hell than force, because "it is a sin peculiar to man," unlike violence, which can be a quality of the beasts as well. Here the issue of conscious choice and free will, as opposed to mere animal instinct, is shown to create ever more abhorrent sins.

Circle 7: the Violent (Cantos XI-XIV)

The Violent Against Others

Dante and Virgil descend a steep and craggy mountain to the banks of the river Phlegothon, where they encounter the frightening Minotaur, furiously gnawing away at himself. Here Dante encounters the "violent against others," represented by the Centaurs, who seem to represent the *condotierri*, or hired mercenaries of their time. In contrast to the ugly violence of the Minotaur, the Centaurs are somewhat attractive figures, perhaps because of their military associations.[7] Dante himself served in the military, with some pride. The Centaurs are shown firing arrows at each other's breasts. However, at the end of the same *canto*, we see some of the most violent sunk up to their eyebrows in "red boiling liquid." A centaur informs Dante, "They are the tyrants who have their hands to blood and plunder..." These include Alexander the Great, the Sicilian tyrant Dionysius and further on, Attila and others.

The Violent Against Themselves (The Suicides) Canto XIII

This *canto* describing the suicides contains some of Dante's most original and poignant imagery. For Dante, the suicides' souls have been turned into trees, perpetually being broken and wounded. When Dante accidentally cracks one of their branches, they cry out in pain. The lifeless shades of their mortal bodies hang from their limbs, an eternal reminder that they have destroyed their own precious lives.

Here he encounters, among others, a Florentine who has just hanged himself. The implication here is that the city of Florence is committing suicide in an unjust civil war.[8]

The Violent Against God: Canto XIV-XVI

As he moves into ever grimmer landscapes, "the doleful wood," he finds more souls in extreme torment. The ground is described as "a dry, deep sand," on which the blasphemous "sinners against God" crawl or stand miserably around, while fire and flame rain down on them for eternity. Their loud cries are fitting for those who "cried out" against God. Most are screaming in pain, but Capaneus, one of the seven classical figures who "laid siege to Thebes" and defied Jove, stands proud and unrepentant through his suffering. Here again we see the significant connection between stubborn pride and rejection of true Godliness, a theme that emerges both for Dante and Dickens.

In *Canto XV* we arrive at one of the sections of Hell most troubling for contemporary readers, the "sodomites." They are included in this circle because, presumably, they have acted against God's "natural order." Yet here Dante encounters a man he knew and deeply respected, the scholar-poet Brunetto Latini, as well as many notable Florentines of his era, suggesting that this particular "sin" was fairly common in Medieval Florence, especially among artists and intellectuals. Again in this *Canto*, we see Dante's ambivalence. He seems torn between his feelings of kindliness towards the sinner and his sense that the "sin" must be condemned. After being greeted as a friend by Latini, Dante inquires plaintively, "Are you here *Ser Brunetto?*" He then begs Latini to sit with him for a while. For his part, Latini addresses Dante as "my son" and asks him solicitously about his life. The meeting with Latini is by far the most amicable and intimate of any of Dante's encounters in Hell. Latini, fifty years Dante's senior, was one of the most noted scholars in Florence. How do we explain how Dante can at the same time "honor his old Master and blacken his memory?" [9] The answer is, with difficulty.

Circle 8 Malebolge: The Fraudulent (Cantos XVII-XXVI)

Dante approaches Circle 8, Fraud *(frode)* with a sense of foreboding at the horrors yet to come. In the previous *Canto*, he prepares us for the ugly images of Fraud, saying "I saw swimming up through that gross and murky air a figure amazing to the stoutest heart..." That monstrous figure, Geryon, is one of the most frightening of Dante's creations. He has "the face of a just man," but "all the rest was a serpent's trunk..." He appears kindly, but is in fact a hideous and dangerous monster. The fraudulent sinners here are trying to fend off flames and the burning soil beneath them. Interestingly, they are all wearing pouches from their necks decorated with their family crests, indicating that these Florentines pride themselves on externals, covering up the darker sins within. Although we will treat him in detail later, it is impossible not to instantly recall one of Dickens' most loathsome "frauds," Sir John Chester in *Barnaby Rudge*, who similarly prides himself on his fake "family crest."

The Circle of Fraud is the longest and most intricate in the *Inferno*, comprising ten subdivisions or pouches (*bolgias*). Together, these regions comprise Dante's "*maleboge*" (evil pockets) and include: 1. Panderers and seducers, 2. Flatterers, 3. Simonists, 4. Soothsayers, 5. Barraters (Grafters), 6. Hypocrites, 7. Thieves, 8. Fraudulent counselors, 9. Sowers of Discord and 10. Alchemists and Falsifiers. Note that these are described in descending order, with each form of fraud more despicable than the one above. Dante's extensive treatment of this sin can only be attributed to the prevalence of fraud of all types in the world in which he lived, a world fraught with hypocrisy and falsity. In Dickens' novels, the vast number of characters representing varieties of fraud can equally be ascribed to his experience of his own hypocritical society.

Bolgia 1: The Panderers (Pimps) and Seducers (Canto XVIII)

In this section, Dante meets the panderers, or pimps, and the seducers. They walk past each other in opposite directions, perhaps to indicate their duplicitous natures. As they walk, their backs are lashed "by horned devils," likely an allusion to the "horns" of the deceived husband. In their group appears a Guelph contemporary of Dante, who supposedly sold his own sister to a wealthy patron. Also we see Jason, mythical hero of the "golden fleece" tale and deceiving husband of Medea, who gets her own revenge by killing his new bride as well as their own children. (Certainly Dante can think up no punishment for Jason worse than the punishment exacted by his wife in Euripides' drama.)

Bolgia 2: The Flatterers

There are only two examples of flatterers in the same *Canto*, Alessio Intermini, another contemporary of Dante, and Thais, a whore of Greek mythology. Their punishment, suitably, is to be buried up to their necks in excrement, indicating perhaps what exuded from their mouths.

Bolgia 3: The Simonists (Canto XIX)

In this rocky landscape, Dante finds a group of sinners buried head down in fiery holes, their legs jutting out wildly above ground. This is the section of Hell reserved for those who have defrauded their religious office by selling it. Here we first encounter Simon Magus himself, who according to the Bible, thought he could buy the same power as Jesus' apostles John and Peter. He is quickly followed by the corrupt popes who, according to Dante, sold their offices for gold. This is, for Dante, another form of "prostitution" and a graver one, because it trades in matters that rightfully belong to God.

Bolgia 4: The Soothsayers (Canto XX)

The soothsayers, punished in true *contrapasso* fashion with their heads twisted backwards now appear weeping. They have pretended to predict the future, which God alone can know. As in similar *cantos*, the soothsayers include characters from the Greek classics, like the blind sage Tiresias, and real individuals from Dante's era like Guido Bonatti, a famed astrologer.

Bolgia 5: The Barraters (Cantos XXI-XXII)

Curiously, the crime with which Dante himself was charged, barratry or sale of public office ("there, no is made "ay" for cash") is treated with a kind of farcical humor. Although the malefactors are dropped into boiling pitch, certainly a form of severe suffering, the devils in this particular *bolgia* behave with riotous vulgarity. Their names are humorous: *Malacoda* (evil-tail), *Barbariccia* (curlybeard), *Ciriatto* (swineface) etc. In this, Dante is apparently playing on the names of famous Florentines he satirizes.[10]

In these *cantos*, we are not very far from the world of Dickens, with his love of satirical naming. According to Sinclair, the grotesque treatment of the barraters, as well as Dante's extensive treatment of them (two and a half *cantos*) demonstrates his shame and outrage at being called a "barrater" and his contempt for those who are actually guilty of this crime.

Bolgia 6: the Hypocrites (Canto XXIII)

The tone of the work turns more serious as we enter the circle of the hypocrites, fittingly enclosed from head to foot in golden cloaks filled with lead. They march somberly in single file. Here Dante encounters Catalano de Malavolti and Loderinghi della Angolo, two "jovial friars," with their cowls concealing their eyes. These two were supposed to protect the city of Bologna, but instead were guilty of corruption and destruction. In the same *bolgia*, we abruptly encounter the more sinister figure of Caiphas, betrayer of Jesus himself, who is stretched out on the ground, crucified with three stakes, a fitting form of *contrapasso*. Hypocrisy is a particularly heinous crime for Dante, as it is for Dickens.

Bolgia 7: The Thieves (Cantos XXIV and XXV)

The brutal descriptions here emphasize that Dante is not describing mere petty theft. He is condemning wholesale social corruption, stealing from society from a position of power and responsibility like today's Wall Street swindlers. These villains are condemned to run naked through swarms of serpents, their hands tied behind their backs with live snakes. The anguish of the sinners, their sighs and groans is such that Dante is forced to comment aloud: "Ah the power of God, how stern it is, pouring forth such strokes for vengeance." Here they encounter Vanno Fucci, the violent leader of the Guelph "blacks." He was supposed to have stolen treasures from the sacristy of the Pisan cathedral, thus committing not only theft, but sacrilege. The horrors of this *bolgia* are emphasized by the metamorphosis of two other thieving Florentines into the bodies of others, all of them transformed into various serpents. Here Dante is once again showing his rage at the corruption of people from his own era, as the five Florentines mentioned were all known to him.

Bolgia 8: The False Counselors (Cantos XXVI-XXVII)

These false counselors are those "who use their high mental gifts for guile." First mentioned is Odysseus himself, who in the *Inferno*, recounts his own story. While the Greeks called him "the wily Odysseus" crediting him for thinking up the idea of the Trojan horse, in general Homer views him as a hero. In Latin translations of *The Odyssey* known to Dante, however, he was viewed more as a villain. For Dante, he was responsible for the defeat of the Trojans, mythical ancestors of the Romans; thereby violating what Dante considered the God-given laws of history. The fact that he used his "great gifts" for evil makes him all the more damnable. False counselors are punished for their sins by entrapment in an individual flaming prison—a moving point of fire. As is typical in the *Inferno*, Dante also encounters a man of his own age, the famous Guido de

Montefeltro (known as "the fox"), an advisor to the Pope who is caught in his own deceptions and later becomes a monk. He was a Ghibelline leader and advisor to Dante's archenemy Pope Boniface. Dante hates him because he urged the Pope to fight against other Christians, instead of what Dante (and his era) considered the "holy cause" of the Crusades.

Bogia 9: The Sowers of Discord (Canto XXVIII)

The mayhem created by those who incite one group against another is graphically illustrated in this section of the *Inferno*, where the "makers of scandal and schism" (Musa) are literally ripped to pieces as their just punishment. Indeed, Dante himself has difficulty finding words for the horrible scene: "Who could ever tell, even with words untrammeled and the tale often repeated, of all the blood and wounds I now saw." One man is ripped apart from his chin "to the part that breaks wind," another holds his bloody head beneath his arm. "Mohamet" is depicted here, mistakenly believed to have been a Christian convert and schismatic, as well as his son-in-law Ali, who was part of the historic division in Islam. The Guelph and Ghibelline division is embodied in the appearance of Mosca dei Lamberti, who helped instigate the bloodshed that plagued Florence for generations. All the above, in Dante's mind, have created a breach in what should be the ultimate unity of the human race.

Bolgia 10: The Falsifiers (Impersonators, Counterfeiters and Al- chemists) (Canto XXIX-XXX)

Here, Dante encounters another form of fraudulent sinner: the impersonators, counterfeiters and alchemists, those who deceive others by pretending to perform miracles. They lie festering in a foul-smelling ditch, covered with scabs and itchy skin. In a word, they are disgusting. These include not merely alchemists, but counterfeiters, those who gull the vulnerable by pretending to be what they are not. There are a series of Italians noted here, one Griffolino among them, who were burned for pretending to perform magic. Their quackery thrives on men's greed and ignorance. While alchemy is not specifically to be found in Dickens, as it was not generally found in 19th century England, we certainly can see a number of deceptive frauds or counterfeiters who profit from the ignorance of others—notably the Ponzi schemer and fake businessman Montague Tigg.

Circle 9: The Traitors (Canto XXXII and XXXIV)

This circle is divided into four types of traitor: traitor to family and friend, traitor to guests, traitor to country or cause, and traitor to patrons and to God. Because it involves a "deep iciness of the heart," treachery has been dubbed "the most anti-social of all sins."[11] The River Phlegethon representing mankind's sins, is portrayed in other *cantos* as "hot blood," whereas in this *canto* it becomes the frozen lake Cocytus.

Held captive in the outer region of the lake named Caina (after the biblical Cain) are those who betrayed their own kin. Dante's contemporary examples of this sin are Napoleone and Alessandro of Mangona, who killed each other fighting over an inheritance. The second division is called Antenora, after the Trojan who betrayed his city to the Greeks. This is the circle of those who have proven traitor to cause or country. Along with figures from literature, such as Ganelon, from the epic poem *The Song of Roland*, we find people from Dante's era who, for Dante, traitorously went over from the Guelphs to the Ghibellines.

Among the traitors noted here are the infamous Ugolino, who apparently betrayed his cause, intriguing against the Ghibellines (of which he was originally a part) and working with various factions to bring about the naval defeat of Pisa by Genoa. He supposedly played one group against the other to advance his own personal interests. The awful punishment for the traitorous is to writhe about, biting each other's flesh, or as in the horrid case of Ugolino, gnawing the very head of his enemy.

Intriguingly, while the traitors' souls are consigned to suffer in Hell, they are also doomed to bodily roam the earth as if they were still alive. Presumably, this is so that they may experience the contempt of the living, who know their betrayals, as well as the torments of the dead. This actually comes closest to the kind of "earthly" damnation experienced by Dickens' villains when they are finally unmasked. The traitors, like

Cain, must endure the torment of exile, utterly cut off from their fellow human beings whom they have chosen to betray.

The third division of Cocytus is called Tolemea, after the Egyptian king Ptolemy XII who slew his guest Pompey. This section represents traitor to guests.

Canto XXXIV: Traitors to Patrons and to God

At last, at the center of the earth in *Judecca*, Dante finally encounters Lucifer himself, a terrifying figure who is frozen from the chest down in a lake of ice. He is both punished and punisher, as he is depicted with three faces, each of which is portrayed as gnawing another sinner against the divine: Judas Iscariot ("the soul who suffers most of all"), who betrayed Jesus, and Brutus and Cassius, who betrayed Julius Caesar, in his own time considered not merely an emperor, but also divine. Lucifer, an imposing giant with three heads, is weeping bloody tears. Dante has at last reached the deepest pit of the Inferno, and as his world is literally "turned upside down," will now proceed up through the mountainous region of Purgatory.

III

Dicken's Inferno: The First Circles

Having all too rapidly made our way through Dante's *Inferno*, we finally gain admission to Dickens' own versions of Hell: the polluted air of London's streets, the miserable workhouses with their dying women and children, the smoke-filled factories, the grim prisons, the lunatic asylum posing as a court of "justice," Chancery in *Bleak House*. The numerous "prisons" in Dickens' novels, both real and symbolic, have a doomed quality and like Dante's *Inferno*, often permit no escape. Here the reader encounters, along with the innocent victims of these sinister institutions, those guilty characters whose unrepented sins cause them to be appropriately punished. For Dickens' villains, the words "Abandon all hope, ye who enter here," can be just as irrevocable as for Dante's.

The "Indifferents"—Jack Maldon, Podsnap, Mrs. Corney, Mrs. Gamp, Jaggers

As we have seen, Dante presents us with a category of miserable souls on the outskirts of Hell itself, called by some translators "the neutrals," by some "the indifferents." Dante explains, "This miserable state is borne by the wretched souls who lived without disgrace and without praise... were not rebels, nor faithful to God, but were for themselves." Similarly, for Dickens, the term was often applied to those who were blithely oblivious to the sufferings of others. He frequently referred to parliamentarians of his time as "the indifferents," openly suggesting that they should all be run out of office. Dickens conveys his general contempt for "indifference" through a relatively minor character, Jack Maldon, the cousin and would-be lover of his married cousin Annie Strong in *David*

Copperfield. After a half-hearted effort to make a new life in India, Maldon has returned to England, and is discussing the daily newspaper with Annie's husband Dr. Strong:

> "Is there any news today?" inquired the Doctor.
>
> "Nothing at all," replied Mr. Maldon. "There's an account about the people being hungry and discontented down in the North, but they are always being hungry and discontented somewhere"
>
> ...
>
> "There's a long statement in the paper, sir, about somebody being murdered," observed Mr. Maldon, "But somebody is always being murdered, and I didn't read it."

David (Dickens) then reflects ironically:

> "A display of indifference to all the actions and passions of mankind was not supposed to be such a distinguished quality of mankind, I think, as I have observed it to be since. I have known it to be very fashionable indeed. I have seen it to be displayed with such success that I have encountered some fine ladies and gentlemen who might as well have been born caterpillars."

Another character that perfectly embodies this quality is Podsnap in *Our Mutual Friend*, curiously enough, believed to be partly modeled on Dickens' life-long friend, literary advisor and official biographer John Forster. Although he and Forster had their quarrels, Dickens maintained he merely used some of Forster's mannerisms, like throwing his arm backwards to dismiss an idea. He denied that Podsnap's personality or moral stance was the same as Forster's.* So who is this Podsnap—a man whose outstanding quality is strong enough to create a noun and chapter heading out of his name—"Podsnappery," a term implying smug complacency about himself and the world in which he lives? In *Our Mutual*

---

* Forster was Dickens' life-long friend, literary agent and editor, and a Unitarian who, like Dickens, had pulled himself up from a modest life (as a butcher's son). He did become more conservative in later years, although he and Dickens remained intimate until Dickens' death. Dickens appointed him both his official biographer and executor of his will.

Friend Podsnap, a member of the coterie of the rich, snobbish Veneerings, is portrayed as self-satisfied and narrow-minded:

> Mr. Podsnap was well to do, and stood very high in Mr Podsnap's opinion. Beginning with a good inheritance, he had married a good inheritance, and had thriven exceedingly in the Marine Insurance way, and was quite satisfied. He never could make out why everybody was not quite satisfied, and he felt conscious that he set a brilliant social example in being particularly well satisfied with most things, and, above all other things, with himself.
>
> Convinced of his own merit and importance, Mr Podsnap settled that whatever he put behind him he put out of existence. There was a dignified conclusiveness—not to add a grand convenience—in this way of getting rid of disagreeables which had done much towards establishing Mr Podsnap in his lofty place in Mr Podsnap's satisfaction. "I don't want to know about it; I don't choose to discuss it; I don't admit it!" Mr Podsnap had even acquired a peculiar flourish of his right arm in often clearing the world of its most difficult problems, by sweeping them behind him (and consequently sheer away) with those words and a flushed face. For they affronted him.
>
> Mr Podsnap's world was not a very large world, morally...

Podsnap, like the "Society" that surrounds him, particularly refuses to hear about the struggling poor. It makes his own life less enjoyable, and besides, he believes that he can do nothing about it. His perspective is the all too common "the poor are always with us" view of his time, as well our own. He is equally indifferent to the sufferings of his former friends, the Lammles. His reaction, when he hears of their financial "smash," is to force the rest of the Veneering guests into silence:

> "Don't ask me, I desire to take no part in the discussion of these people's affairs. I abhor the subject. It is an odious subject, a subject that makes me sick, and I—" And with his favourite right-arm flourish which sweeps away everything and settles it forever, Mr. Podsnap sweeps these inconveniently unexplainable wretches who have lived beyond their means and gone to total smash, off the face of the universe.

This smug personality type can be found in nearly all of Dickens' novels. The original title of *Little Dorrit*, "Nobody's Fault," alludes to the vast indifference of society at large to human suffering, especially that of the poor. In general, he presents the rich as indifferent to such suffering, from the Veneerings in *Our Mutual Friend* to the Tite Barnacles in *Little Dorrit* and the ruthless factory owner Bounderby in *Hard Times*, who accuses workers that ask for a modest raise of only "wanting to eat oysters."

However, Dickens finds moral indifference at all ends of the social spectrum. Mrs. Corney, the small-time manager of *Oliver Twist*'s oppressive workhouse, comfortably enjoys her position of power over her desperate charges, although she is not overtly abusive. When an old workhouse nurse who attended Oliver's mother during childbirth is dying and Mrs. Corney is asked to go to her side, she refuses, remarking, "What's that to me. I can't keep her alive, can I?" She relishes her cozy little teas in her own apartment, while her charges in the workhouse literally starve. Mrs. Corney eventually marries Mr. Bumble, making his life a living hell. She does commit the crime of concealing the proof of Oliver's true parentage when she inadvertently discovers it. Still we will not drop Mrs. Corney into a darker section of the *Inferno*, that of fraud. Her main sin is that of indifference, not outright malice.

Then there is Mrs. Gamp, the alcoholic nurse in *Martin Chuzzlewit* whose peculiarly inventive English makes her one of Dickens' greatest and most hilarious creations. While her character is unique, Dickens regarded her as an example of the poorly trained nurses of the time (Dickens' *Preface* to the novel). Mrs. Gamp has absolutely no concern for the sick people with whom she is entrusted; her only interest is in getting paid and well wined and dined—preferably wined:

> "...I don't deny it Mr. Chuzzlewit, that I never could have kep myself up but for a little drain of spirits, which I seldom touches, but could always wish to know where to find, if so dispoged, never knowin' what may happen next, the world, the world bein' so uncertain."

In her alcoholic ramblings and constant references to an apparently nonexistent friend Mrs. Harris, readers generally find "Sairey" Gamp to be more humorous than evil. The fact is, however, she is utterly indifferent to her patients. She is also sometimes charged with the laying out of the dead, for whom she cares equally little:

> "Ah so the gentleman's dead, sir! Ah! The more's the pity." She didn't even know his name. "But it's what we all must come to. It's as certain as being born, except that we can't all make our calculations as exact. Ah! Poor dear!..." "Ah," repeated Mrs. Gamp, for it was always a safe sentiment in cases of mourning.

Mrs. Gamp will eventually be discharged from her duties which are no longer needed, and humiliated in front of those who have come to believe that "Mrs. Harris" doesn't really exist.

There are few among Dickens' characters that are neither good, redeemable, or outright evil, so the population of this particular circle is relatively limited. Nevertheless, we might consider here the sinister, yet oddly engaging Jaggers, the lawyer who links Pip in *Great Expectations* with his secret patron Abel Magwitch. Jaggers defends the worst of criminals, and through his brilliance, even gets cold-blooded murderers off without punishment. He does this, not out of any feelings of compassion, but rather for money and a sense of pride and power. He is apparently respected and feared by the entire criminal class of London. Jaggers does perform a good deed for Pip (for which he is amply compensated) and in a sense attempts to do the same for Estella, by placing her as a baby in a home with the wealthy, but crazed Miss Havisham. Of course Havisham, a woman whose main goal in life is to wreak misery on the male species because of her own romantic disappointment, proves horribly destructive to the beautiful Estella, who as a result of her upbringing cannot love. Is Jaggers good or bad? We never know for sure, and Dickens never comments directly on him. Nevertheless, a lengthy description of Jaggers' office suggests how Dickens (like Pip) views him:

> Mr. Jaggers's room was lighted by a skylight only, and was a most dismal place—the skylight, eccentrically pitched like a broken head, and

the distorted adjoining houses looking as if they had twisted themselves to peep down at me through it. There were not so many papers about, as I should have expected to see; and there were some odd objects about, that I should not have expected to see—such as an old rusty pistol, a sword in a scabbard, several strange-looking boxes and packages, and two dreadful casts on a shelf, of faces peculiarly swollen, and twitchy about the nose. Mr. Jaggers's own high-backed chair was of deadly black horsehair, with rows of brass nails round it, like a coffin; and I fancied I could see how he leaned back in it, and bit his fore-finger at the clients. The room was but small, and the clients seemed to have had a bad habit of backing up against the wall: the wall, especially opposite to Mr. Jaggers's chair, being greasy with shoulders. I recalled, too, that the one-eyed gentleman had shuffled forth against the wall when I was the innocent cause of his being turned away.

Jaggers' fundamental amorality places him naturally at the outer edge of the *Inferno*. Although there are moments when he acts kindly, as when giving Pip advice about his over-spending, he is generally surrounded by an atmosphere of dread. Pip cannot stand to be around him socially, and even Jaggers' genial assistant Mr. Wemmick only maintains his sanity by maintaining a strict division (complete with drawbridge) between his personal world with his beloved "aged P" (parent) and the law office where he collaborates in Jaggers' darker schemes.

And what is the punishment meted out to these characters? Nothing too terrible, to be sure, certainly by comparison with Dante's "neutrals" who are "devoured by worms and stung by wasps." Podsnap is finally put in his place by one of his former friends, the good-hearted Twemlow, when he insists on deriding Eugene's marriage to the lower class Lizzie. Twemlow, for the first time, stands up against his friend's insufferable snobbery:

> "I say…if such feelings on the part of this gentleman induced him to marry this lady, I think he is the greater gentleman for this action, and makes her the greater lady."

Podsnap takes his refusal to agree with him poorly:

"I should like to know,' sneers Podsnap, whether your noble relation would be of such an opinion." **

At this point, "a canopy of wet blanket seems to descend on the company…" and the rest of the social snobs fall to arguing amongst each other.

Mrs. Corney will face the law for concealing information, and is doomed to a miserable marriage and a life of poverty in the workhouse, along with her husband Mr. Bumble. Mrs. Gamp will be exposed and fired. Finally, Jaggers is forced to experience the undoing of all his arrangements: Pip's loss of his "inheritance," the capture of his benefactor, Estella's impulsive, resentful marriage to an abusive husband, and perhaps finally, a sense of his own moral isolation from society. At the very least, he must eventually come to terms with a sense of his own powerlessness.

In general, the fitting punishment for "the indifferents" is that the rest of the world becomes equally indifferent to them.

Circle 1: Limbo—Jo, Hugh, Barnaby Rudge, Louisa Grandgrind, Estella

Dante was naturally more sympathetic to those who lived at a time when Christianity was unavailable than to those who ignored its teachings. His first circle of the *Inferno*, Limbo, is peopled by notable "heathens" he generally respects, such as Virgil himself. So where is the moral equivalent from Dickens' era when Christianity in all its forms, from Roman Catholic and Anglican to Unitarian and Dissenting Protestant, was presumably accessible to everyone? However, the reality is not quite so simple.

In the period when Dickens' novels are set, the late 18th and early 19th centuries, the desperately poor and their children often received little or no education, and were largely ignored by established religion. One his-

---

** It hardly stretches the point to compare Podsnap with today's commentators who would "sweep away" those unfortunates who bought mortgages they couldn't afford—even though, like the Lammles, they were often encouraged to do so by unscrupulous bankers.

torian describes part of late 18th century England in the following terms: "...those industrial areas where the traditional forms of ecclesiastical organization had broken down and where a brutal paganism flourished amid squalor and vice." [1] Despite the many evangelical movements of the 19th century, some members of the rural and urban underclasses continued to languish in conditions of abuse and profound ignorance. The only religious officials they do encounter are so callous that their moral preaching appears merely as the grossest hypocrisy. Dickens regarded the educational plight of poor children in the Ragged Schools of his time as "careless maintenance from year to year...of a vast hopeless nursery of misery, ignorance and vice; a breeding place for the hunks and jails." (1843, *The Daily News*)[2]

In other words, it is possible to find in Dickens' world characters lacking any genuine spiritual education. A classic example is the pitiable Jo, the street urchin in *Bleak House*. Jo, based on a real boy, is a victimized child, who dwells either on the streets, or in the hopeless slum personified in the novel as "Tom-All-Alone's." Here is Dickens' description of this hellish place:

> Darkness rests upon Tom-All-Alone's. Dilating and dilating since the sun went down last night, it has gradually swelled until it fills every void in the place. For a time there were some dungeon lights burning, as the lamp of life hums in Tom-all-Alone's, heavily, heavily, in the nauseous air, and winking—as that lamp, too, winks in Tom-all-Alone's—at many horrible things. But they are blotted out. The moon has eyed Tom with a dull cold stare, as admitting some puny emulation of herself in his desert region unfit for life and blasted by volcanic fires; but she has passed on and is gone. The blackest nightmare in the infernal stables grazes on Tom-all-Alone's, and Tom is fast asleep.

Jo has been abandoned by the society at large. He is ignorant of the world around him, and even of himself:

> "Name, Jo. Nothing else that he knows on. Don't know that everybody has two names. Never heerd of such a think."

Jo sweeps his crossing all day long, unconscious of the link, if any link there be. He sums up his mental condition when asked a question by replying that he "don't know nothink."

Jo's pathetic, outcast state is emphasized throughout the novel. Ironically, at one point the homeless waif sits to eat his meager breakfast on the steps of "the Society for the Propagation of the Gospel in Foreign Lands." Dickens' satiric portrayal of missionaries like Mrs. Jellyby and Mrs. Pardiggle who are obsessed with saving souls in Africa, while ignoring the souls in their own homes and on their very doorsteps, makes it clear that charity should begin at home.

Treated as a criminal simply for being homeless, chased by the police, and finally dying of pneumonia, Jo is told by the police one last time to "move on" once he is released from the hospital. The kindly humanitarian Dr. Woodcourt attempts to give him last rites. But Jo knows no prayers:

> "Jo! Did you never know a prayer?"
> "Never know'd nothink, sir"
> "Not so much as one short prayer?"
> "No sir. Nothink at all. Mr. Chadband's he was a praying wunst a Mr. Snagsby's, and I heerd him, but he sounded as if he wos a speakin to hisself, and not to me."

When Woodcourt finally gets him to repeat a short prayer, we might assume that Jo is somehow "saved." However, his dazed repetition of sacred words is without meaning. Dickens implies that this poor boy consigned to a hell on earth—not of his own choosing—may face no real reprieve in the afterlife. Dickens' outraged commentary on Jo's death suggests how thoroughly and cruelly Jo has been abandoned by organized religion and society at large:

> Dead, your Majesty! Dead! Right Reverends and Wrong Reverends of every order. Dead, men and women, born with heavenly compassion in your hearts. And dying thus around us every day.

Dickens indignantly reminds us that Jo is not alone in his plight. Physically and spiritually neglected children roam throughout his novels.

In *Barnaby Rudge*, the rough stableman Hugh never knew his father (his mother is dead), and has been raised like an animal, without any education either intellectual or moral. Because of this he acts instinctually and sometimes violently. When he nearly assaults the pretty Dolly Varden, to whom he is attracted, he warns her not to tell anyone:

> "All about here know me, and what I dare to do if I have a mind. If ever you are going to tell, stop when the words are on your lips and think of the mischief you'll bring, if you do, on some innocent heads that you wouldn't want to hurt a hair of. Bring trouble on me, and I'll bring trouble and something more on them in return. I care no more for them than for so many dogs; not so much—why should I? I'd sooner kill a man than a dog any day."

Significantly, Hugh relates more to animals than to humans, especially the horses he tends and his pet dog. The same can be said for the intimate relationship between his young friend Barnaby Rudge, and his pet raven Grip. (Dickens himself loved animals, especially birds. He had two pet ravens named Grip, as well as a bird named Dick after himself, and deeply mourned their passing.) Like Jo, when Hugh is about to die, he refuses to profess a faith he doesn't have in order to save himself:

> "That gentleman yonder"—pointing to the clergyman—"has often spoken to me of faith, and strong belief. You see what I am—more brute than man, as I have often been told—but I have faith enough to believe, and did believe as strongly as any of you gentlemen can believe anything, that this one life would be spared. See what he is!—Look at him!"

Here Hugh is referring to his cellmate young Barnaby Rudge, for whom in a kind of noble simplicity, Hugh would lay down his own life. His last compassionate thoughts are for his dog, begging one of his jailors to take him from his house and care for him. Are these generous sentiments enough to save Hugh from damnation? It's up to the reader to decide. Hugh makes it clear in this final speech, however, that his lack of religious education has made him what he is. At the very least Hugh is no hypocrite, which cannot be said for those who falsely proclaim their faith in this and many other Dickens novels. He rejects the offer of last rites:

> "I fear," observed the clergyman, shaking his head, "that you are incorrigible."
>
> "You are right. I am," rejoined Hugh sternly. You make merry-making of this (last rites) every month; let me be merry too."

As for his simple-minded friend Barnaby, it is a somewhat different story. He has a devout and loving mother, but is mentally incompetent and therefore unable to distinguish right from wrong. It is no accident that both he and Hugh are swept up in the anti-Catholic crusade. The more violent and lucid Hugh will be hung for his role in the bloodshed; Barnaby Jr. will mercifully be spared at the last minute. Like his pet raven Grip, Barnaby is too impaired to understand what he is doing. When Grip croaks out random slogans of the anti-Catholic movement, "I'm a devil, I'm a Polly, I'm a kettle, I'm a Protestant. No Popery!" Barnaby ignorantly praises him for his bit of wisdom. "Well said, Grip!" In fact, Grip, who becomes stubbornly mute after Barnaby is arrested, starts unaccountably shrieking out at the end of the novel, "I'm a devil, I'm a devil!" Who knows? Grip may have more of a conscience than some of the humans in the book.

Although she hails from the comfortable middle class, Louisa Gradgrind in *Hard Times*, like Jo and Hugh, has been deprived of any religious or spiritual education. She has been raised by her father the schoolmaster Gradgrind in an emotional void. Schooled in the materialist philosophies of Malthus, Hobbes and Bentham, she has been taught to respect "the facts, only the facts." Although economically comfortable, unlike Jo, Louisa is truly a lost soul. She might well be placed in the domain of "the sullen wrathful," (see Colon, above), but Louisa is also suited to the circle of Limbo. Yes, she is sometimes "sullen," angry at being pushed into marriage with a man she doesn't love, the rich, pompous Josiah Bounderby. However, she is not angry so much as depressed over her spiritually deprived condition.

While not totally lacking a conscience like her brother Tom, Louisa doesn't know how to love, either God or her fellow humans. Although by the end of the novel she has softened and become aware of her plight, she will never really be "saved." For Dickens, "salvation" generally means a loving marriage, a husband and children. This, Louisa will be denied:

> Herself again—a wife—a mother, lovingly watchful of her children, ever careful that they should have a childhood of the mind no less than a childhood of the body, knowing it to be a more beautiful thing, and a possession, any hoarded scrap of which is a blessing and a happiness to the wisest? Did Louisa see this? Such a thing was never to be.

In many ways, the ending of *Hard Times* is the harshest of all Dickens' novels. The honest factory worker Stephen Blackpool, one of the few admirable characters in the book, dies miserably; Gradgrind himself realizes his philosophical errors, but is forced to face the fact that he has morally destroyed his own children. Tom superficially "repents" and goes into exile in Australia. However, he never shows profound contrition and therefore it is difficult to assign him even the relative comfort of Purgatory. Louisa is alone. Only Sissy Jupe, the penniless orphan girl taken in by Gradgrind, but previously raised by warm-hearted performers in a traveling circus, is capable of love, and thus for Dickens has earned some kind of future happiness.

The proud, beautiful Estella in *Great Expectations* is another character whose false upbringing deforms her into a woman incapable of any human or spiritual feeling. Raised by the demented Miss Havisham as an instrument of her disappointment with men, Estella's appointed role in life is to make all men suffer. She cruelly flirts with Pip, the novel's protagonist, but repeatedly rebuffs him, eventually marrying a man who abuses her—clearly a form of *contrapasso*. When Miss Havisham finally seeks some minimal affection from Estella, she is met with cold indifference and brutal honesty:

> "You stock and stone!" exclaimed Miss Havisham. "You cold, cold heart!"

"What?" said Estella, preserving her attitude of indifference as she leaned against the great chimney-piece and only moving her eyes; "Do you reproach me for being cold? You?"

"Are you not?" was the fierce retort.

"You should know," said Estella. "I am what you made me. Take all the praise, take all the blame, take all the failure; in short, take me."

After some reflection, Estella ponders the mystery of her emotional life in terms of her upbringing:

"I began to think….that I almost understand how this comes about. If you had brought up your adopted daughter wholly in the dark confinement of these rooms, and had never let her know there was such a thing as daylight by which she had once seen your face—if you had done that, and then, for a purpose had wanted her to understand the daylight and know all about it, you would have been disappointed and angry?"

Dickens actually wrote two different endings to this novel. In the original, more psychologically credible one, Estella remains a lost soul, recognizing her inner emptiness but unable to change it. On dubious advice from friend and fellow writer Edward Bulwer-Lytton, Dickens made the decision to alter the ending, showing a penitent and redeemed Estella, who realizes that she loves Pip and will stay with him after all. This of course is consistent with the "happy endings" that generally mark Dickens' novels, but arguably feels less authentic than the original ending.

True, Dickens is not specifically speaking of Christian teaching or the lack of it, like Dante in his description of the souls deprived of Christian salvation, but the meaning is much the same. Estella, like Louisa and the benighted child Jo, has been raised without any access to a spiritual, emotional or moral life. They are what their society and families have made them. One cannot entirely blame them, as they are "more to be pitied than scorned." At times, Dickens, unlike Dante, presents his characters as products of their environment, in a sense more consistent with modern sociology or even Marxism than Catholicism.

At the same time, Dickens' characters like Dante's have free will, and inevitably make moral choices. Thus they must be ultimately judged by their own decisions. This can be seen in the difference between Louisa and Tom Gradgrind. While raised in the same spiritually hollow philosophy, Louisa is capable of showing some heart when she gives a little money to the desperate worker Stephen Blackpool. Tom, on the other hand, thinking only of himself, is willing to set Stephen up for a theft he himself committed. While Louisa may find herself in Limbo, her brother should be relegated to the Thieves.

Much has been made of the fact that Dickens himself rarely attended church, although he did begin to attend more seriously after the tragic death of his sister-in-law. However, he thought it important enough to write a book on Jesus' life and teachings for his own children *(The Life of Our Lord)* showing that he valued true religious and moral education. It is merely the prattling of pious hypocrites that he objects to, as we shall see later. He takes the Bible, especially the New Testament, quite seriously—quoting it constantly throughout his novels, and deliberately misquoting it in the mouths of false Christians.

Circle 2: The Lustful—Steerforth, Rosa Dartle, Bradley Headstone

For Dante, Circle 2, the Lustful, moves us into the world of active sin. Up to this point, the sins in the *Inferno* have been largely passive. At the same time, the sins in Circle 2 are still of "incontinence" or weakness, rather than malice. Passionate, adulterous lovers hurt others, but not deliberately. They have no wish to harm other people; they simply cannot help themselves.

Unfortunately, any discussion of sexual love in the works of Charles Dickens proves deeply problematic. Dickens is long past medieval notions of courtly love, with tempestuous lovers like Lancelot and Guinevere throwing their world into turmoil through adulterous passion. The literature of the Middle Ages—from the *lais* of Marie de France to Chaucer's *Canterbury Tales*—is filled with tales of open, often joyous sexuality. Dickens, however, lived in the age of Queen Victoria (on whom he had a youthful crush) where sexuality and unseemly displays of passion were largely unacceptable, in one's personal life or in fiction. Even in France, a more sexually open country, Dickens' contemporary

Gustave Flaubert was brought up on charges for daring to write a novel about adultery, the great *Madame Bovary*, even though his main character is harshly punished in the end. Because of the censorship laws of his time, Flaubert only narrowly escaped prison.

Dickens was surely aware of the problem of censorship. However, he was also a man who kept his own deeper feelings buried from public view, and even to some extent, from his writing. Biographer Peter Ackroyd astutely comments:

> His was a passionate nature kept severely under control, and there was a sense in which he was always too hard and too driven a man to be a sensuous one. In his novels, sexuality remains unconscious, but everywhere apparent; when directly expressed, it tends to be thwarted or blocked off. [3]

Ackroyd suggests that Dickens' early experiences of life in prison and as an observer of London's mean streets, had shown him the ugly and humiliating side of sex:

> …sex in Dickens is almost entirely linked with the idea of confusing class boundaries, for example of bringing down its victims, of consigning them to the same dirt and squalor and disease which his vision of London visits upon the poor." [4]

In her excellent book on Dickens' mistress Nelly Ternan, Claire Tomalin describes Dickens' London in these terms:

> In the 1850's the sights of the London streets were something a nice young woman simply had to shut her mind to, even if she could not always shut her eyes to the drunkenness, violence and prostitution. [5]

While he may have indeed feared the more degrading aspects of sex, Dickens was always sympathetic to the plight of "fallen women."

Dickens own sexual experiences remain shrouded in mystery. As a young man, he became infatuated with a girl named Maria Beadnell, who eventually rejected him for someone with more money. This four year mainly one-sided romance proved an anguishing experience at the time. It is fictionalized in his semi-autobiographical novel *David Cop-*

perfield through the character of David's wife Dora, with whom David is similarly infatuated, but then somewhat disillusioned. The theme is taken up again in *Little Dorrit*, where Arthur Clennam's encounter with his former "grand passion" Flora Finching, now grown old, plain and silly, mirrors Dickens' own disappointing re-encounter with Beadnell in later years. In short, this is the love of youthful idealization and disillusionment—nothing, however, "sinful" about it.

Then, Dickens married. Sadly, the marriage to Catherine Hogarth, though long and fruitful, was not a success. Although they lived together for years and were companionable for many, they grew apart emotionally. He eventually came to feel they had nothing in common, although this evidently did not keep him out of her bedroom (she bore him ten children). He did, however, idolize her younger sister Mary, who lived with them in the early years of their marriage, and had the virtue of dying young and beautiful, while Catherine grew less attractive and more irritable with endless childbirth and child-rearing. According to some biographers, she was always somewhat difficult and suffered from severe post-partum depressions. Of course the truth of any marriage is impossible to know, especially after a century and a half. Catherine Dickens has been portrayed by some as the innocent victim of a selfish husband, by others as a neurotic shrew. Likely neither is true, although living with a driven genius like Dickens could never have been easy, and his rejection of her in later life was obviously cruel.

Meanwhile, Mary would be recreated in countless idealized young women characters, all beautiful, virtuous, kind, and pure. No biographer has ever hinted at anything remotely adulterous about this relationship, although a modern observer might accuse him of a kind of "emotional adultery" in his apparent adoration of the young sister-in-law who literally died in his arms. He actually wore her ring on his finger for the rest of his life and asked to be buried next to her, something he would be denied when other relatives were buried with her.

There is also no evidence that Dickens had affairs during most of his marriage. But in his forties, he met a young actress Ellen (Nelly) Ternan, fell deeply in love with her and eventually separated from his wife, living much of the time with Ternan in various undisclosed locations, sometimes under an assumed name. Since he was conflicted enough to be ashamed of this relationship, the true details remain obscure. He destroyed most of the letters between himself and Ternan before he died, and his closest friends remained loyally mute about the relationship. There is real evidence from existent letters to friends and diaries (and more recent infra-red readings of blacked out lines) that she may have borne him a child who died young. Most biographers like Tomalin, are now convinced this relationship was physically consummated; only a few are not. In any case, it seems to have been a true romantic passion, yet one that was not unmixed with pain and frustration.

So what part does passion play in his novels? Very little, it would appear at first glance. Explicit sexuality, of course, is absent, as in most 19th century novels. However, in addition to his many virtuous romantic attachments ending in happy marriage, Dickens creates characters that are driven to distraction and cruelty by unbridled lust. It is surely no accident that these individuals appear especially in his later novels, at a time when Dickens' himself was obsessed with Ternan. At the end of his life, he creates several characters whose infatuations literally veer into insanity. Many biographers feel that these characters are, in part at least, self-projections of their author.

One of Dickens' earliest examples of lust is Steerforth, David's idolized best friend in *David Copperfield*, written at the mid-point of Dickens' career (1847) and well before his encounter with Ternan. It appears that although he was living in a stable marriage at this time, Dickens could still relate emotionally to romantic obsession. He did become intensely preoccupied for a time with a young woman, Augusta de la Rue, whom he repeatedly treated for neurasthenia through the use of hypnotism, to the extreme annoyance of his wife.

Steerforth's heedless abduction of the innocent "little Em'ly," niece to David's beloved childhood nurse Peggotty, leads to general disaster: her disgrace and separation from her loving family, the agony and death of her virtuous fiance Ham, and Steerforth's own demise. Steerforth's name might indicate someone direct and "in control." In fact, it suggests rather the impetuous selfishness of his character. The wealthy and spoiled Steerforth has always done just what he wanted—damn the consequences. He secretly seduces Emily and runs away with her, although he has no intention of marrying her. Intriguingly, Steerforth is often depicted in association with tempestuous weather, just like the lovers in Dante's second circle of the *Inferno*. He loves the open ocean, abducts Emily in a boat, and eventually dies in a shipwreck, washed up on shore alongside Emily's betrothed Ham, who has bravely attempted to save his life. The final tempest that destroys both men is indeed so fierce it seems to take on supernatural proportions:

> As the receding waves swept back with a hoarse roar, it seemed to scoop out deep caves in the beach, as if its purpose was to undermine the earth. When some white-headed billows thundered on, they dashed themselves to pieces before they reached the land, every fragment of the late whole seemed possessed by the full might of its wrath, rushing to be gathered to the composition of another monster. Undulating hills were changed to valleys, undulating valleys (with a solitary storm bird sometimes skimming through them) were lifted up to hills, masses of water shivered and shook with a booming sound, every shape tumultuously rolled on, and as soon as made, changed its shape and place, and beat another shape and place away, the ideal shore on the horizon, with its towers and buildings, rose and fell, the clouds flew fast and thick, I seemed to see a rending and upheaving of all nature.

This apocalyptic vision of natural disaster might well come straight out of Dante's *Canto III*. Steerforth's demise, drowning as he clings desperately alone to his own pleasure boat, can be seen as a genuine form of *contrapasso*. He has willfully allowed himself to follow his desires, and in the end, caught up in their uncontrollable nature, is destroyed by them.

There is yet another character in this novel, so close to Dickens' heart that he called it his favorite, who represents the "Hell" to which romantic passions can drive an unhappy lover. This is the strange and unique creation Rosa Dartle, Mrs. Steerforth's longtime companion, who has been desperately in love with Steerforth since his youth. Some suggest that at one point he may have seduced her, but this is never made explicit. Her name itself suggests "a rose with thorns," a love connected with pain. Indeed, she is often cruel to Steerforth, who responds in kind. On her lip she bears a scar from when, in a fit of anger, the young Steerforth threw a hammer at her. The scar, we soon learn, goes far deeper than Rosa's skin. Steerforth remarks to David, who has first noticed it, "She has borne that mark ever since, as you see…and she will bear it to her grave, if she ever rests in one, though I can hardly believe she will ever rest anywhere."

Rosa, too, is driven by her unrequited passion for Steerforth, but instead of loving, it makes her cruel—to Steerforth, his mother, little Emily, and even the gentle Mr. Peggotty. After Steerforth runs away with and then abandons Emily, Rosa goes to visit her, hurling her poison at the pathetic, lost young girl:

> "I have come to look at you. What, are you not ashamed of the face that has done so much?" The resolute and unrelenting hatred of her tone, its cold, stern sharpness, and its mastered rage, presented her before me as if I had seen her standing in the light. I saw the flashing black eyes, and the passion—wasted figure, and I saw the scar with its white track, cutting through her lips, quivering and throbbing as she spoke.

Finally, she can no longer contain herself:

> Rosa sprang from her seat, recoiled, and in recoiling struck at her (Emily) with a face of such malignity, so darkened and disfigured by passion that I had almost thrown myself between them.

For perhaps the first time in *David Copperfield* Dickens fully exposes the demonic, destructive aspect of love. Of course, in this novel both the foolish romanticism of youth and the darker passions of unhealthy attachment are counterbalanced by the serene, steadfast love of Agnes Wickfield, whom David treats as a "sister" until the very end of the book, when he realizes that his feelings for her run much deeper. Still, Agnes remains a far less compelling figure than Steerforth, Emily or Rosa. Indeed, she seems to represent the idealized, tranquil love that Dickens aspired to, but probably never achieved in his own life.

As for Dickens personally, matters seem to only get worse after the writing of *David Copperfield*. Far from finding peaceful satisfaction in his adulterous relationship with Nelly Ternan, Dickens was evidently prey to jealousy, guilt, and fear of discovery. His last two novels, *Our Mutual Friend*, and the unfinished *The Mystery of Edwin Drood* portray two of his darkest characters, both succumbing to romantic obsession to the point of violence.

The first is the schoolmaster Bradley Headstone in *Our Mutual Friend*, who immediately becomes infatuated with Lizzie, the lovely young daughter of Thames boatman Gaffer Hexam. This infatuation grows steadily more destructive, as he realizes that Lizzie's affections have turned elsewhere, towards the wealthy and handsome Eugene Wrayburn.

As Ackroyd suggests, passion here is indeed mixed with the "confusion of class boundaries." For Headstone, jealousy of Wrayburn is mingled with a bitter sense of his own social inferiority. He has become a respectable schoolmaster by slowly dragging himself out of a lower social class, while Wrayburn possesses the entitled ease of the upper classes. This peculiar inversion of Dickens' usual sympathies—in general it is the hardworking poor, not the idle rich who earn his affection and admiration—suggests that those critics who perceive a personal identification with Headstone's torment may be on to something. Nor is Wrayburn himself a particularly likeable character. He is somewhat lazy, careless and selfish—a bit of the Steerforth in him; that is, until he actually falls in love with Lizzie, and is nearly murdered because of it.

For Bradley Headstone, his first encounter with Lizzie ignites the flame that will burn ever more intensely throughout the novel, until all morality and sanity have been consumed from his soul. He has just been introduced to her by her brother Charley, his pupil, and immediately is beset with romantic fantasies. He remarks to Charley almost casually,

> "Some man who had worked his way might come to admire—your sister—and might even in time bring himself to think of marrying your sister—and it would a sad drawback and a heavy penalty upon him if, in

overcoming in his mind other inequalities of condition…this inequality and this consideration remained in full force."

Ironically, Headstone is alluding to the social inequality between himself and Lizzie, but his comments could also apply to Eugene Wrayburn, his own social superior. Wrayburn fleetingly appears in this same scene, spurring Headstone to inquire with his first pangs of jealousy, "Then he knows your sister?" For her part, Lizzie, normally a warm and open person, flinches when Headstone first offers her his arm:

> Her hand was just within it, when she drew back. He looked round with a start, as though he had detected something that repelled her, in the momentary touch.

This little scene, apparently so innocent, foreshadows the disaster to come.

From this point, we eventually come to Lizzie's rejection of his marriage offer, and his wildly jealous response:

> His head bent for a moment, as if under a weight, and then he looked up again, moistening his lips, "I was going on with the little I had left to say. I knew all this about Mr. Eugene Wrayburn. All the while you were drawing me to you. I strove against the knowledge, but quite in vain. It made no difference to me. With Mr. Eugene Wrayburn in my mind, I went on. With Mr. Eugene Wrayburn, I spoke to you just now. With Mr. Eugene Wrayburn in my mind, I have been set aside and I have been cast out."

The helpless, obsessive nature of Headstone's feelings is all too clear. His frenzied talk and refusal to accept Lizzie's rejection on its own merits frighten her, as well they should. By the end of the novel he is driven to stalk Wrayburn and Lizzie, masochistically searching out signs of their attachment. Ultimately, he tries to murder Wrayburn, clubbing him over the head and throwing him into the river.

His *contrapasso* will be that Lizzie, who has thus far resisted Wrayburn's advances, finds and saves the drowning man, marrying him at his bedside as he struggles for life. Headstone's true punishment comes when he learns of this marriage:

> For the he saw that through his desperate attempt to separate these two forever, he had been the means of uniting them. That he had dipped his hands in blood to mark himself a miserable fool and tool. That Eugene Wrayburn, for his wife's sake, set him aside and left him to crawl along his blasted course. He thought of Fate, or Providence, or be the directing Power what it might, as having put a fraud upon him—overreached him—and in his impotent mad rage bit, and tore, and had his fit.

In the end, Headstone regrets his crime, but only because it hasn't succeeded. In an attempt to cover it up, he finds himself obliged to dispose of his accomplice Roger (Rogue) Riderhood, sending them both tumbling into the river, locked in each other's arms. Another form of *contrapasso*: he meets the fate he originally designed for Eugene. Will he find himself in the circle of those destined for doomed passion, for murder or for suicide? The reader must decide. However, it is so overwhelmingly clear that his passion for Lizzie is the main force driving Headstone, it is fitting to leave him here among the obsessive lovers.

As for John Jasper, in *The Mystery of Edwin Drood*, his passion for his pupil Rosa (a name Dickens connects with romance in at least three novels: *David Copperfield*, *Bleak House* and *Edwin Drood*) almost certainly leads to cold, premeditated murder of his own nephew Edwin.*** For this, his besetting sin, we will visit him in another, deeper circle of Hell, yet he deserves to be at least mentioned here, because the driving force behind his act is also uncontrolled passion.

Even Pip, the hero of another late novel, *Great Expectations*, is victim to a frustrated romantic obsession with the beautiful, unattainable Estella. However, since Pip's essential moral nature is not destroyed by passion, he can't be placed in Hell at all. Similarly, Sydney Carton, in *A Tale of Two Cities*, written when Ternan was apparently still resist-

---

*** Since this novel was unfinished before Dickens' death, some claim that the identity of the murderer was unknown or even that Drood is still alive. However Dickens told several people that the murderer was Jasper, as we shall see later in the book.

ing a full sexual relationship with Dickens, represents another version of romantic frustration. He too, however, will be "redeemed" by his noble self-sacrifice at the end of the novel. We will encounter both of these characters in our chapter on Purgatory.

Circle 3: The Gluttonous—Mr. Pumblechook, Mr. Wopsle

For Dante, this particular circle of Hell is one of the shortest and least compelling. He seems to include it for theological reasons as a sin condemned by the Church rather than any profound personal concern with the flaw. (Italians, after all, have been known to enjoy a good meal from time to time.) For Dickens as well gluttony appears to be a relatively minor vice, sometimes disgusting, but only truly despicable when paired with more serious vices, like cruelty or indifference. His gluttons generally tend to be humorous rather than malevolent. The truth is, Dickens himself enjoyed many an excellent meal once he had achieved success. He was no ascetic, and in fact, deplored the stance of the Calvinists and Sabbatarians, who opposed natural human pleasures like eating, drinking, dancing or his beloved theatricals. His affectionately drawn Pickwickians (*The Pickwick Papers*) are constantly dining and drinking with good companions as Dickens himself frequently did with his numerous friends and acquaintances.

Like some of his characters, however, Dickens also knew what it was to go hungry while others gorged. Both Wackford Squeers and his son Wackford Jr. in *Nicholas Nickleby* feast on good food, while abetting the starvation of their pathetic charges. Since Squeers Sr. is not merely a glutton, but an abuser, whose violent beatings terrify his victims, we must consider his "besetting sin" to be in the realm of violence and revisit him later.

Two characters who might well belong among the gluttons are Pip's Uncle Pumblechook and Mr. Wopsle in *Great Expectations*. We first encounter them both at the Christmas dinner table of Pip's older sister and her husband Joe, feasting and drinking, all the while lecturing Pip about the evils of gluttony. Pip describes them at the table:

(Pumblechook) "Look at Pork alone. If you want a subject, look at Pork."

"True, sir. Many a moral for the young," returned Mr. Wopsle,—and I knew he was going to lug me in before he said it, "might be deduced from that text."...

"Swine," pursued Mr. Wopsle, in his deepest voice, and pointing his fork at my blushes, as if he were mentioning my Christian name, "swine were the companions of the Prodigal. The gluttony of the Swine is put before us, as an example to the young." (I thought this pretty well in him who had been praising up the pork for being so plump and juicy.) "What is detestable in a pig is more detestable in a boy."

Meanwhile Pip, who is having some difficulty getting a bite to eat himself, writhes in agonies of fear, lest they learn the fact that he has secretly given Pumblechook's pork pie to the convict he has just met on the moors. This is a pivotal moment in the novel, as the convict is Abel Magwitch, who will ultimately become Pip's benefactor as well as a kind of curse on his life. However, for Wopsle and Pumblechook, their total preoccupation is with food.

During a later visit with Pip, Pumblechook again preaches to Pip over breakfast, stuffing himself while Pip gets virtually nothing to eat. Meanwhile he is trying to quiz Pip on math:

> I was hungry, but before I had swallowed a morsel, he began a running sum that lasted all through the breakfast. "Seven?" "And four?"....And so on. And after each figure was disposed of, it was as much as I could do to get a bite or a sup, before the next guess came; while he sat at his ease guessing nothing, and eating bacon and hot roll in (if I may be allowed the expression) a gorging and gourmandizing manner.

Even Wopsle and Pumblechook's gluttony is compounded by other sins; in Wopsle's case, false moralizing, in that of Pumblechook, false friendship. When Pip comes into his secret inheritance, Pumblechook claims to be his bosom friend and "patron"; when he loses it again, he will have nothing more to do with him. Nevertheless, the close association of these characters with overeating makes this circle an appropriate setting for them.

Periodically, we encounter other gluttons in Dickens' novels, as in his pointed reference to Reverend Chadband's "fat smile," but as noted, in general, these are paired with other, far more serious vices. Flora Finching, Arthur Clennam's old flame in *Little Dorrit,* has an over-attachment to both food and alcohol, yet as she is more silly than evil, she can't really be placed in Hell at all, but rather in Purgatory.

In the final analysis, Dickens' approach to gluttony is neither ascetic nor epicurean. It is more like "the middle path" prescribed by the Buddha. As mentioned above, he invariably enjoyed good food and drink himself. But he also saw the damage over-indulgence, especially of alcohol, could cause. In fact, if we included alcoholism in the category of gluttony (as Dante does in *Purgatory*) we would be forced to consider characters like Jenny Wren's destructively alcoholic father in *Our Mutual Friend,* and the alcoholic wife of Stephen Blackpool in *Hard Times,* who create nothing but misery for all around them.

IV

Venturing Deeper into Hell

Circle 4: The Avaricious and the Prodigal—(Ebenezer Scrooge),
Ralph Nickleby, Krook, Nell's grandfather, Harold Skimpole, the
Chuzzlewits

As in Dante's *Inferno*, in Dickens' world "here are to be found far more
people than elsewhere." Avarice, a sin he particularly despised, was epi-
demic in 19th century England, as it is today. Not a single Dickens'
novel fails to include at least one or indeed many examples of this vice.
Although the rich tend to suffer most from this particular malady of the
soul—characters such as Ralph Nickleby, Josiah Bounderby, Fascination Fledgeby and of course, Ebenezer Scrooge—there are also the poor,
like Krook in *Bleak House* or Silas Wegg in *Our Mutual Friend*, whose
greedy obsessions prove disastrous.

Since Scrooge is Dickens' archetypal miser, we should consider him
briefly here, even though he eventually repents and is thus found among
the "saved". Yet his character perfectly embodies the darker aspects of
avarice and the suffering it causes both to the sinner and to those around
him. Throughout his life, Scrooge has done serious harm to those who
loved him and worked for him, like the woman he first loved and his underpaid employee, the humble Bob Cratchit, even though as a true penitent he cannot technically not be relegated to Hell. Noting Dante's distinction between "the avaricious and the prodigal," we see that Scrooge
is clearly among the hoarders of wealth, not the spenders. Nevertheless,

the fact that they find themselves in the same circle indicates their close affinity.

Dickens' Christmas novellas like *A Christmas Carol* were intended both as entertainment and as conscious morality tales. Their lessons are more obvious and simplistic than in his longer novels. However, he is able to plumb his character's souls in some of these works nearly as well as in his longer novels. At the beginning of the book, we see Scrooge as a lonely, angry man who has deliberately cut himself off from his fellow humans:

> Nobody ever stopped him in the street to say, with gladsome looks, "My dear Scrooge, how are you? When will you come to see me?" No beggars implored him to bestow a trifle, no children asked him what it was o'clock, no man or woman ever once in his life inquired the way to such and such place of Scrooge…
>
> But what did Scrooge care! It was the very thing he liked. To edge his way along the crowded paths of life, warning all human sympathy to keep its distance, was what the knowing ones called "nuts" to Scrooge.

He lost true love in his youth because of his obsession with money, mistreats his employee Bob Cratchit, refuses to donate to the poor, and generally leads a mean miserable existence. He even rejects the invitation of his own nephew on Christmas, responding to the nephew's hearty "A Merry Christmas, uncle," with a sour, "Good afternoon!"

Scrooge's isolation from humanity caused by his obsession with accumulating money eventually brings him the painful and frightening visitations from the three Christmas "ghosts." These experiences can, in a sense, be seen as warning descents into the "Hell" that awaits him if he does not change his ways. In many respects the journey Scrooge must take into past, present and future accompanied by Marley's ghost is similar to Dante's guided tour of the *Inferno*. As we all know, in the end Scrooge sees the error of his ways and finds redemption. Scrooge has made his way into so many popular versions of the story and cartoons, down to Disney's humorous "Scrooge McDuck," that it is now sometimes difficult to take him seriously. The same, however, cannot be said for the misers in Dickens' longer, more complex novels.

Ralph Nickleby, Nicholas Nickleby's uncle shares Scrooge's characteristic obsession with money and his lack of real human connection with friend or family. Nickleby is a money-lender whose relationships are primarily based on financial gain. While he grudgingly accepts some little responsibility for his nephew Nicholas, Nicolas's widowed mother and his sister Kate, he does so only at the least possible cost. He places Nicholas in a job working for the evil Wackford Squeers at the school for abandoned children, Dotheboys Hall. When he consigns Nicholas to the tender mercies of Squeers, he leaves Squeers with these words:

> "If any caprice of temper should induce him (Nicholas) to cast aside this golden opportunity before he has brought it to perfection, I consider myself absolved from extending any assistance to his mother and sister."

Kate is put to work at minimum wage as a seamstress in the dressmaking establishment of the bizarre Mantalinis, where she is constantly assailed by the lecherous Mr. Mantalini.

When Nicholas inevitably comes into conflict with the abusive Squeers, Ralph Nickleby sides with Squeers against his nephew, and becomes Nicholas's bitter enemy. He attempts to force Madeline Bray (the girl Nicholas loves) into a marriage with a vicious old man, by hiding the truth of her inheritance and making her father utterly dependent upon himself.

But Ralph Nickleby's worst action is the (partly unintentional) sacrifice of his own son, the pathetic cripple Smike. When Smike was a baby, he was first abandoned by Nickleby, who had married the child's mother for money and refused to make the marriage public. When she eventually left him, Ralph placed the child in the care of a friend named Brooker, who told him that it had died. Smike, however, had not died. He had been entrusted to Squeers, to be starved, beaten and humiliated. Ignorant of the fact that Smike is actually his own son until the very end of the novel, Ralph persecutes him with a vengeance simply because he is a friend of Nicholas, who has dared to defy him. When Smike dies of his life-long abuse, Ralph finally learns the awful truth: he has helped destroy his own child. Brooker ("broker?") the man who helped Ralph to give away his son and was responsible for concealing the true story from him, has his own guilt to bear. When asked by those listening to his final confession, "What reparation can you make?' Brooker responds:

> "None gentlemen, none...This confession can bring nothing upon me but new suffering and punishment; but I make it and will abide by whatever comes. I have been made the instrument of working out this dreadful retribution upon the head of a man, who in the hot pursuit of his bad ends, has persecuted and hunted down his own child to death. It must descend on me too—I know it must fall—my reparation comes too late, and neither in this world nor in the next can I have hope again!"

Here we have the intriguing notion that some remorse can actually come "too late" for redemption. Smike has died unnecessarily, due to his father's coldness and obsession with money which led him to disavow his marriage and his infant child, as well as Brooker's stubborn silence about the truth. Ralph leaves the scene of this revelation "slinking off like a thief" into the darkness and the cold, ironically passing a dismal pauper's burial ground.

In utter chill and desolation, Ralph now resembles Scrooge, as he hurries alone towards his home. He thinks of what might have been, had he actually known that his son was alive. Could he have become a different sort of person? Would he have been able to love? But the thought that torments him most is that his own child died in the presence of Nicholas, Smike's beloved protector and friend, instead of himself, his own father. Imbued with despair, as well as a desire to revenge himself on Nicholas and his friends ("Is there no way to rob them of further triumph, and spurn their mercy and compassion?") he hangs himself from an iron hook on the ceiling of his bedroom. Greed has finally led him to what for a Catholic like Dante would be an even greater sin—suicide. However, it is clear that the driving force for Ralph has indeed been avarice, so it is to this circle that we should finally consign him.

A more minor character, but certainly an embodiment of "hoarding", is the rag and bottle merchant Krook in *Bleak House*. He accumulates everything: money, valuables, old letters, used clothes. We know little about him except that he is greedy, sneaky and a drinker. He conspires with Smallweed, Tulkinghorn and others to get the letters that will prove Lady Dedlock's questionable past, which ultimately destroys her. He is a shady character, whose main claim to fame may actually be his *contrapasso*-like death from "spontaneous combustion," probably a combination of his over-consumption of alcohol, and the old papers and rags that fill his over-crowded home. (Dickens apparently became convinced from various newspaper articles that spontaneous combustion of a human was scientifically possible. Today's scientists would disagree.)

At this point, we might recall Dante's distinction between two types of avarice: the hoarder and the prodigal or spendthrift. For the prodigal, there is a character who at first seems an unlikely candidate for the *Inferno*: Nell's grandfather in *The Old Curiosity Shop*. Depicted throughout the novel as a gentle and affectionate old man, unlike the harsh Ralph Nickleby, it is nonetheless clear that his greedy addiction to gambling, his wasteful spending of all he has and all Nell earns, leads directly to her destruction. Indeed, selfish parents—or in this case, grandparents—are legion in Dickens' novels, from the humorous but irresponsible Mr. Micawber, to the drunken father of the "doll's dressmaker" Jenny Wren in *Our Mutual Friend* and little Dorrit's debt-ridden father in *Little Dorrit*. All these characters are selflessly supported by their loving, long-suffering children. Obviously they express Dickens' deep feelings of resentment towards his own parents, who he felt abandoned him yet whom he supported for most of his life.

Curiously, neither Nell, nor Dickens himself explicitly condemns the old man whose gambling addiction dooms little Nell to wandering and begging, although plenty of characters along their journey do, reproaching him bitterly for his lack of concern for his granddaughter. The original fictional narrator of the story, Master Humphrey, a character Dickens eventually discards after a few chapters, chides the old man for leaving Nell alone in a dangerous place on a dark night. In reflecting on this encounter with the strange old man and child, he muses:

> "His affection for the child might not be inconsistent with villainy of the worst kind; even that very affection was in itself an extraordinary

contradiction, or how could he leave her thus? Disposed as I was to think badly of him, I never doubted that his love for her was real."

Nell clearly adores her grandfather, staunchly defending him against all criticism. However, after one of his gambling binges, for the first time she sees him in a very different light:

> And at the table sat the old man himself, his white face pinched and sharpened by the greediness which made his eyes unnaturally bright, counting the money of which his hands had robbed her.

Indeed, there is at least one scene in the novel where the kindly old man, who has crept furtively into his granddaughter's room to steal her last savings, suddenly appears even to her as a kind of monster:

> She had no fear of the dear old grandfather, in whose love for her this disease of the brain had been engendered; but the man she had seen that night, wrapt in the game of chance, lurking in her room, and counting the money by the glimmering light, seemed like another creature in his shape, a monstrous distortion of his image…

It is curious that Dickens here uses the modern term "disease" to describe the addiction to gambling, seemingly viewing it more as an illness than a sin. Yet the fact remains, it is Nell's own "loving grandfather" even more than her diabolic enemy Quilp, who destroys her. He has forced her to run with him from his creditors, beg on the roads, and urged her to steal even from the kindly people who have taken them in—all to feed his gambling habit. He has stolen the very little she has put aside for their survival. True, he seems to repent towards the end of the novel, after Nell has suffered the first attack of the wasting illness that will ultimately kill her. He suddenly becomes considerate and protective of her, traits that are largely absent through most of the book, but it is far too late. By the time he and Nell reach their final resting spot, a gloomy old church attached to a cemetery, she is clearly doomed.

Will he be punished for his selfishness and greed? In this world, of course, when the precious child for whose sake he claims to be gambling has died of poverty and exposure to the elements. Dickens has him die of grief soon after, and put to rest in a grave next to his granddaughter. Will they be reunited in heaven? Given the grandfather's selfish and destructive behavior, it is doubtful.

Harold Skimpole, the eternal house guest of the generous John Jarndyce in *Bleak House*, is a different type of "prodigal." He uses his fake charm and child-like pose to worm money out of Jarndyce and everyone else, money he stubbornly refuses to earn himself. He covers his greed with protestations of innocence with the ways of the world, actually claiming that he is doing his benefactors a favor by taking their money:

> "Then, for heaven's sake, having Harold Skimpole, a confiding child petitioning you, the world, an agglomeration of practical people of business habits, to let him live and admire the human family, do it somehow or other, like good souls and suffer him to ride his rocking horse!....I almost feel as if YOU ought to be grateful to ME for giving you the opportunity of enjoying the luxury of generosity."

Early in the novel, Skimpole appears annoying, yet relatively harmless. His host John Jarndyce and Jarndyce's ward Esther Summerson treat him with tolerant affection, at least initially. In the course of the novel, however, we discover a darker aspect to Skimpole's character. First, he drives the desperately ill Jo away from the house so as not to be infected by his illness. Then he conspires with the lawyer Vholes to encourage Richard Carstone in his hopeless and destructive lawsuit. Indeed, we might actually drop him into the deeper circle of fraud, except for the fact that Dickens himself treats him with a certain light-hearted tolerance.* He will eventually be cast out of Jarndyce's heavenly home, but nothing worse.

In truth, the sheer number of greedy characters in Dickens novels could fill a book all by itself, not to mention a very crowded circle of Hell. It is impossible to mention them all. However, we can hardly leave the circle of the avaricious without a passing nod at the rapacious Chuzzlewit clan (*Martin Chuzzlewit*). Although Dickens considered the "be-

---

* This repellent character, like Podsnap, has been partially modeled on another of Dickens' friends Leigh Hunt, who unlike Forster, resented the implied caricature.

setting sin" and theme of this novel to be that of selfishness, the Chuzzlewit family, with the possible exception of young Martin himself, is also driven by greed. In the case of the patriarch, old Martin, the form of avarice is hoarding. He holds on to his money for dear life, fearing (correctly) that most of his family is only waiting for him to die so that they can inherit. Similar to Scrooge and Ralph Nickleby, he is so obsessed by this suspicion that he is unable to trust anybody. His brother Anthony has raised his own son Jonas to worship money, ultimately driving him to murder and himself to a form of suicide. Cousin Seth Pecksniff, the arch hypocrite, pretends to love Martin only to get his hands on his cash. Aptly named cousin Chevy Slyme joins with the unscrupulous Montague Tigg to defraud the rest of the family. Indeed, the entire Chuzzlewit family—nieces, nephews, aunts and uncles—all sit around flattering the old man for much of the novel, so eager are they to become his inheritors. In the case of the unhappy Chuzzlewits, money is indeed "the root of all evil," as Pecksniff himself once hypocritically opines. By the end of the novel, they are all suitably chastised: with public humiliation, poverty, imprisonment, or in the case of Tigg, death.

Circle 5: The Wrathful—Roger (Rogue) Riderhood, Hortense, Miss Wade, Edith Dombey

In Dickens' novels, anger is generally combined with other weaknesses such as greed or envy, or as for Rosa Dartle, unfulfilled passion. Anger springs from these emotions and often leads to acts of violence, in some cases, outright murder. Yet there are certain characters driven by an inexplicable, generalized resentment towards the rest of humanity, a resentment that may simmer along silently beneath the surface, or boil over in overt rage. Dante distinguishes between the "repressed" and the "openly wrathful." Some of Dickens' characters, however, move all too easily between the two.

One such character is Roger (Rogue) Riderhood, the boatman in *Our Mutual Friend*. Like Lizzie's father, Gaffer Hexam, Riderhood makes his living by scavenging the remains of shipwrecks. When we first encounter him, he is already expressing his resentment of Hexam, who has just picked up some valuable articles from a dead body he covets for himself:

> "He's (the dead man) had touches enough not to want to make no more, as well as I make him out, Gaffer! Been knocking about with a pretty many tides, aint he pardner? Such is my out of luck ways, you see! He must have passed me when he went up last time, for I was on the look-out below bridge here. I a'most think you're like the wultures, pardner, and scent em out."

His use of the term "pardner" is more bitter than affectionate, and Gaffer responds with his own anger at Riderhood, a man who robs not only the dead which Gaffer considers ethical, but the living. Riderhood is, of course, afflicted with the sin of greed as well as anger, but resentment and jealousy dominate all his relationships.

When he nearly drowns, and his friends and daughter Pleasant (not a bad character, as her name suggests) are grieving over his presumed body, he miraculously comes back to life. However, in contrast to how a man "reborn" might act, he exhibits his customary foul temper:

> "Well Riderhood," says the doctor, "How do you feel?"
> He replies gruffly, "Nothing to boast on." Having, in fact, returned to life in an uncommonly sulky state.
> "I don't mean to preach: but I hope," says the doctor, gravely shaking his head, "that this escape may have a good effect upon you, Riderhood."
> The patient's discontented growl of a reply is not intelligible...

Even when his loving daughter tries to help him into his coat and an upright position, he maintains his defiant, angry attitude. Dickens continues:

> Then, getting on his unsteady legs, leaning heavily upon her, and growling "Hold still can't you? What! You must be a-staggering next, must you?"

Indeed, as he plots against everyone in the novel, from his supposed "partner" Gaffer, to the hero of the novel John Rokesmith (Harmon), to

Bradley Headstone with whom he initially collaborates solely to do harm to Eugene Wrayburn, Riderhood is in a chronic state of anger:

> As the Rogue sat, ever and ever again nodding himself off his balance, his recovery was always attended by an angry stare and growl, as if in the absence of any one else, he had aggressive inclinations towards himself.

In this, Dickens' last completed novel, there is the constant return to the symbolic theme of water; water as a source of regeneration and rebirth for some, like the hero of the novel John Rokesmith, who once nearly drowned, but recovered and is living under an assumed identity, or Wrayburn, who will nearly drown, only to be saved both physically and spiritually by Lizzie Hexam. However, for Riderhood, a near drowning results, not in redemption, but in the continuation of his anger towards all humanity. The fact that he often expresses himself in an animalistic "growl," says it all. His punishment, a form of *contrapasso*, is to be finally truly drowned, clutched in the grip of Bradley Headstone whom he is blackmailing and who has attempted to betray him as well. Believing in the false superstition that once a man "has been drowned he cannot be drowned again," Riderhood feels himself secure from Headstone's rage. In the chapter, entitled "What was caught in the traps that were set," the two men go down, like fish in a net they have both made, tumbling into the water in each other's arms:

> Riderhood went over into the smooth pit backwards, and Bradley Headstone upon him. When the two were found, under the ooze and the scum behind one of the rotting gates, Riderhood's hold had relaxed, probably in falling, and his eyes were staring upward. But he was girdled still with Bradley's iron ring and the rivets of the iron ring held tight.

In addition to Dickens' many wrathful men, the Murdstones, Sikes, Jonas Chuzzlewits, whose anger ultimately erupts into violence, we find a small band of angry females parading through the novels. Such women stand in sharp contrast to Dickens' infinitely sweet-tempered heroines, to whom even mild expressions of resentment or irritability are utterly foreign. One feminist critic attributes his angry women to sexual and social repression, and sees Dickens' portrayal of them as evidence of his own sexist attitudes. "As befits women who all in some way or other challenge social norms and conventions in Dickens' novels and indeed in 19th century novels generally, all are dark, proud, passionate, unhappy and repressed..."[1] This view holds the women to be rebels against an unfair social order, unfairly criticized by Dickens himself for their rebellion. While not without merit, this approach shows the difficulty in judging a 19th century moralist like Dickens by modern Freudian or feminist standards.

True, a few of his enraged women characters, like Rosa Dartle or Miss Havisham in *Great Expectations* are products of romantic or sexual frustration. Yet Dickens also creates strong female characters who manage to live quite contentedly in single, sexless lives. Even heroines like Agnes, Amy Dorritt or Esther Summerson in *Bleak House*, are reconciled to peaceful lives of good works without romance, until of course, they are rewarded with love and marriage at the end of the novels.

So let us pause for a moment to acknowledge a woman who is certainly a joyously fulfilled example of single womanhood (and one of my personal favorites among all Dickens' women), Aunt Betsey Trotwood, David's adoptive mother in *David Copperfield*. Like the embittered Miss Havisham, Aunt Betsey was once disappointed in love, yet she lives quite contentedly in a platonic friendship with a demented, childlike man named Mr. Dick. She is capable of temper tantrums, as when donkeys trample her beautiful lawn ("Donkeys, Donkeys!") or of righteous indignation, when the Murdstones abuse her darling David, and Uriah Heep nearly destroys the lives of everyone she loves. Yet she has one of the biggest and kindest hearts in all of Dickens. She will surely be found in heaven, with all her flaws, and nowhere near the circle of the wrathful. We might acknowledge, in passing, a similar strong single woman, the indomitable Miss Pross in *A Tale of Two Cities*, who will defend her "darling" Lucie Manette to the death. Aunt Betsy and Miss Pross are both outraged by injustice, and as fiercely protective as mother tigers. But theirs is not the sin of "wrath." It is rather the same moral outrage against injustice that so often animates Dickens himself.

The motives for destructive anger in Dickens' women are actually as varied as those of his male characters. Yet in neither gender can Dickens approve of chronic rage; whatever its provocation, he portrays it as immoral and inhuman. For Madame Defarge in *A Tale of Two Cities*, a woman who merrily knits while the bloody heads of aristocrats roll off the guillotine, the cause is social and personal resentment. Her sister was raped and died at the hands of the aristocrat St. Evremonde, and the rest of her family subsequently destroyed by him. Thus she vows revenge on him, his family and his entire class. Since her anger erupts into extreme violence, we will discuss Madame Defarge, one of Dickens' most memorable villains, in that deeper circle.

There are also women like Riderhood, who hold an inexplicable grudge against the world. They simply hate everybody. One such character is Hortense, Lady Dedlock's French maid in *Bleak House* (modeled after a real-life Swiss murderess). She hates Lady Dedlock for replacing her with a younger and more beautiful maid, but even prior to this, she was apparently always angry. In fact, she has been dismissed because she is in lawyer Tulkinghorn's words, "the most implacable and unmanageable of women." She hates Tulkinghorn for not finding her the position she wants, even though he offers her ample payment for her services in his schemes against Lady Dedlock. But her anger at him goes far beyond any actual slights, and seems a more generalized aspect of her personality. When Tulkinghorn offers her money, she erupts in fury:

> "Two sovereigns! I have not change them, I re-fuse them I de-spise them, I throw them from me!" Which she literally does, taking them out of her bosom as she speaks and flinging with such violence on the floor that they jerk up again into the light before they roll away into corners and slowly settle down there after spinning vehemently.

As with Riderhouse, her anger is expressed in a singular manner of speech:

> "I AM rich," she returns, "I am very rich in hate. I hate my Lady, of all my heart. You know that?"
> "Know it? How should I know it?" (Tulkinghorn)

"'Because you have known it perfectly before you prayed me to give you that information. Because you have known perfectly that I was en-r-r-r-r-raged!" It appears impossible for mademoiselle to roll the letter "r" sufficiently in this word, notwithstanding that she assists her energetic delivery by clenching both her hands and setting all her teeth.

Eventually this rage spills over into violence, when she shoots Tulkinghorn through the heart. This, of course, would be her "besetting sin," as outright violence is worse than anger in anyone's universe. Yet as her dominant emotional state throughout the novel is rage, it seems appropriate to focus here on this aspect of her character. Her hatred for all explodes in her last scene, when she is arrested by the mild-mannered police detective Bucket, who has finally unraveled the mystery of Tulkinghorn's murder. Although Bucket advises her that silence is the wiser course, she spits out her anger, first at Bucket, then at both Lord and Lady Dedlock:

Mademoiselle Hortense eyes him with a scowl upon her tight face, which gradually changes into a smile of scorn. "You are very mysterieuse (to Bucket). Are you drunk?"

Her rage against Bucket intensifies, although he continues to speak to her quite calmly and reasonably:

"Ah my God, you are a great idiot," cries Mademoiselle with a toss of her head and a laugh. "Leave me to pass downstairs, great pig." With a stamp of her foot and a menace.

And finally:

Mademoiselle, with that tigerish expression of the mouth and her black eyes darting fire upon him, sits upright with her hands clenched and her feet too, one might suppose—muttering, "O you Bucket, you are a Devil."

She even vents her fury on poor Sir Leicester Dedlock who, so far as we know, has never actually wronged her:

"He is a pure abused!" cries Mademoiselle. "I spit upon his house, upon his name, upon his imbecility!" All of which she makes the carpet represent.

As for Lady Dedlock, whom she has successfully helped destroy, she still feels nothing but pure hatred.

"You'd bite her, I suspect," says Mr. Bucket.
"I would," making her eyes very large. "I would love to tear her limb from limb."

While Hortense's rage is virtually a personality disorder, it does derive, at least in part, from a sense of class resentment. Although he seems to heartily dislike his own creation, Dickens, who suffered his own periodic sense of social inferiority, taps into her emotions rather easily.

In the mysterious Miss Wade who moves in and out of *Little Dorrit* while never central to its plot, the anger is less overtly violent than that of Hortense, yet she expresses a similar class resentment. Intriguingly, although she is a relatively minor character, Miss Wade is given her own chapter, written in the first person from her point of view, "The History of a Self-Tormentor." Some see her as a rare example of homosexuality in Dickens, because of her peculiarly symbiotic relationship with the servant girl Tattycoram. However there is no explicit evidence of this in the novel. In using the term "self-tormentor" to describe her, Dickens suggests that her rage is mainly self-directed.

In this personal history, Miss Wade speaks of an early attachment to a female friend unfairly broken up by the girl's mother because of their social differences. After this, she describes several disappointed romantic attachments with men, all broken, according to her, because she was merely a governess. One of these is with Henry Gowan, a rich, careless young man, who plays with her feelings and may have seduced her, then drops her for the spoiled and beautiful Pet Meagles. When Miss Wade steals away the servant girl Harriet (or Tattycoram as she is condescendingly called by the Meagles family) from the Meagles, it seems that she empathizes with Tattycoram's endurance of the family's insufferable paternalism. But then she herself abuses Tattycoram. They are described by

Dickens as "two natures, constantly tearing each other to pieces." Here we see how a life of anger creates nothing but misery for all concerned. Indeed Tattycoram exhibits her own anger from the first moment she encounters Miss Wade, and indicates the source of her fear:

> "I am afraid of you."
>
> "Afraid of me?"
>
> "Yes. You seem to come to me like my own anger, my own malice, my own—whatever it is—I don't know what it is. But I am ill-used, ill-used, ill-used!"...
>
> The visitor (Miss Wade) stood looking at her with a strange attentive smile. It was wonderful to see the fury of the contest in the girl, and the bodily struggle she made as if she were rent by the Demons of old.

These two women bring out the worst in each other, each stoking the other's resentments. They create a kind of mutual Inferno, recalling Sartre's famous description of Hell in his play *"Huis Clos,"* ("No Exit") *"l'enfer, c'est les autres."* (Hell is other people.)

Just as he understands the pernicious effects of society on his characters, Dickens often intuits how evil personal influences can bring out the worst in a person, while the good can bring out the best. In short, for him morality is not a strictly individual matter. Throughout the novels, we encounter "pairings" of characters: Silas Wegg with Mr. Venus, Uriah Heep with Mr. Micawber, Riderhouse with Headstone, Miss Miggs with Mrs. Varden, Miss Havisham with Estella, who reinforce each other's worst tendencies. By the same token, the influence of "angels" like Nell, little Dorrit, Agnes and others, brings out the good in all they meet.

As for Dickens' "sullen" women, those whose anger is mainly repressed, perhaps his finest portrayal is Edith Skewton (Granger) Dombey, the unhappy second wife of businessman Paul Dombey in *Dombey and Son*. As seen through most of the novel, Dombey is incapable of real affection; his only important tie is to the son who was to become his heir and partner, yet who tragically dies young. He totally ignores his loving and devoted daughter Florence. After his wife dies, he meets Edith Skewton Granger, a beautiful widow whose mother is bent on selling her to the highest bidder, and is immediately determined to make her his wife.

Edith is frequently described as "cold," like Dombey himself, but her coldness is actually a form of suppressed anger. When about to be introduced to Dombey by her scheming, flirtatious mother Mrs. Skewton, ironically named "Cleopatra," she is described thus:

> Edith, so beautiful and stately, but so cold and repelling. Who, slightly acknowledging the presence of Major Bagstock (Dombey's friend), and directing a keen glance at her mother, drew back the curtain from a window, and sat down there looking out.

When Cleopatra tries to engage her in false social chatter, Edith rebukes her:

> "It is certainly not worthwhile, Mama," said Edith, looking round "to observe these forms of speech. We are quite alone. We know each other."
>
> The quiet scorn that sat upon her handsome face—a scorn that evidently alighted on herself, no less than them—was so intense and deep, that her mother's simper, for the instant, though of a hardy constitution, drooped before it.

Edith is fully aware of her mother's schemes to snag her a rich husband, and has nothing but contempt, both for her mother and herself. She will marry Dombey, miserably, because he is incapable of any real tenderness or respect for her feelings. From the first, she evidently despises the marriage. When James Carker, Dombey's duplicitous assistant, gives her some flowers after the wedding ceremony, "there is something in the momentary action of her hand, as if she would crush the flowers it holds and fling them, with contempt, upon the ground." But she controls the angry impulse, and instead puts her arm through her new husband's in submission to her fate. She will try to be a good wife to Dombey although she doesn't love him, but her efforts are doomed by Dombey's own character flaws.

The only authentic feeling she has—and it is profound—is for Dombey's neglected young daughter Florence, for whom she comes to feel a genuine maternal affection. Florence even calls her "mother." Yet

Dombey's rejection of Florence and treatment of herself as a prized possession only makes her hate him the more.

Meanwhile, the duplicitous Carker, whom we will visit later in a deeper circle, secretly attempts to seduce her. Eventually, she will leave Dombey and run away with Carker, not out of love, but to revenge herself on both men who have conspired to break her ties with the one person she actually cares for, Florence Dombey.

Finally, when she confronts Carker with the truth of her feelings, her "sullen" and repressed anger erupts into overt rage. She stands before him, queen-like, and speaks out from the depths of her soul:

> "I am a woman," she said, confronting him steadfastly, who from her very childhood has been shamed and steeled. "I have been offered and rejected, put up and appraised, until my very soul has sickened. I have not had an accomplishment or grace that might have been a resource to me, but it has been paraded and vended to enhance my value, as if the common crier had called it through the streets."

In this passage Dickens, who is sometimes taken to task for sexism, portrays in powerfully sympathetic terms the suffering caused by the treatment of woman as commodity, to be sold like a slave in the marriage market. Florence Dombey's *"cri de coeur"* can almost be seen as the fictional equivalent of Frederick Engel's *The Origins of the Family, Private Property and the State* in its passionate denunciation of "bourgeois marriage" based on money rather than love.

At first Carker is dazzled by her indignant speech, ignorant of the fact that her anger targets him as much as Dombey. But she soon clears up that little misconception:

> "And thus—forced by the two (Dombey and Carker) from every point of rest I had—forced by the two to yield up the last retreat of love and gentleness within me, or to be a new misfortune on its innocent object—driven from each to each, and beset by one when I escaped the other—my anger rose almost to distraction against both. I do not know against which it rose higher—the master or the man!"

After running away with Carker to France, she abandons him as well, threatening to stab him if makes any attempt to touch her. Fortunately, she is not obliged to kill him; he will meet his fate by accident.

At the very end of the novel, Edith appears one last time to visit Florence, who is now happily married. Is Edith redeemed? Probably not, since she says she has no regret for what she has done, and in fact, would do it again. Her punishment will be to live out the rest of her life in a lonely self-exile.

There is another, more minor character in the same novel, Alice Marwood, a reformed prostitute whose situation and sullen anger directly parallel Edith's. Alice Marwood's mother is a working class equivalent of Cleopatra Skewton. She also manipulates her daughter's love life for monetary gain. Alice states it plainly: "She was covetous, and poor, and sought to make a sort of property of me." One link between the two women is James Carker himself; he was the man who once seduced and abandoned Alice. When a desperate Dombey is seeking out his absconded wife and Carker, Alice drops a hint as to where they have gone. However, she instantly regrets her action, fearing that it will result in violence against Carker. She tries to warn Carker that Dombey is pursuing him. In this, more selfless act, there may actually be some form of redemption for Alice Marwood. Is she meant as a parallel for Edith, or a softer version of the same sin? It is not entirely clear.

It might initially seem unfair that more women than men can be found in this circle. Certainly this is not because Dickens' women as a group are any angrier than his men. Rather, Dickens' wrathful men, like Bill Sikes, Quilp or Jonas Chuzzlewit, are socially freer to act out their rage. Thus they are often doomed to inhabit deeper parts of Dickens' Inferno, among the Violent or even the Traitors.

V

Circles of Malice

Circle 6: the Heretics—Reverend Stiggins, Reverend Chadband, Revered Honeythunder, the Murdstones, Mrs. Clennam

The term "heresy," a theological error so grave that in Dante's era heretics might be tortured or burned at the stake, would obviously have a very different connotation for a 19th century liberal Protestant like Dickens. One definition of heresy, "denial of a revealed truth by a baptized member of the Roman Catholic Church" (Merriam-Webster) would brand all Protestants including Dickens himself as "heretics." However, if we understand the word in its broader sense, the abuse or misuse of true Christian teachings, it isn't difficult to find "heretics" in Dickens' world. For Dickens, these are often hypocritical men of the cloth who use religion as a club to attack the helpless, utterly lacking the basic spirit of love for others taught by Christ himself. Such clerics: Stiggins (*The Pickwick Papers*), Chadband (*Bleak House*), Honeythunder (*The Mystery of Edwin Drood*) either practice the very sins they condemn, or terrify their flock with thoughts of hellfire rather than inspiring them with God's love and mercy. They seem to have totally ignored Christ's own admonition to "judge not that ye be not judged."

Then there are non-clerical fanatics like the Murdstones in *David Copperfield*, Miss Miggs in *Barnaby Rudge*, and Mrs. Clennam in *Little Dorrit*, who preach piety to hide their basic hard-heartedness and lack of true Christian charity. Let us consider a few choice examples of these various types of "heretic."

An early version of the hypocritical cleric is the red-nosed Reverend Stiggins, friend to Sam Weller's stepmother in *The Pickwick Papers*. A prodigious drinker and eater, Stiggins finds ways to use his clerical position as "the shepherd" (Dickens' ironic title for him) to pry money out of devout and gullible women, all the while accusing the rest of the world of sinful behavior, especially Sam's good-natured father. Like the devout Miss Miggs in *Barnaby Rudge*, he persistently stirs up trouble between husband and wife. He loves to attack others as "sinful," while reserving various choice vices for himself.

His brother of the cloth, Reverend Chadband in *Bleak House* is even more repellent. From the moment we first encounter him, he literally oozes self-importance and falsity from every pore:

> "Peace, my friends," says Chadband, rising and wiping the oily exudations from his reverend visage. "Peace be with us! My friends, why with us? Because," with his fat smile, "it cannot be against us, because it must be for us; because it is not hardening because it is softening; because it does not make war like the hawk, but comes home to us like the dove. Therefore, my friends, peace be with us! My human boy, come forward!"
>
> Stretching forth his flabby paw, Mr. Chadband lays the same on Jo's arm and considers where to station him. Jo, very doubtful of his reverend friend's intentions and not at all clear but that something practical and painful is going to be done to him, mutters, "You let me alone. I never said nothink to you. You let me alone."

Jo, as simple as he is, instinctively senses the unsavory intentions of Chadband and recoils from his touch, just as Lizzie Hexam recoils from the touch of Headstone. In fact, Chadband is in league with the lawyer Snagsby and others who are trying to worm information out of him pertaining to his knowledge of Lady Dedlock's secret past and "love child" Esther Summerson. Chadband responds quickly to Jo:

> "No, my young friend," says Chadband smoothly, "I will not let you alone. And why? Because I am a harvest-labourer, because I am a toiler and a moiler, because you are delivered over unto me and are become as a precious instrument in my hands."

Chadband employs high-flown Biblical rhetoric to manipulate the unsuspecting boy and impress those around him. We will later see that when he has no more used for Jo, he will cast him out into the streets, ordering him like all the others "to move on."

He actually blames poor Jo for his lack of religious education:

> "We have here among us, my friends," says Chadband, "a Gentile and a heathen, a dweller in the tents of Tom-all-Alone's and a mover-on upon the surface of the earth. We have here among us, my friends," and Mr. Chadband, untwisting the point with his dirty thumb-nail, bestows an oily smile on Mr. Snagsby, signifying that he will throw him an argumentative back-fall presently if he be not already down, "a brother and a boy. Devoid of parents, devoid of relations, devoid of flocks and herds, devoid of gold and silver and of precious stones. Now, my friends, why do I say he is devoid of these possessions? Why? Why is he?" Mr. Chadband states the question as if he were propounding an entirely new riddle of much ingenuity and merit to Mr. Snagsby and entreating him not to give it up.

In addition to a marked lack of Christian compassion, Reverend Chadband has a secondary vice, gluttony. When he visits his friends' homes he immediately sets to work at the table. Dickens takes great delight in an ironic twist on the Biblical term "vessel," as he frequently does in disposing of religious hypocrites:

> Guster, much impressed by regarding herself for the time as the handmaid of Chadband, whom she knows to be endowed with the gift of holding forth for four hours at a stretch, prepares the little drawing-room for tea. All the furniture is shaken and dusted, the portraits of Mr. and Mrs. Snagsby are touched up with a wet cloth, the best tea-service is set forth, and there is excellent provision made of dainty new bread, crusty twists, cool fresh butter, thin slices of ham, tongue, and German sausage, and delicate little rows of anchovies nestling in parsley, not to mention new-laid eggs, to be brought up warm in a napkin, and hot buttered toast. For Chadband is rather a consuming vessel—the persecutors say a gorging vessel—and can wield such weapons of the flesh as a knife and fork remarkably well.

Yet another hypocritical cleric is the Rev. Honeythunder in *The Mystery of Edwin Drood*. We first encounter him through his letter to Minor Canon Crisparkle in which he is already "denouncing a public miscreant...," in this case the orphaned immigrant brother and sister Neville and Helena Landless who have just arrived from Ceylon "on the subject of their defective education, and they (should) give in to the plan proposed; as I should have taken good care they did, whether they liked it or not." Honeythunder calls these young adults "inmates," which says a lot about the kind of "Philanthropy" he is proposing for them. This self-styled "Philanthropist" with his loud voice and bullying manner actually has a scheme for "making a raid on all the unemployed persons in the United Kingdom, laying them every one by the heels in jail, and forcing them, on pain of prompt extermination, to become philanthropists."* As the novel evolves, Honeythunder takes a decidedly un-Christian stand against the falsely accused Neville Landless. His philanthropy, according to Dickens, was "of the gunpowderous sort that the difference between it and animosity was hard to determine." Dickens explicitly satirizes Honeythunder's brand of religion, showing it to be the direct opposite in all respects from Christ's in The Sermon on the Mount, which tells us to "love your neighbor as yourself," and "pray in secret":

> You were to love your brother as yourself, but after an indefinite interval of maligning him (very much as if you hated him) and calling him all manner of names. Above all, you were to do nothing in private, or on your own account. You were to go down into the offices of the Haven of Philanthropy and put your name down as a Member and a Professing Philanthropist. Then you were to pay up your subscription, get your card of membership and your riband and medal, and were evermore to live upon a platform, and evermore say what Mr. Honeythunder said...

---

* An early provision of Massachusetts Welfare Reform "charitably" required single mothers on welfare to abandon their own children to sub-standard child care, so they might have the privilege of doing unpaid "community service." And what would Dickens make of "Christian" candidate Newt Gingrich's recent proposal to take poor children out of school and force them into low paid janitorial jobs, "for their own good"?

As his name suggests, Honeythunder is a caricature who has been wrongly taken by some to symbolize Dickens' hatred of all clericals. However, from the beginning of the novel, he is pointedly contrasted to Minor Canon Crisparkle, who in keeping with his luminous name is neither loudmouth nor bully, but on the contrary, a soft-spoken and compassionate human being. He comes to the aid of the falsely accused Neville Landless, as well as the orphan Rosa Bud when she is threatened by John Jasper; in short, Crisparkle is Dickens' version of a true Christian:

> Mr. Crisparkle, Minor Canon, early riser, musical, classical, cheerful, kind, good-natured, social, contented, and boy-like...

Crisparkle gradually helps Neville Landless subdue his fiery temper through patience and consideration. Eventually he will collaborate with kindred spirits like Rosa's kindly guardian Mr. Grewgious and the mysterious Dick Datchery, to save Rosa from the clutches of the obsessed John Jasper. We can only speculate about what eventually happens to Honeythunder, since the novel is only half complete.

As for non-clerical "heretics," few can compare with Mr. Murdstone, David Copperfield's cruel step-father and his equally "stony"-hearted sister. From the moment they appear in David's household, they work to break the spirits of his young and weak-minded mother, and attempt to break him as well. After her death, their behavior only grows worse. Eventually, they will pack David off to work in a warehouse, just as Dickens' own parents sent him to the blacking factory at an early age. In a sense, the Murdstones may represent for Dickens the darker side of his own parents, while the feckless but good-hearted Mr. Micawber, who like John Dickens winds up in debtor's prison, embodies their more lovable traits. Even as the Murdstones mentally and physically abuse David, they incessantly preach Christian morality. When David's mother marries Murdstone, the Phiz illustration** of his home significantly depicts

---

**   Walder notes that original illustrations of Dickens' novels, especially those by Phiz (Hablot Brown) often showed a home with a painting on the wall from the Bible, a scene paralleling the action in the novel itself. Since Dickens himself approved these drawings, we may infer that he also approved their symbolic significance.

a painting on the wall of Abraham's sacrifice of Isaac. Another famous illustration takes place in a gloomy church. Dickens' portrayal of the Murdstones in church is a denunciation of the crueler aspects of Calvinism:

> The gloomy taint that was in the Murdstone blood darkened the Murdstone religion, which was austere and wrathful...Again, the dreaded Sunday comes round, and I file into an old pew first, like a guarded captive brought to a condemned service. Again, Miss Murdstone, in a black velvet gown that looks as if it had been made out of a pall, follows close upon me; then my mother; then her husband....Again, I listen to Miss Murdstone mumbling the responses, and emphasizing all the cruel words with dread relish. Again, I see her dark eyes roll round the church when she says "miserable sinners," as if she were calling the whole congregation names...Again I wonder with sudden fear whether our good old clergyman can be wrong, and Mr. and Miss Murdstone be right, and all the angels in heaven can be destroying angels.

Here the Murdstones' religiosity is contrasted with the true religion of the "good old clergyman." Once again, Dickens isn't attacking all clergymen, only those who pervert the true spirit of Christianity. Without stretching the point, one might actually associate the Murdstones not merely with Calvinism, which Dickens detested, but with the medieval "heresy" of Manicheanism, which held good and evil to be locked in an equal combat, always with the emphasis on "evil." In a late introduction to *Oliver Twist,* Dickens states emphatically his own conviction that "good is always more powerful than evil."

We can also see that the Murdstones' sin has brought us down into a circle of "malice," just as in Dante. Their maltreatment of David is cold and deliberate. David sums it up thus:

> "I was not actively ill-used. I was not beaten or starved (although he is in earlier parts of the novel), but the wrong that was done to me was done in a systematic passionless manner. Day after day, week after week, month after month I was coldly neglected..."

Finally, there is an allusion to Murdstone as a man who sets himself up as a "false idol." The wife of the kindly Dr. Chillip who attends the Copperfield family in David's youth, makes the following perceptive comment about him:

> "Mr. Murdstone sets up an image of himself and calls it Divine Nature."

A similar example of the Bible-toting individual who seems to worship herself as a "false idol" is Mrs. Clennam in *Little Dorrit*. She is incapable of showing affection even to her son Arthur, for reasons that become clearer as the novel's mystery unfolds. From the first, she is described by Dickens as "cold."

Arthur has just come to see his mother after a twenty year absence, seeking the clue to a mystery about his childhood and wanting to help settle his dead father's estate. His mother receives him in the same indifferent manner with which she treated him as a child:

> She gave him one glassy kiss, and four stiff fingers muffled in worsted.

She is even worse than before and has become a complete shut-in, nearly oblivious to the world around her:

> "Does it snow?"
> "Snow, mother, and we only in September?"
> "All seasons are alike to me," she returned with a grim kind of luxuriousness. "I know nothing of summer and winter, shut up here. The Lord has been pleased to put me beyond all that."

Mrs. Clennam represents a dehumanized version of Christianity; she is perpetually poring over her Bible, but practices none of the charity embodied in it. Arthur's dead father has left him a gold watch, with the words "Never Forget" inscribed upon it. Arthur suspects that perhaps the family has deeply wronged some innocent party in the settlement of the family estate, and of course he is right. For those readers who will enjoy unraveling this secret, it is not necessary to reveal the plot. Although Mrs. Clennam comes to repent her part in a deception that has harmed, among others, little Dorrit herself, at the end of the book she continues to rationalize it as part of a fight against "evil." Her theological debate with little Dorrit at the end of the novel lays out two sharply different versions of Christianity:

> "I have done," said Mrs. Clennam, "what it was given me to do. I have set myself against evil; not against good. I have been an instrument of severity against sin. Have not mere sinners like myself been commissioned to lay it low in all time?"
>
> "In all time?" repeated little Dorrit.
>
> "Even if my own wrong had prevailed with me, and my own vengeance had moved me, could I have found no justification? None in the old days when the innocent perished with the guilty, a thousand to one? When the wrath of the hater of the unrighteous was not slaked even in blood, and yet found favor?"
>
> "O, Mrs. Clennam," said little Dorrit. "Angry feelings and unforgiving deeds are no comfort and no guide to you and me. My life has been passed in this poor prison (the Marshalsea prison), and my teaching has been very defective, but let me implore you to remember later and better days. Be guided only by the healer of the sick, the raiser of the dead, the friend of all who were afflicted and forlorn, the patient Master who shed tears of compassion for our infirmities. We cannot but be right if we put all the rest away, and do everything in remembrance of Him. There is no vengeance and no infliction of suffering in His life, I am sure."

Little Dorrit, standing "in the softened light of the window," is juxtaposed against "the black figure in the shade," Mrs. Clennam. Her simple theology invokes the teachings of Jesus in the Sermon on the Mount against the bloody and wrathful punishments of sinners invoked by Mrs. Clennam. "The later and better days," little Dorrit refers to, are apparently the days after Jesus arrived, with his philosophy of "turn the other cheek," explicitly opposed in the gospels to the old "an eye for an eye."

For Dickens, Mrs. Clennam is guilty of denying the true teachings of Jesus. She will suffer the literal collapse of "The House of Clennam" built on false pride and false religion. Her final punishment or *contrapasso* will be actual physical paralysis after falling in a stroke next to the rubble of her home. Dickens pronounces her final sentence: "She lived and died a statue," yet another oblique allusion to false idols.

In brief, Dickens revered true religion, but detested religious hypocrites, a point made explicit in his late preface to *The Pickwick Papers*:

> Lest there be any well-intentioned persons who do not perceive the difference...between religion and the cant of religion, piety and the pretence of piety, a humble reverence for the great truths of the Scripture and the audacious and offensive obtrusion of its letter and not its spirit in the commonest dissensions and meanest affairs of life, to the extraordinary confusion of ignorant minds, let them understand that it is always the latter, and never the former, which is satirized here.

Today's politicians who preach hatred in the name of religion might perhaps take heed.

Circle 7: the Violent

For Dante, this circle is divided into three parts: the violent against others, the violent against self, and the violent against God. For Dickens, there is no character that could actually be deemed "violent against God." Even Dante resorts to a mythological character Capaneus who defied the Greek gods, to find an example for this sin (strange, perhaps, since those who killed Christ were in Christian terms certainly "violent against God"), so we will only consider the first two categories of this sin and leave out the last. This has the added benefit of omitting Dante's "sodomites" who in any event, never appear in Dickens' novels.

The Violent against Others—Mr. Bumble, Wackford Squeers, Bill Sikes, Barnaby Rudge Sr., Rigaud-Blandois, Mme. Defarge

Violence against others can take many forms, from severe neglect and beatings to outright murder, both tragically prevalent in Dickens' novels as they were in his society. The term "abuse" was obviously not in common usage either in Dante or Dickens' era, nor was the psychological concept as we understand it today. Victorian society approved child and wife beating as both legal and moral. Yet at least one physician has called

Dickens' *Oliver Twist* a "textbook study of abuse" in all its forms—mental and physical, institutional and individual. Speaking of *Oliver Twist* "Dr. Brennan says that the recognized consequences of abuse, including absconding passivity, depression, poor self-image and vulnerability to anyone who shows them what appears to be love, are very well illustrated by the text." (*British Medical Journal,* Nov. 20, 2001.)[1] Dickens instinctively grasped how the abuse of power, the strong against the weak, worked psychologically, and he invariably condemned it. In a late introduction to *Oliver Twist*, he argues that abusers like Bill Sikes and his girlfriend Nancy do exist in the real world, while demonstrating how they and their victims think. Like so many abused women, Nancy refuses to leave Bill, believing that their "love" is stronger than his abuse, that she belongs with him and may save him yet:

> It has been observed of Nancy that her devotion to the brutal housebreaker does not seem natural. And it has been objected to Sikes in the same breath—with the same inconsistency, as I venture to think—that he is surely overdrawn, because in him there are none of the redeeming traits which are objected to as unnatural in his mistress. Of this latter objection, I would merely remark, that I fear that there are in the world some insensible and callous natures that do become utterly and incurably bad...

As for Nancy, Dickens remarks,

> IT IS TRUE. Every man who has ever watched these melancholy shades (abused women), must know it to be so. From the first introduction of the poor wretch, to her laying her blood-stained head upon the robber's breast, there is not a word exaggerated or overwrought. It is emphatically God's truth, for it is the truth He leaves in such depraved and miserable breasts; the hope yet lingering there; the last fair drop of water at the bottom of the weed-choked well.

In this same introduction, Dickens rebuts critics who doubt the existence of the real prototype for the depraved area of London where Fagin resides, Jacob's Island. This long passage expresses all of Dickens: the moralist (yes, Virginia, there are evil people), the psychologist (Nancy still seeks a "drop" of affection from her abuser and murderer) and the social realist (the criminal world is sordid and wretched, not romantic as portrayed in melodramas). In all of these, he is appealing in capital letters to "THE TRUTH" against those critics of his work who brand him as too dark and negative.

First, let us look at the merciless beatings meted out to Oliver and other workhouse children, simply for the crime of asking for "more." It is worth mentioning that at least one of these abusers is Mr. Bumble, a beadle and therefore a minor officer of the Church. Dickens describes Oliver's punishment for the crime of begging for food, with bitter irony:

> Let it not be supposed by the enemies of 'the system' that during the period of his solitary incarceration, Oliver was denied the benefit of exercise, the pleasure of society, or the advantage of religious consolation. As for exercise, it was nice cold weather, and he was allowed to perform his ablutions every morning under the pump, in a stone yard, in the presence of Mr. Bumble. Who prevented his catching cold, and caused a tingling sensation to pervade his frame, by repeated applications of the cane. As for society, he was carried every other day into the hall where the boys dined, and there sociably flogged as a public warning and example.

It's made clear that this institutional abuse of children was perfectly acceptable at the time. Bumble considers he is merely doing his duty. For Dickens, however, it is clearly a form of violence to the bodies and minds of his helpless charges. Bumble's fitting punishment is to marry a strong-willed woman, Mrs. Corney, who will eventually humiliate him in front of the very workhouse inmates he has beaten—to their utter delight. Once married to the intrepid Mrs. Corney, Mr. Bumble dares to declare himself master of the workhouse and demand total submission from his new wife. She does not respond well at all:

> Mrs. Corney that was had tried the tears, because they were less troublesome than an actual assault, but she was quite prepared to make trial of the latter mode of proceeding...The first proof he experienced of the fact, was conveyed in a hollow sound, immediately succeeded by the sudden flying off of his hat to the opposite end of the room...the expert

lady, clasping him tightly around the throat with one hand, inflicted a shower of blows (dealt with singular vigour and dexterity) upon it with the other. This done, she created a little variety by scratching his face and tearing his hair...

Both Mr. and Mrs. Bumble (the former Mrs. Corney) will be punished by ending up as workhouse inmates themselves. Mr. Bumble loses his "porochial" position as beadle, and she loses hers as head of the workhouse because of their conspiracy to conceal Oliver's mother's belongings. They sink into abject poverty. Once again, we see that those who have treated others badly will get their certain come-uppance in this world, regardless of what might occur in the next.

Still, Bumble is not the worst of Dickens' child abusers. Wackford Squeers, the headmaster of Dotheboys Hall ("Do-the-boys-Inn"?),*** in *Nicholas Nickleby* richly deserves that title. At the hands of Squeers, the beating and starving of helpless children become even more vicious and sadistic. Many children literally die under his tender care. One youth, ironically misnamed Bolder, is beaten simply for the "crime" of having warts on his hand:

> As Squeers spoke, he caught up the boy's hand by the cuff of his jacket and surveyed it with an edifying aspect of horror and disgust. "What's do you call this sir?" demanded the schoolmaster, administering a cut with the cane to expedite the reply.
>
> "I can't help it indeed sir," rejoined the boy, crying. "It's the dirty work I think sir—at least I don't know, sir, but it's not my fault."
>
> "Bolder," said Squeers, tucking up his wristbands and moistening the palm of his right hand to get a god grip of the cane, "you're an incorrigible young scoundrel, and as the last thrashing did you no good, we must see what another will do towards beating it out of you."
>
> With this, and wholly disregarding a piteous cry for mercy, Mr. Squeers fell upon the boy and caned him soundly: not leaving off indeed, until his arm was tired out.

***   Dotheboy's Hall was an example of the real Yorkshire Schools that existed in Dickens' time. Eventually, they were exposed as hell-holes and closed down.

Squeers will eventually be punished by the law for manipulation of a family will, jailed and "transported" for his crime (note: he is not legally accountable for the merciless beatings). His wife, son and daughter, who have all participated in the beatings, will be themselves beaten by the angry students of Dotheby's when they hear of Squeer's fate, but then are calmed down and told by Nicholas' friend, the kindly John Browdie, "not to beat the women." Dotheboys will be closed and its little inmates freed, helped by John and other good-hearted souls.

Then there is the most serious form of "violence against others," cold-blooded murder. Murderers appear in virtually all Dickens' novels: Bill Sikes in *Oliver Twist*, who kills the only person who truly loves him, his mistress Nancy; Barnaby Rudge Sr. in the novel *Barnaby Rudge*, who has killed his patron and protector and escaped punishment by casting the blame on another; Jonas Chuzzlewit in *Martin Chuzzlewit*, who attempts to murder his own father and then murders his co-conspirator Montague Tigg, the wife-killer Rigaud in *Little Dorrit*, Hortense in *Bleak House*, Orlick in *Great Expectations*, Madame Defarge, in *A Tale of Two Cities*, Bradley Headstone in *Our Mutual Friend*, and finally John Jasper in *The Mystery of Edwin Drood*. Their motives vary from greed to jealousy to revenge, but in nearly all of the cases (Bill Sikes perhaps an exception) their murders are planned and premeditated. In the circle of the violent, we are now clearly in the territory of "malice."

Three of these characters, Bill Sikes, Jonas Chuzzlewit and Barnaby Rudge, are especially intriguing, because we experience their psychological torment after their crimes are committed. They will be pursued by the demons of their own minds, yet are never truly penitent in a Christian sense. For Dickens, they will most certainly be damned, both in this world and the next.

Bill Sikes is presented by Dickens as a generally brutal man, even feared by the malevolent Fagin. He regularly beats his mistress Nancy and his dog aptly named "Bullseye," eventually beating Nancy to death, first with a gun, then with a club, for "betraying him" by helping Oliver. Ignoring her desperate prayers for mercy, both for herself and his own soul, he repeatedly clubs her, even after she is already bloodied and dying. Critics now believe that the scene of Nancy's horrific murder, once considered too melodramatic to be credible, was actually inspired by a real life incident, the violent murder of a prostitute named Eliza Grimwood. Like Nancy, Grimwood was apparently on her knees when she was murdered and stabbed repeatedly even after she was already dead. The dramatic scene of Nancy's murder was a gruesome favorite of Dickens, one that he obsessively reenacted when acting out readings from his works towards the end of his life. The emotions it evoked in him, in the opinion of many biographers, were so extreme they damaged his health and may have even helped lead to his premature death.

Later, more sanitized versions of this murder, from early films to the musical *Oliver*, downplay the extreme violence of the scene as written by Dickens:

> The housebreaker (Sikes) freed one arm, and grasped his pistol. The certainty of immediate detection if he fired, flashed across his mind even in the midst of his fury; and he beat it twice with all the fury he could summon, upon the upturned face that almost touched his own.
>
> She staggered and nearly fell: nearly blinded with the blood that rained down from a deep gash in her forehead; but raising herself with difficulty on her knees...breathed one prayer of mercy to her Maker.
>
> It was a ghastly figure to look upon. The murderer staggering backward to the wall, and shutting out the sight with his heavy hand, seized a heavy club and struck her down.

From here on in the novel, Sikes is no longer referred to as "the housebreaker" or Bill Sikes, but simply as "the murderer." The memory of this bloody scene, even further elaborated by the author, will pursue him as he tries to flee from the law. It is reenacted again and again in his mind, and he fancies he sees Nancy herself, especially her eyes, following him. Of course, it is his own conscience taking shape, terrifying him with his bloody deed. In the end, as he tries to escape the police by letting himself down from a rooftop with a rope, he suddenly sees "those eyes" and accidentally hangs himself.

Barnaby Rudge, the partially eponymous character of a novel in which he rarely appears, (the novel is actually named for his son, Barnaby Jr.) has murdered his employer and faked his own death. This murder has apparently been motivated by sheer greed, although we never know either the identity of the murderer or his motive until the end of the novel. Edgar Allan Poe, who reviewed the novel in his capacity as literary critic, believed that the identity of the murderer was not all that mysterious, and could be guessed early on in the book.[2] In this he may be right; Dickens was not a mystery writer in the classic "whodunit sense." He drops hints about the identity of his villains quite early in the novels. Dickens' principal concern is with the moral condition of the murderer, in the case of Rudge, uniformly bad. Rudge has a kind-hearted wife, who protects him for a time. She even tries to save his soul, although she is aware of the gravity of his crime, telling their son,

> "He has shed the blood of one who loved him well, and trusted him
> and never did him wrong in word or deed....But although we shun him,
> he is your father dearest, and I am his wretched wife. They seek his life
> and he will lose it. It must not be by our means, nay, if we could win him
> back to penitence, we should be bound to love him yet."

Despite her best efforts, Rudge cannot be brought to repent. His main concern is how to keep out of the hands of the law. There is some awareness of his guilt, however, when he looks upon his son Barnaby, whose mental disability he sees as a kind of punishment for his own crime:

> The murderer, full of anxious thoughts, looked after him, and paced
> up and down, disquieted by every breath of air that whispered amongst
> the boughs, and by every light shadow thrown by the passing clouds
> upon the daisied ground...In the intense selfishness which the constant
> presence before him, and their consequences here and hereafter,
> engendered, every thought of Barnaby as his son, was swallowed up and
> lost. Still, his presence was a torture and a reproach; in his wild eyes,
> there were terrible images of that guilty night; with his unearthly aspect,
> and his half-formed mind, he seemed to the murderer a creature who
> had sprung into existence from his victim's blood.

Like Bill Sikes, also branded "the murderer," Rudge feels some guilt, but not enough to truly repent his crime. Once he is caught and in prison awaiting the gallows, he still refuses to soften, despite the urgent pleas of his wife. Nor does he particularly care about the son who is also in prison because of his unwitting participation in the riots. Barnaby Sr. will be hung. Yet we do see him suffer psychologically. This is as close to the experience of a "conscience" that characters like Barnaby Rudge and Bill Sikes may come.

Barnaby Rudge like *Martin Chuzzlewit* is named after two characters with the same name, each flawed in some way. The younger Rudge gets caught up in the violent Gordon riots, but his mental defects make him innocent under the law, and in Dickens' mind, before God (see Limbo).

Dickens first contemplated calling the novel *Gabriel Vardon* (an earlier spelling) after the warm-hearted locksmith at its moral center, but for some reason, he chose not to. We can only speculate that the sinful characters in this novel—of which there are many—are in many respects more fascinating to Dickens than the good, or rather that sin itself is more interesting and complex than virtue. Many readers of Dante feel similarly about his *Divine Comedy*; the *Inferno* is generally considered more compelling than either the *Purgatorio* or the *Paradiso*.

Jonas Chuzzlewit in the novel *Martin Chuzzlewit* is another murderer who is hounded by fear of capture, yet also lacks sincere repentance. However, since his own father is the object of his planned murder, he belongs in an even deeper section of the *Inferno*: Traitors to Family, where we will meet up with him later.

Then there is the cold-blooded murderer Rigaud in *Little Dorrit*, whom we first encounter in prison.**** This character is based on an actual figure named Lacenaire in 19th century France, known for his personal elegance and cool demeanor as he neatly dispatched his victims with a knife. In *Little Dorrit* he is at first in prison awaiting execution for killing his own wife, but he somehow cleverly escapes. Rigaud will become involved with Mrs. Clennam through his desire for her fortune, and is ultimately killed when her house collapses upon him. Rigaud's death is, of course, another form of *contrapasso*; his craving to possess Mrs. Clennam's wealth leads him to be buried beneath it.

**** The original for this character was the prototype for the character Lacenaire in the classic French film *The Children of Paradise*.

We cannot leave the circle of the violent without considering one of the most extreme of all Dickens' murderers, who just happens to be a female: the bloodthirsty Madame Defarge in *A Tale of Two Cities*. Madame Defarge is unique and fascinating on many counts. First, she is one of the rare violent women in Dickens—perhaps even worse than his male murderers, because unlike them, she is a mass killer. While Jonas kills out of greed and fear of discovery, Sikes out of anger at betrayal, and Jasper out of lust and jealousy, she kills or aims to kill all aristocrats or anyone with a drop of St. Evremonde blood, refusing even to spare the innocent child of Lucie and Charles Darnay. Her bloodlust is generalized and political, similar to today's terrorists who kill both the innocent and the guilty. This is politically motivated murder, and it is coldly plotted in advance.

For Madame Defarge, there is a personal element as well; her sister was raped and died at the hand of the arrogant nobleman St. Evremonde, her family destroyed as a result. Her craving for revenge knows no bounds. Her best friend and fellow murderess is given the symbolic nickname "Vengeance."

At the same time, the first third of the novel actually creates some sympathy for her and her fellow revolutionaries. Unlike his close friend Thomas Carlyle, whose book on the French Revolution formed the basis for *A Tale of Two Cities*, Dickens was equally enraged at the abuses committed by the nobility, particularly St. Evremonde himself, who is depicted as totally callous. When he is murdered by a desperate father whose child has been run over by his carriage, while he drives by unconcerned, Dickens virtually applauds the poor man's act of revenge. Dickens vividly portrays the injustice and cruelty of the nobles who randomly imprisoned anyone they disliked or feared, and feasted in luxury while denying bread to the masses.

The bloodbath that follows when the people finally rise up is, for Dickens, partial retribution for their decades of arrogance and oppression.

Madame Defarge herself is initially depicted as a somewhat attractive figure, despite her sinister brooding over past wrongs. From high school reading of the novel, I remembered her as an angry old woman. Yet in fact, she is described by Dickens as rather young, with flashing dark eyes and a rose in her hair. She also has an indomitable will; her fiery nature stands in contrast with Lucie Manette, one of Dickens' most pallid and passive heroines. It is fitting that Madame Defarge will eventually be killed, not by Lucie, but by the indomitable Miss Pross, Lucie's life-long nurse and protector who is defending Lucie and her child. Pross, with her flaming red hair, powerful body and temper, is initially described by Dickens as being "like a man." This was evidently considered a compliment. The final encounter between these two women, when the older Miss Pross overcomes the younger and more powerful Madame Defarge, physically embodies Dickens' conviction that "love is stronger than hate."

While sympathetic to the wrongs they have endured, Dickens never downplays the ruthlessness of Madame Defarge and her fellow revolutionaries. After Charles Darnay has been unjustly imprisoned due to her manipulation of the legal process, Dr. Manette returns from a visit to the prison where his son-in-law is being held. What he sees there is so horrific he keeps the details from Lucie:

> So much of that dreadful time as could be kept from the knowledge of Lucie was so well concealed from her that not until long afterwards.... did she know that eleven hundred defenseless prisoners of both sexes and all ages had been killed by the populace; that four days and four nights had been darkened by this deed of horror and that the air around her had been tainted by the slain.

Unlike her husband Ernest, who still feels some lingering loyalty to his old friend Doctor Manette, Madame Defarge is without a drop of mercy for anyone. She would eradicate the nobility from the face of the earth, the innocent along with the guilty. Early in the novel, she is already plotting their extinction:

> "It does not take a long time," said Madame, "for an earthquake to swallow a town. Eh well! Tell me, how long it takes to prepare the earthquake?"
>
> "A long time, I suppose," said Defarge.

"But when it is ready, it takes place, and grinds to pieces everything before it. In the meantime, it is always preparing, even though it is not seen or heard…" She tied a knot with flashing eyes, as if it throttled a foe.

"I tell thee," said Madame, extending her right hand, for emphasis, "that although it is a long time on the road, it is on the road and coming."

When her moment of vengeance comes, she is pitiless. The governor of the Bastille has been taken by the mob and Madame Defarge takes part in the blows against him:

> (Madame Defarge) was so close to him when he dropped dead under it, that, suddenly animated, she put her foot upon his neck, and with her cruel knife—long ready—hewed off his head.
>
> The hour was to come, when Saint Antoine was to execute his horrible idea of hoisting men up for lamps to show what he could be and do. Saint Antoine's blood was up, and the blood of tyranny and domination was down—down on the steps of the Hotel de Ville where the governors body lay—down on the sole of the shoe where she had trodden on the body to steady it for mutilation.

After this, the frenzied mob, including Madame Defarge, carry the heads of murdered prisoners around on pikes.

Dickens not only condemned random killing; he also had serious questions about capital punishment. He never totally opposed it, but often wrote critically of it in his newspaper and journal articles and in at least two novels (*A Tale of Two Cities, Barnaby Rudge*) he portrays the crowds that delight in public hangings with disgust. In fact, the hang-man Dennis in *Barnaby Rudge*, who joins the anti-Catholic mob, will wind up being hung himself, clearly a form of *contrapasso*. Like Dickens, we may understand the desire for revenge that animates those who have been deeply wronged, but Dickens makes it clear what disasters can occur once people yield to this desire.*****

***** From Dickens' blood-thirsty revolutionaries we might reflect upon the fatal flaw in our current wars. Killing by suicide bombs or drones still takes innocent human lives. Like Dickens, we may understand the thirst for revenge from people who have been deeply wounded. Yet the simple dictate of the Ten Commandments, "Thou shalt not kill," remained Dickens' ultimate moral code.

The Violent Against Self—Tom Jarndyce, Ralph Nickleby

For the Catholic Church, suicide has always been a mortal sin. According to some historians, this is because in the early days of Christianity believers were so eager to get to heaven, some took it upon themselves to hasten the process. This unhappy trend had to be discouraged. As we have seen, Dante has a special circle in his *Inferno* for the suicides. For a liberal Protestant like Dickens, suicide itself was not necessarily a "sin." However, it could be morally questionable, especially when mingled with other sins. As we have seen, Ralph Nickleby hangs himself in part to hurt others—so they will not have the "satisfaction" of seeing him brought to justice for his financial crimes, or even feel pity for him. As with many other "sins," Dickens naturally intuits a psychological element that would eventually be made explicit by modern psychiatrists and psychologists. In his classic work *Man Against Himself,* Karl Menninger suggests that suicide is just as often an act of anger as it is of despair, a view that is now widely accepted by psychiatrists. Bradley Headstone's "suicide-homicide" is also an act of rage, as he plunges both himself and Riderhood into a watery grave.

There are few other suicides in Dickens. One character who is mentioned, but never appears in the novel, is Mr. Jarndyce's dead brother Tom in *Bleak House*, who did kill himself in despair over the fruitless lawsuit Jarndyce vs. Jarndyce. An old man recounts his story:

> "Tom Jarndyce was often in here. He got into a restless habit of strolling about when the cause (his lawsuit) was on, or expected, talking to the little shopkeepers and telling them to stay out of Chancery, whatever they did. 'For,' he said, 'it's being ground to bits in a slow mill. It's being roasted at a slow fire; it's being drowned by drops; it's going mad by grains.' He was as near making away with himself, just where the long lady stands, as near could be."

Soon, he does "make away with himself" with a pistol. However, Tom Jarndyce is an example of someone whose "hell" is already experienced in this world, before his actual sin is committed.

Tom Jarndyce's folly is an object lesson to his brother John, a tragic loss and a warning against greed. Unfortunately, this lesson is never learned by Jarndyce's nephew Richard who, although not technically a suicide, allows that same lawsuit to progressively destroy his mind and health, leading to his eventual death. In this sense, Dickens comes close to the spirit of Dante; for him, life itself is precious and should never be thrown away, especially not for money. The financier Merdle (*Little Dorrit*) will commit suicide apparently to escape punishment when his fraudulent dealings are about to be revealed, but since suicide is not his "besetting sin," we will consider him later. Similarly, Jonas Chuzzlewit will commit suicide to evade an inevitable hanging. He too belongs in an even deeper circle of Hell, as a Traitor to Family.

Violence in all its forms was clearly antipathetic to Dickens. While he understood and experienced anger in his own life, towards his parents, his society and even sometimes his friends and family, there is no evidence from his letters, the testimony of his children or even his deserted wife, that he ever resorted to any form of violence. Some might claim that he acts it out in his fiction (note to himself on Jo in *Bleak House*— "kill him!") But in his personal life and his social activism he generally opposed violence, even those forms that were legally sanctioned by society, like capital punishment or the beating of children.

VI

Fraud in All its Ugly Forms

Circle 8 of the *Inferno*, Fraud, is its second deepest and most intricate. Dante divides his circle into ten subdivisions or *"bolgias,"* to demonstrate the many distinct and varied types of fraud. While some of Dante's specific examples, such as the alchemists and soothsayers, may lack an exact counterpart in 19th century England, Dickens' world has at least as many frauds as appear in the *Inferno*. It's a society filled with fakers, impersonators, con men and hypocrites. Dickens comprehensively catalogues various types of fraud in his description of Leicester Square, a neighborhood largely inhabited by scoundrels in *Bleak House*. One inhabitant, Mr. George, a retired soldier, is actually an honest, trustworthy character in the novel. However, the same cannot be said for his villainous neighbors:

> Behind dingy blind and curtain, in upper story and garret, skulking more or less under false names, false hair, false titles, false jewelry, and false histories, a colony of brigands lie in their first sleep. Gentlemen of the green-baize road who could discourse from personal experience of foreign galleys and home treadmills, spies of strong governments that eternally quake with weakness and miserable fear, broken traitors, cowards, bullies, gamesters, shufflers, swindlers and false witnesses...all with more cruelty in them than there was in Nero, and more crime than is in Newgate. For howsoever bad the devil can be in fustian or smock frock...he is a more designing, callous, and intolerable devil when he sticks a pin in his shirt-front, calls himself a gentleman...

In short, the worst fraud is the most deeply disguised. In this sense, we see how characters like Rigaud-Blandois, Montague Tigg and Sir

John Chester, who dress up as gentlemen, can be more dangerous than those who appear in more simple and obvious guise. And their crimes are more malicious, because more craftily designed.

We also see why fraud is placed in such a deep circle of the *Inferno*, even deeper than violence, for murder can arise from uncontrolled passion, as it does with Bradley Headstone. It is a quality shared by animals that may kill out of fear or necessity. Fraud, on the other hand, is always malicious and coldly calculated.

Bolgia 1: the Panderers and Seducers—Fagin, Cleopatra Skewton, Miss Havisham, Sir Mulberry Hawke, James Harthouse

Here we find two types of fraud that are sadly common to all ages and nations. Prostitution is often charitably dubbed "the oldest profession," and of course panderers or pimps who sell women's bodies for profit have existed in virtually every society. Today, they are even glorified in some pop songs, like the revolting, "It's a hard life for a pimp," that was actually nominated for an Academy Award a few years ago. Fortunately, it didn't win.

So why is this particular sin placed in the category of fraud and not greed, since money is its object? Perhaps because it can be veiled as "pleasant," or harmless; or because the pimp so often succeeds in his aims by persuading his victim that he "loves her." Or because pimps can still dress themselves in fancy clothes and jewelry and parade themselves with pride before the public.

Some of Dickens' pimps are criminals who ply their trade illegally; others are parents or relatives who "sell" their daughters into loveless marriage for their own profit. Fagin in *Oliver Twist* is clearly of the former type. The novel implies that he took Nancy in when she was a young girl, and forced her into both thievery and prostitution. Like pimps around the world he keeps her, in part at least, by persuading her that he is her "friend." Bill Sikes then takes over, keeping Nancy in line by threats as well as his perverse form of "love."

In a sense, Fagin is also a "panderer" of the young boys he snatches and uses as thieves. They do the stealing; he takes their money. There is a false, fatherly tone in the way he addresses Nancy and the children he sends out to steal, whom he often refers to as "my dears." When he first meets Oliver, he greets him jovially:

> "We are very glad to see you, Oliver, very," said the Jew. "Dodger, take off the sausages; and draw a tub near the fire for Oliver."

This warm welcome is very enticing for an orphan boy who has just recently been starved and beaten in a workhouse. Oliver is at first cheered by the companionship of this little "family," until, of course, he realizes how he is actually to be used.

When Oliver manages to escape from Fagin's clutches, Fagin will conspire with others, including Nancy, to get him back. Once a child has fallen into his clutches, he is never permitted to leave for fear of bringing the law down on the whole operation.

Fagin will end in prison and eventually is hung. Like most of Dickens' true villains, his final thoughts are of himself, not his victims. He is obsessed with the dreadful thought of death by hanging, something he has casually observed for other men, but can't bear for himself:

> At one point he raved and blasphemed; and at another howled and tore his hair. Venerable men of his own persuasion had come to pay beside him, but he had driven them away with curses. They renewed their charitable efforts, and he beat them off.
>
> Saturday night. He had only one night more to live. And as he thought of this—the day broke—Sunday.
>
> It was not until the night of this last awful day, that the withering sense of his helpless, desperate state came in its full intensity upon his blighted soul; not that he had ever held any defined or positive hope of mercy, but that he had never been able to consider more than the dim probability of dying so soon.

Dickens' portrayal of Fagin's last moments goes on for several pages and accomplishes two seemingly contradictory things. Because we enter into Fagin's thoughts and fears, the scene actually engenders some sympathy for the despised man. We come to share his terror at the finality of death by execution. At the same time, Dickens graphically illustrates the "Hell" that Fagin must suffer because of his evil deeds. Like Dante, Dickens is often able to damn his villains thoroughly, yet at the same time show some compassion for their suffering. It is also interesting that Dickens mentions a prison visit by "venerable men of his own persuasion," suggesting that had Fagin been able to repent even with Jewish prayers, he could have been saved. To some degree, this comment may mitigate the accusations of anti-Semitism justifiably heaped on *Oliver Twist*.

Then there are those parents who "pander" their daughters in legal matrimony for their own enrichment. One of these, as we have seen, is Cleopatra Skewton in *Dombey and Sons* who receives the deserved contempt of her daughter Edith, and eventually dies. In *The Old Curiosity Shop*, Nell's greedy brother Frederick seeks to sell her off to his friend Dick Swiveller, but is thwarted in his attempt by her escape with their grandfather. Ralph Nickleby nearly forces the hapless old man Bray to give away his daughter Madeleine into marriage with the hideous miser Gride, just to pay off a debt, but this plot—as all Ralph's plots—is eventually foiled. In *David Copperfield*, the conniving Uriah Heep enmeshes Mr. Wickfield in his net by using his alcoholism against him, very nearly getting him to give away his lovely daughter Agnes to him. Here again, the evil plot fails and true love wins out in the end.

Seth Pecksniff in *Martin Chuzzlewit* cheerfully marries off his daughter Mercy (ironically nicknamed Merry) to the malignant Jonas Chuzzlewit for Jonas' fortune. Merry, unfortunately, is all too willing to comply. Her youthful vanity persuades her that she can control her evil-tempered husband. Alas, she will be proven wrong when Jonas turns her married life into a living hell, and she quickly becomes anything but "merry." Eventually, she will be freed of Jonas, but only after being suitably tempered by suffering. In general, Dickens seems so attached to the ideal of loving marriage, he has difficulty allowing his heroines to be permanently trapped into marriages of convenience.

Before leaving the "panderers," we might also consider Miss Havisham in *Great Expectations*. While she doesn't exactly "sell" her ward Estella like other Dickens' parents, she manipulates Estella's beauty to accomplish her own wrongful end: revenge. When she was a young woman, Miss Havisham was abandoned at the altar by a heartless suitor, Arthur Compeyson. Because of this early disappointment, she raises her ward Estella in a gloomy mansion and teaches her how to make all men suffer. She actively encourages her to seduce poor Pip, just to make him miserable. Miss Havisham's punishment will be to never know any real love herself. As we have seen, even Estella rebuffs her belated attempts to seek a drop of affection. Finally, Miss Havisham will be accidentally burned alive amidst the crumbling relics of her own failed wedding day, objects she has obsessively kept through the years. This too can be seen as a form of *contrapasso*. Although by the end of the novel she comes to repent the damage she has wrought, endlessly repeating, "What have I done! What have I done!" her regrets come too late. She has already managed to ruin Pip's life and Estella's, as well as her own.

As for "the seducers," we have already encountered Steerforth in *David Copperfield*. However, he seems to genuinely love Emily, although social class prevents him from marrying her. Therefore, it is kinder to leave him above in the circle of the "lustful." There are others, however, whose motives are less sincere. The slimy old lecher Sir Mulberry Hawke in *Nicholas Nickleby* can hardly keep his hands off Nicholas' sister Kate.

Hawke is introduced to Kate by her uncle Ralph, who doesn't quite intend for her to be molested, but rather used as attractive bait for his dubious financial deals. When he discovers Hawke actually assaulting her, he becomes furious.

Yet he has deliberately left Kate alone with Hawke. She is nervously attempting to read a book, while Ralph and his riotous friends disport themselves in the next room:

> ...she had read through several chapters without heed of time or place, when she was terrified by hearing her name pronounced by a man's voice close at her ear.
>
> The book fell from her hand. Lounging on an ottoman close beside her was Sir Mulberry Hawke, evidently the worse—if a man be a ruffian at heart, he is never the better—for wine.

"What a delightful studiousness!" said this accomplished gentleman. "Was it real, now or only to display the eyelashes..."

"Do me the favor to be silent now, sir," replied Kate.

"No, don't," said Sir Mulberry, folding his crush hat to lay his elbow on, and bringing himself closer to the young lady, "upon my life, you oughtn't to. Such a devoted slave of yours, Miss Nickleby—it's an infernal thing to treat him so harshly, upon my soul it is..."

Kate hastily rose; but as she rose, Sir Mulberry caught her dress, and forcibly detained her.

"Let me go sir," she cried, her heart swelling with anger. "Do you hear? Instantly—this moment!"

"Sit down, sit down," said Sir Mulberry, "I want to talk to you."

Then Kate utters the unfortunate phrase that leads one editor to dismiss the entire scene as an example of the sheerest melodrama: "Unhand me sir, this instant."[1] While there are certainly elements of classic melodrama in the scene, there is also realism in the way Hawke attempts to use flattery to win over Kate. (This author can attest from personal experience that some old seducers act very much like Hawke towards young and vulnerable girls.)

Unlike Mulberry Hawke, James Harthouse in *Hard Times* appears at first an amiable and attractive young man; yet he deliberately sets out to seduce Louisa Gradgrind Bounderby who is trapped in an unhappy marriage. Like Steerforth, he is almost unaware of his purpose, at least at first, giving way to his own desires, but he is just as manipulative. He is subtle in his approach, and therefore in some ways more dangerous than a blatant seducer:

He had established a confidence with her, from which her husband was excluded...he had artfully, but plainly assured her, that he knew her heart in its last most delicate recesses; he had come so near to her through its tenderest sentiment; he had associated himself with that feeling; and the barrier behind which she had lived had melted away. All very odd, and very satisfactory!...

When the Devil goeth about like a roaring lion, he goeth about in a shape by which few but savages and hunters are attracted. But when he is trimmed, smoothed and varnished according to the mode; when he is aweary of vice and aweary of virtue, used up as to brimstone and used up as to bliss; then, whether he take to the serving out of red tape or the serving out of red fire, he is the very Devil.

Harthouse poses a threat to Louisa because he understands her cynicism, and uses it to his advantage. She is especially vulnerable to him because she has been married off to a man she does not love. About to yield to Harthouse, she abruptly runs away to beg her father for help, even as she realizes that he and his materialistic philosophy cannot help her:

> "This night, my husband being away, he has been with me, declaring himself my lover. This minute he expects me, for I could release myself of his presence by no other means. I do not know that I am sorry, I do not know that I am ashamed, I do not know that I am degraded in my own esteem. All I know is that your philosophy and your system will not save me. Now, father you have brought me to this. Save me by some other means!"

In the end, her father, though sincerely grieved by her plight, cannot "save her." His own philosophy renders him helpless in matters of the soul. That task will be left to Sissy Jupe, the warm-hearted servant girl who has become Louisa's friend, and nurses her back to some semblance of calm after her close call with perdition.

A more obvious seducer is the lecherous dwarf Quilp in *The Old Curiosity Shop*. He makes lewd advances not merely to little Nell, but to every female he encounters, including his tough-minded co-conspirator Sally Brass. However, because he is so cosmically evil, Quilp must ultimately be dropped into a much deeper pit of Hell.

In general, Dickens treads with delicacy on the world of prostitution, rife in London during his lifetime. It's an ugly subject, and he obviously prefers to spare the sensibilities of his readers. However, it's clear that his sympathies are always with the "fallen women," and not with their "panderers," the men who use or sell them. Martha, in *David Copperfield*, is like little Em'ly, a young woman who has been sexually active outside of marriage and thus condemned by society. It is implied that she may have become a prostitute. Yet she is as sympathetically drawn as Emily herself, and a picture of Mary Magdalene on the wall graces one of the illustrations in which Martha appears. Dickens' most heart-felt charitable project was his establishment with philanthropist Angela Burdett Coutts of Urania Cottage, a rehabilitation home for prostitutes. Into this effort he poured more than eleven years of time, money and personal attention to the women themselves, encouraging them in letters and in person to never give up on their lives, to start anew, learn a trade or marry. Many of them did just this, in England or in emigration to Australia, South Africa or America. However, the men who use them receive little sympathy from Dickens, either in his novels or his life.

The profound feelings of guilt that evidently weighed on Dickens towards the end of his life included not only his abandoned wife, but the secret mistress Nelly whom he loved, but would never marry. He went to extreme lengths to make certain that the outside world would never have cause to consider Nelly Ternan "a fallen woman," even though his own moral sense (and desire to preserve his own image) kept him from divorcing his wife in order to marry her.[2]

Bolgia 2: The Flatterers—The Lammles, the Veneerings, the Friends of the Veneerings, the Friends of the Merdles

Probably the two most shameless flatterers in all of Dickens are Seth Pecksniff in *Martin Chuzzlewit*, a man who nauseatingly fawns on old Martin in order to become his chief inheritor, and Uriah Heep in *David Copperfield* whose "umble" protestations of reverence for "Master Davey" mask much darker designs. However, these two are guilty of far worse sins than flattery, so we won't dwell on them here.

A purer form of flattery is found most prominently in the "Society" world of *Our Mutual Friend*, where the appropriately named "Veneerings" (all glossy surface, no real feeling) and their "hundred dearest and oldest friends" engage in a society of mutual flattery for their own sense of pride and social advantage. The interactions of this world are not without humor. For example, when Podsnap and his wife are first invited to the Veneerings, they mistake Mr. Twemlow, a less important guest, for their host, and fall upon him enthusiastically:

A too, too large smiling man, with a fatal freshness on him, appearing with his wife, instantly deserts his wife and darts at Twemlow with:

"How do you do? So glad to know you. Charming house you have here. I hope we are not late. So glad of the opportunity, I am sure."

By the time he realizes his mistake, he has managed to offend everybody; Twemlow, who considers Veneering a fool, Veneering "who is not at all complimented by being supposed to be Twemlow, who is dry and weazen and some thirty years older," and Mrs. Veneering who "equally resents being the wife of Twemlow." In short, these pretentious snobs receive their come-uppance almost immediately. Not much in the way of a major *contrapasso,* but fitting nonetheless.

On a more serious note, when the social-climbing Lammles enter the Veneering's world, they too incessantly flatter their hosts, as well as each other. In this world, all is false; there is no authentic friendship or love. Once a person has lost his or her money or social position, he will be coldly dropped from favor. For the Lammles, this leads to a miserable marriage, as they have each deceived the other about their fortunes. In fact, both are penniless, but they have entered into marriage, each thinking the other was rich. Immediately after the elaborate wedding ceremony thrown by their "best friends", the Veneerings, the awful truth emerges, and they fall to attacking each other bitterly:

"Then you married me on false pretenses."

"So be it. Next comes what you mean to say. Do you mean to say you are a woman of property?"

"No."

"Then you married me on false pretenses."

"If you were so greedy and grasping that you were over-willing to be deceived by appearances, is it my fault, you adventurer?" the lady demands, with great asperity.

Dickens obviously has great fun toying with these characters, quickly turning their flattery into insult, their snobbery into contempt.

The Lammles' *contrapasso* is to be forever bound to each other in poverty and mutual dislike. Meanwhile, the lordly Veneerings, who are flattered by all, will ultimately be abandoned by their "hundred oldest and dearest friends," when they themselves face financial ruin.

Similarly, the legion of fawning "friends" who crowd around the wealthy Merdles in *Little Dorrit* will mostly lose the money they have invested with the duplicitous banker.* When little Dorrit's father receives his unexpected inheritance, he too becomes enamored of Merdle and the entire world he stands for. Meanwhile, he begins to disdain his old friends, and even to some degree his loving daughter Amy (little Dorrit), because she refuses to "rise" to his level of social pretense.

William Dorrit's flattering of the "great man" Merdle reveals the pathetic deterioration of his mind, and quickly turns more tragic than humorous. Merdle has just shown up while Dorrit is at breakfast, still in his dressing gown. The object of this visit is matrimony. Merdle's stepson is infatuated with little Dorrit's sister Fanny, and plans to marry her. William Dorrit is beside himself with unctuous pleasure:

> "Mr. Merdle, this is—ha—indeed an honor. Permit me to express the—hum—sense, the high sense I entertain of this—ha, hum—highly gratifying act of attention. I am well aware, sir, of the many demands on your time, and its—ha—enormous value...That you should—ha—at this early hour bestow your priceless time on me, is—ha—a compliment that I acknowledge with the greatest esteem." Mr. Dorrit positively trembled in addressing the great man.

The profound irony of this scene is that he too has been persuaded to invest with Merdle, and will soon lose all his money. His selfish daughter Fanny (like Lear's Goneril and Regan) who craves wealth and social position, will make her lucrative match, and is doomed to a miserable marriage with a man she despises. William Dorrit's fate—foreshadowed here in his deteriorating speech, filled with "ha's" and "hums,"—is to succumb to dementia, and in front of the very Society he so fervently hoped to impress. At a party with the Merdles and the rest of this group, he suddenly reverts mentally to his days in debtor's prison, becoming the

---

* A similar fate was met by some of the false and even the true friends of the American financier Bernard Madoff. This seemed most tragic in the case of a widow who, because her late husband trusted him, invested all her money with Madoff and was left penniless.

pathetic William Dorrit of old. At this point, little Dorrit, the daughter who sincerely loves her father will stand by him as she has always done, much like the mad Lear's faithful daughter Cordelia consoles him at the end of Shakespeare's tragedy. Dickens, while not by temperament a tragic author, loved Shakespeare, and it's hard not to see elements of Lear in William Dorrit's unhappy end.

Bolgia 3: the Simonists—Catholic Clerics in "A Tale of Two Cities"

The crime of simony, or paying for a church office (named for the Biblical character Simon Magus, who offered money to be named one of Jesus' apostles) was undoubtedly a more serious problem in the all-powerful medieval Church than in 19th century England. Nevertheless, in its broader sense of "trafficking in religious things for money," simony existed both as a sin and a punishable crime under the 19th century Church of England. Dickens' contemporary Anthony Trollope, in his series *Barchester Chronicles*, focuses far more than Dickens on the clerical world, where characters are sometimes rightfully accused of simony. Mr. Bumble in *Oliver Twist*, as we have seen, uses his relatively minor position as beadle for financial gain, as does the preacher Stiggins. However, these characters are relatively insignificant in the religious order of things.

There are many hypocritical and cold-hearted Protestants clerics in Dickens' novels, as we have seen, yet for institutional church corruption, Dickens looks back to Catholic France of the 18th century in *A Tale of Two Cities*. At the beginning of the novel, Dickens condemns the entire world of the nobility, including:

> ...military officers destitute of military knowledge; naval officers with no idea of a ship; civil officers without a notion of affairs; brazen ecclesiastics of the worst world worldly, with sensual eyes, loose tongues and looser lives; all totally unfit for their several callings, all lying horribly in pretending to belong to them, but all nearly or remotely of the order of Monseigneur, and therefore foisted on all public employments from which anything was to be got...

The interpenetration of the feudal aristocracy with all institutions of French society, including the Church, creates some of the injustices that eventually spawn a bloody revolution.

The monetary fraud we find in Dickens' society naturally lies more with its secular and political institutions than with its churches. These will be described in deeper *bolgias*.

Bolgia 4: the Soothsayers

Like simony, soothsaying was relatively rare in 19th century England. Nevertheless, we find a few references to the practice in Dickens' novels. In *A Tale of Two Cities*, set in 18th century France, Dickens catalogues the various types of frauds assembled around the French court, including a group of soothsayers called the Convulsionists:

> The leprosy of unreality disfigured every human creature in attendance upon Monseigneur. In the outermost room were half a dozen exceptional people who had, for a few years, some vague misgiving in them that things in general were going rather wrong. As a promising way of setting them right, half of the half dozen had become members of a fantastic sect of Convulsionists, and were even then considering whether they should foam, rage, roar and turn cataleptic on the spot—thereby setting up a highly intelligible finger-post to the Future, for Monseigneur's guidance.

With profound irony, Dickens implies that these "false prophets" fail absolutely to diagnose the true malady of the regime, the oppression of the masses. They are unable to predict the bloody revolution that is imminent.

While not exactly soothsaying, the role of the quacks in America, who promise young Martin Chuzzlewit and his friend Mark Tapley a land flowing with milk and honey, certainly falls into the category of false prophecy. The land purchased by the guileless pair turns out to be a dreary, disease-infested swamp:

> A flat morass, bestrewen with fallen timber; a marsh on which the good growth of the earth seemed to have been wrecked and cast away,

that from its decomposing ashes vile and ugly things might rise; where the very trees took the aspect of huge weeds begotten of the slime from which they had sprung...this was the realm of Hope through which they had moved.

Dickens took much criticism for his harsh portrayal of American con artists in this novel. However, he rightly responded that he was no easier on the fakers, hypocrites and scoundrels in his own society.[3] The danger for an Englishman coming to America was, of course, the fact that he didn't really know it, and thus was more easily gulled by false promises. Martin does meet a few decent people in America who try to warn him against frauds, like the kindly Mr. Bevan, but with his typical pride, he refuses to take their sensible advice. He will eventually learn, through a process of suffering unto near death, that his attitudes have been wrong. Young Martin Chuzzlewit is among a number of Dickens' protagonists who must go through "Hell" (in an ironically entitled dismal swamp called "Eden") and Purgatory to come to self-awareness and eventual redemption.

Bogia 5: the Barraters—Chancery in "Bleak House" and its Lawyers, Vholes, the Circumlocution Office in "Little Dorrit," the Barnacles, the Electioneers in "The Pickwick Papers"

Unlike simony, more characteristic of a society with an all-powerful central Church, barratry or graft can be found in most times and places.** Barratry is of course the very crime for which Dante was unfairly condemned and punished by exile. Dickens' England, at least as he depicts it, is a society rife with this form of corruption.

The two institutions that best represent barratry on a grand scale in Dickens' novels are undoubtedly the Court of Chancery in *Bleak House* and the Circumlocution Office in *Little Dorrit*, both modeled on real life, although some of Dickens' critics denied this. In these cases, it is less

---

** As of this writing, the powerful former speaker of the Massachusetts House of Representatives is serving a prison term for "sale of his office" for cash, as is the former governor of Illinois, for attempting to sell President Obama's Senate seat. In fact, it's arguable that our entire Congress is currently filled with barraters.

the corrupt individuals than the institutions themselves that are criminal. However, each has its own particularly odious human representatives. In the Court of Chancery, lawyers and judges enrich themselves by maintaining a system where no plaintiff can ever win his suit; it simply doesn't matter to them whether justice prevails so long as they get paid. In describing the endless, futile lawsuit Jarndyce vs. Jarndyce that has lined the pockets of hundreds of lawyers and judges while despoiling its claimants, Dickens goes on for pages—indeed entire chapters. Throughout years and even generations, this dispute over a family will has utterly destroyed the Jarndyce family. The following diatribe gives a small idea of Dickens' horror at the institution and the lawsuit:

> How many people out of the suit Jarndyce vs. Jarndyce has stretched forth its unwholesome hand to spoil and corrupt would be a very wide question. From the master upon whose impaling files reams of dusty warrants in Jarndyce vs. Jarndyce have grimly writhed into many shapes, down to the copying-clerk in the Six Clerks Office who has copied his tens of thousands of Chancery folio pages under the eternal heading, no man's nature has been made better by it. In trickery, evasion, procrastination, spoliation, botheration, under all sorts, under false pretences of all sorts, there are influences that can never come to good…Shirking and sharking in all their many varieties have been sown broadcast by the ill-fated cause; and even those who have contemplated its history from *the outermost circle of such evil* (italics mine) have been insensibly tempted into a loose way of letting bad things alone to take their own bad course, and a loose belief that if the world go wrong it was in some off-hand manner never meant to go right.

Is it purely accidental that Dickens speaks of the realm of evil created by Chancery in Dante's own terms? The "outer circle" seems to signify those indifferent or careless functionaries who allow "the evil" to go on, as opposed to the inner circle of more deliberate malice. In this darker circle we would surely find the aptly named Vholes, a conniving lawyer who drains the last of Richard Carstone's small savings, encouraging him to pursue the hopeless case that will eventually take his very life. He is likely named for the vole, a small rodent like a mouse or rat, who "will burrow under plants or ground cover they are particularly fond of and eat away until the plant is dead." (Wikipedia)

Here as in other Dickens' novels, characters corrupt each other. Richard has been introduced to Vholes by the feckless Skimpole:

> "Vholes bribed me perhaps? He gave me something and called it a commission. Was it a five pound note? Do you know, I think it MUST have been a five pound note!"

Like the little animal that bears his name, Vholes slowly eats away at his client. He is even compared by Esther to a vampire:

> So slow, so eager, slow bloodless and gaunt, I felt as if Richard were wasting away beneath the eyes of this advisor, and there was something of the Vampire in him.

Vholes encourages Richard to pursue his own separate lawsuit in the Jarndyce vs. Jarndyce case, persuading him that he can gain more by relying solely on him. As Richard quickly spends down the little inheritance he has left and breaks with his true friends and family—John Jarndyce and Esther—he uses up all his youth, hope and his life, dying like the pitiful Miss Flyte, another hopeless claimant in the case. The number of characters killed, naturally and unnaturally, by the lawsuit and the Court of Chancery that spawned it, makes the crime of barratry even more serious for Dickens than it is for Dante, who as we have noted, treats barratry somewhat comically. By the end of the case, all the Jarndyce money has been used up by the litigators, and the claimants are all either ruined or dead.

In *Little Dorrit*, it is the Circumlocution Office and its rich representatives, the Barnacles and Stiltstalkings that destroys fortunes and lives. The Circumlocution Office is the vast bureaucracy to which people with any type of business must appeal. As its name implies, to enter this office is to enter a world of doublespeak, evasion and endless waiting; nothing will ever be resolved, no problem ever solved. In short, it is totally corrupt.

Arthur Clennam first approaches the office to seek information about his father's will. He suspects that somebody—perhaps little Dorrit herself—has been abused in the administration of the will. However, he finds himself in a kind of madhouse, a hall of mirrors:

> Numbers of people were lost in the Circumlocution Office. Unfortunates with wrongs, or with projects for the general welfare (and they had better have had wrongs at first, than have taken that bitter English recipe for certainly getting them), who had in slow lapse of time and agony had passed safely through other public departments; who according to rule, had been bullied in this, overreached by that, and evaded by the other; got referred at last to the Circumlocution Office, and never reappeared in the light of day.

Clennam is sent from person to person, shuttled from one office to another, getting nothing but bureaucratic evasion. Finally, he winds up seeing Tite Barnacle's son Ferdinand, who can give him no answers either. He is not very bright, but as a Barnacle, he is a respected part of the Circumlocution royalty:

> The Tite Barnacle Branch, indeed, considered themselves in a general way as having vested rights in that direction, and took it ill if any other family had much to say to it. The Barnacles were a very high family, and a very large family. They were dispersed all over the public offices, and held all sorts of public places. Either the nation was under a load of obligation or the Barnacles were under a load of obligation to the nation. It was not quite unanimously settled which...

Of course Dickens, dripping with irony, knows very well who is under obligation to whom. The Barnacles are profiting handsomely from their useless public office—sheer patronage. Meanwhile, the bureaucracy of the Circumlocution Office makes it impossible for honest entrepreneurs like Arthur and his business partner and friend Daniel Doyce to ever get a chance to succeed. In this respect, Dickens is clearly on the side of the entrepreneurial and creative capitalist, and against the stifling bureaucracy of the government and its profiteers.

The wealthy Veneerings in *Our Mutual Friend* are also guilty of doling out patronage, buying and selling political office to benefit themselves and their friends:

> A new race of intimate friends has sprung up at the Veneerings since he went into Parliament for the public good, to whom Mrs. Veneering is very attentive…Boots says that one of them is a Contractor who (it has been calculated) gives employment, directly and indirectly to five hundred thousand men….Buffer says that another of them hadn't a sixpence eighteen months ago, and through the brilliancy of his genius in getting those shares issued at eight-five, and buying them all up with no money and selling them at par for cash, has now three hundred and seventy-five thousand pounds…

It is not clear how any of these people are punished in this life, except that they will be doomed to "friendships" that are shallow and cold, and to speculative deals that often fall through. The Veneerings themselves "go smash" and are forced to retreat to Calais to live off of Mrs. Veneering's diamonds, without, of course, their "intimate friends" who will find they "always despised them" once their true finances are revealed.

Another form of "barratry," electoral fraud, is described with high comedy in Dickens' first novel *The Pickwick Papers*. Voters are literally given money to vote for the preferred candidate in a local election, while the opposing voters are given so much alcohol and drugs that they collapse and are unable to make it to the polls.

> "They keep 'em locked up till they want 'em," resumed the little man. "The effect of that is to keep us getting at them, and even if we could, it would be no use, for they keep them very drunk on purpose."

Meanwhile, the other party is giving away "five and forty green parasols" to the women, so they will vote for their side. In fact, such dubious practices existed not merely in England, but in America at the time. Some biographers surmise that Edgar Allan Poe, who was found drunk in a distant city during an election, wearing another man's clothes at the time of his death, may have been the victim of a common electoral scam.

Dickens, from his early days as a journalist reporting on Parliament, and throughout his life as both journalist and novelist, was a particularly harsh critic of the British government and its institutional corruption. Some forms of this corruption, like his depiction of the local election in *Pickwick*, are humorous. Others such as the corrupt legal system embodied by the Court of Chancery are justifiably depicted as deadly.

Bolgia 6: the Hypocrites—Seth Pecksniff, Christopher Casby, "Fascination" Fledgeby

Hypocrisy in all forms abounds in Dickens' world, from the phony Samaritan Mrs. Jellyby in *Bleak House* who is full of concern for starving Africans, yet virtually starves her own children, to *David Copperfield*'s treacherous friend Uriah Heep. There is some difficulty in distinguishing the hypocrites from their less heinous cousins the flatterers (see above) and even more malevolent relatives, the impersonators (see below). The purest embodiment of hypocrisy in all of Dickens is undoubtedly Seth Pecksniff in *Martin Chuzzlewit*. Posing as a virtuous man, mouthing moral axioms, pretending to patronize struggling young architects, Pecksniff constantly schemes to get more money into his own pocket. No character in Dickens, however, insists upon his own high-mindedness as fervently and frequently as Pecksniff. Illustrations of the man depict him with his head tilted heavenward, a pious little smile on his lips. When his former pupil John Westlock, who is leaving after being royally fleeced by Pecksniff, comes to say goodbye, Pecksniff continues to preach at him airily:

> "You will shake hands, sir?"(Westlock)
> "No, John," said Mr. Pecksniff, with a calmness quite ethereal, "no, I will not shake hands, John. I have forgiven you. I have already forgiven you, even before you ceased to reproach and taunt me. I have embraced you in the spirit, John, which is better than shaking hands."

Pecksniff always manages to act as though he is the long-suffering, wronged party, even when he clearly is in the wrong. Pecksniff's true character is made clear from the very beginning:

Mr. Pecksniff's professional engagements, indeed, were almost, if not entirely, confined to the collection of rents with which pursuit he occasionally varied and relieved his graver toils, can hardly be said to be a strictly architectural employment. His genius lay in ensnaring parents and guardians, and pocketing premiums. A young gentleman's premium being paid, and the young gentleman come to Pecksniff's house, Mr. Pecksniff borrowed his case of mathematical instruments...entreated him from that moment, to consider himself one of the family...

In this, of course, he also belongs among the avaricious, as we have noted earlier. Even the evil Jonas Chuzzlewit, his son-in-law, is more honest than the oily Pecksniff, and indeed at one point in the novel actually calls him out as "a hypocrite."

When he first appears in the novel, Pecksniff has "generously" taken young Martin under his wing, supposedly to train him in the field of architecture. In fact, he is only doing this to endear himself to old Martin, young Chuzzlewit's rich grandfather, whose fortune he hopes to inherit. As soon as he thinks that the old man has disowned his grandson, he throws Martin out of the house without a penny. He treats another "apprentice," the good-hearted Tom Pinch, as his poorly paid slave, although Pinch himself doesn't quite realize this until the end of the novel. Moreover, it is made clear from the outset that Pecksniff knows next to nothing about architecture; he takes in his charges for what they can pay him and teaches them nothing. In fact, he steals whatever they do produce and takes credit for it himself:

> ...there were cases on record in which the masterly introduction of an additional back-window, or a kitchen door, or half a dozen steps or, even a water-spout, had made the design of a pupil Mr. Pecksniff's own work, and had brought substantial reward into that gentleman's pocket. But such is the magic of genius, which changes all it handles into gold!

He also attempts to seduce old Martin's innocent young ward, perhaps not accidentally named Mary, like Dickens' sister-in-law, who died at closely the same age of eighteen. Mary Graham is an orphan who has been devoted to old Martin's welfare, even though he has told her she won't inherit a penny of his money in order to keep her honestly attached to him. Mary is in love with young Martin and he with her, but Pecksniff, who is old enough to be her father, still pursues her.

Pecksniff, however, doesn't deceive everyone. His students, including Martin, soon see him for what he is. Eventually he will be unmasked and publicly humiliated by the older Martin Chuzzlewit in a scene that gives great satisfaction to the reader, especially since Pecksniff staunchly maintains his hypocritical façade to the very end. Old Martin has long understood Pecksniff's true nature, but pretended otherwise just to see how far Pecksniff would go, and to test the love of his grandson, young Martin. He is finally so overcome with pent up fury, he takes his walking stick and strikes Pecksniff to the ground:

> "Listen, hypocrite! Listen smooth-tongued, servile, crawling knave!" said Martin. "Listen you shallow dog. What! When I was seeking him, you were already spreading your nets; you were already fishing for him, were ye? When I lay ill in this good woman's house, and your meek spirit pleaded for my grandson, you had already caught him, had ye? Counting on the restoration of the love you knew I bore him, you designed for one of your two daughters! Or failing that, you traded him as a speculation which at any rate should blind me with the luster of your charity and found a claim upon me! Why even then I knew you. And I told you so. Did I not tell you I knew you even then?"
>
> "I am not angry, sir," said Mr. Pecksniff softly. "I can bear a great deal from you. I will never contradict you, Mr. Chuzzlewit."

Pecksniff's determination to maintain his false front only further inflames the old man. Old Martin will not be deterred in his goal of total exposure and punishment of the slimy Pecksniff:

> "Hear me, rascal!" said Mr. Chuzzlewit. "I have summoned you here to witness your own work. I have summoned you to witness it, because I know it will be gall and wormwood to you! I have summoned you to witness it, because I know the sight of everybody here must be a dagger in your mean, false heart!"

For his own admittedly selfish ends, old Martin has been testing everyone to see who truly loves him: Pecksniff, young Martin, his assorted money-grubbing relatives, and even his devoted ward Mary. Once again, there is something Lear-like in this scenario, although since we are in the world of Dickens and not Shakespearean tragedy, it all comes out well in the end. In fact, it is more like the ending of one of Shakespeare's comedies, where everything that is topsy-turvy, immoral and unfair in the scheme of things will eventually be set right. The deceitful Pecksniff, who has attempted to turn the old man against his grandson and win his fortune for himself, will be beaten, insulted, banished and reduced to abject penury. He will wind up begging his relatives for small sums of money. Young Martin will be recognized as a good man and heir to old Martin's fortune; Mary will be rewarded by obtaining young Martin's hand in marriage by the now God-like old Martin. For comparisons with Shakespeare we might look to comedies like *The Tempest* or *All's Well That Ends Well* or even darker "comedies" like *A Winter's Tale* or *Measure for Measure*. The essence of classical comedy is, of course, the happy ending. At the same time, Pecksniff's *contrapasso*, poverty and utter humiliation, comes close to the spirit of Dante.

Another Dickens hypocrite ultimately unmasked is Christopher Casby, the ruthless landlord of the impoverished district Bleeding Heart Yard (*Little Dorrit*). Casby appears to be a benevolent elder, resembling the Biblical "patriarch" Dickens ironically dubs him, in part due to his fatherly demeanor, in part to his flowing white mane of hair. He uses a front, a basically decent man named Pancks, to collect his rents and "bleed" the poverty-stricken inhabitants of their last shilling.

While Pancks does the dirty work of exacting the rents, and is therefore despised by most of the inhabitants, Casby circulates about the Yard like a lord, greeting everyone amiably. He doesn't fool all of them of course; however, he initially fools Arthur Clennam, who knows him only as the father of his first love, Flora Finching. Arthur visits their house again after many years abroad to seek help for little Dorrit. Naturally, as the widowed Flora is eager to reprise her long lost romance, Casby receives Arthur hospitably. His genial appearance temporarily deceives Arthur as to his true character:

Confronting him, in the room in which he sat, was a boy's portrait, which anybody seeing him would have identified as Master Christopher Casby, aged ten...sitting (on one of his own legs) on a bank of violets, moved to precocious contemplation by the spire of the village church. There was the same smooth face and forehead, the same calm blue eyes, the same placid air. The shining bald head, which looked so very large because it shone so much; and the long grey hair at its sides and back, like, which looked so very benevolent because it was never cut, were not, of course to be seen in the boy as in the old man...Patriarch was the name which many people delighted to give him.

Here Dickens directly takes on the pseudo-science of phrenology which was so popular in the 19th century. Phrenology held that you could understand a person's character by the "bumps" on his head. Unfortunately the benign-looking bumps on Casby's skull conceal a calculating, ruthless brain.

Casby pushes Pancks once too often to squeeze more money out of his starving tenants, and the kindly Pancks finally rebels. What is his revenge on the "Patriarch?" He will expose Casby's hard-heartedness to the whole Yard:

> "What do you pretend to be," said Mr. Pancks. "What's your moral game? What do you go in for? Benevolence, aint it? You benevolent!" Here Mr. Pancks, apparently without the intention of hitting him, but merely to relieve his mind and expend his superfluous power in wholesome exercise, aimed a blow at the bumpy head, which the bumpy head ducked to avoid. This singular performance was repeated, to the ever increasing admiration of the spectators at the end of every succeeding article of Mr. Panck's oration.....speaking as a sufferer by both, I don't know that I would as soon have the Merdle lot as your lot. You're a driver by disguise, a screwer by deputy, a wringer and squeezer and shaver by substitute. You're a philanthropic sneak. You're a shabby deceiver!"

At this point, all the residents of "Bleeding Heart Yard" burst out laughing. Many have already seen through Casby's hypocrisy; only Arthur and "some old ladies in the neighborhood" were truly blinded by his benevolent appearance. At the end of Pancks' long peroration, in which he blames himself as well for participating in Casby's deception ("I am a grubber!"), Pancks gives the Patriarch his fitting *contrapasso*; he takes out a scissors and cuts off his precious white mane.

Another Dickens hypocrite takes even longer to unmask, because his disguise is so clever. "Fascination" Fledgeby in *Our Mutual Friend* is a money-lender who appears trustworthy by using his Jewish assistant, the elderly Riah, as his front. Everyone believes that Riah is the unscrupulous money-lender, Fledgeby merely a friendly financial advisor. Dickens makes it clear that the stereotype of the "greedy Jew" held by most of his countrymen makes it all too easy for them to be duped by Fledgeby, who poses as an honest businessman, then fleeces them. Among his many victims are his society friends the Lammles. Riah himself is apparently innocent of how he is being used, but once he becomes aware of the charade he flees from Fledgeby.

Since Fledgeby is charming, rich, and above all, not Jewish, no one suspects that he is behind the double-dealing that eventually ensnares and ruins them. His friend Twemlow, who has also lost money from Fledgeby's schemes, finally broaches his situation to Sophronia Lammle, the one person who sees through Fledgeby:

> "Unfortunately, madam," returns Twemlow, "the one money obligation to which I stand committed, the one debt of my life…has fallen into Mr. Riah's hands."
>
> "Mr. Twemlow," says Mrs. Lammle, fixing his eyes with hers: which he would prevent her doing if he could, but he can't; "it has fallen into Fledgeby's hands. Mr. Riah is his mask. It has fallen into Fledgeby's hands. Let me tell you this, for your guidance. The information may be of use to you, if only to prevent your credulity, in judging another man's truthfulness by your own, from being imposed upon."

At first Twemlow refuses to believe her, because she has "no proof," just as her own husband has refused to believe her. But here Dickens shows his faith in a woman's instinct over male rationality. Sophronia, who has also been ruined by Fledgeby, yet has managed to save her young friend Georgianna Podsnap from marrying him, rebukes Twemlow for his naivete:

"My husband, who is not over-confiding, ingenuous, or inexperienced, sees this plain thing no more than Mr. Twemlow does—because there is no proof! Yet I believe five women out of six, in my place—would see it as clearly as I do."

Once Lammle himself realizes that his enemy is not Riah, but rather Fledgeby, he physically assaults the moneylender. Jenny Wren, who appears on the scene soon after, compounds this punishment by throwing a can of pepper in Fledgeby's eyes, temporarily blinding him, just as Society has been "blinded" to his true character.

It is here worth noting that Dickens, sometimes castigated for his "insipid goodies," can also create women who are sharper than their male counterparts. Some of these, like Sally Brass in *The Old Curiosity Shop*, might be immoral in other respects; others like Esther Summerson in *Bleak House*, are pure hearted heroines, but both can see through a fraud more quickly than a man. In Esther's case, she intuits Harold Skimpole's dishonesty much earlier than her benevolent patron John Jarndyce and begins to avoid the man.

In stark contrast to Fledgeby, Riah is portrayed as a kind and honest old man with a long flowing white beard, a genuine "patriarch" of the Jewish faith. He eventually breaks with Fledgeby once he becomes aware of his schemes, and later will help hide Lizzie Hexam from both the murderous Headstone and Eugene Wrayburn, whom she loves but distrusts. In a sense, Riah is not only a contrast to Fledgeby, but to Casby, whose own flowing white locks belie a villainous mind, as well as to Fagin, whose crafty, sinister appearance actually expresses his true character. Riah is, as already noted, the idealized Jew that Dickens offers us to compensate for Fagin.

Taken as a whole, Dickens' fakers prove the old adage that appearances can be deceiving. They are all illustrations of the New Testament "wolves in sheep's clothing." Happily for Dickens' readers, his hypocrites are ultimately unmasked, and are punished by exposure, humiliation and often beating before those they have sought to defraud.

Bolgia 7: the Thieves—Merdle, Tom Gradgrind

Theft takes many forms in Dickens' novels. His primary concern, however, is not with small time criminals like the charming Artful Dodger in *Oliver Twist*, or those many among the London destitute who were forced to steal for mere survival. The Dodger is a cunning pickpocket, but he is also a child who has been abandoned and taken in by the manipulative grown-up Fagin. According to Dickens, petty theft was often treated far too harshly by the judicial system of his time. Dickens' true-life account of a desperately poor mother named Mary Jones who was caught stealing a piece of cloth, then hung for her crime is heart-rending:

> The woman's husband was pressed, their goods seized for some debts of his, and she with two small children, turned into the streets a-begging. It is a circumstance not to be forgotten that she was very young (under nineteen) and most remarkably handsome. She went to a linen-draper's shop, took some coarse linen off the counter, and slipped it under her cloak; the shopman saw her, and she laid it down: for this she was hanged. (Preface to *Barnaby Rudge*)

Dickens makes it quite clear that any "crime" referred to here was certainly not that of theft.

Even Tom Gradgrind (*Hard Times*) who steals from a bank, then deliberately throws suspicion on Stephen Blackpool, is a relatively minor example of this sin. Nevertheless, Tom's cold-blooded act leads to the persecution and destruction of a particularly honest and decent man. Tom deserves to be relegated to the Circle of the Thieves, although his punishment is "transportation," to Australia, common at the time, but comparatively light as "infernal" punishments go.

Like Dante, Dickens is mainly concerned with grand theft, the criminal who robs from all society. In this, there is no better example than the financier Merdle, the prototype for today's Bernard Madoff, although unfortunately such swindlers need no prototype. In fact, the character of Merdle was based on a real person of Dickens' era, the fraudulent banker John Sadleir. When his dishonest financial schemes were exposed, he slit his throat.[4] Merdle is clearly in the world of Fraud, as he manages to deceive everyone with his financial schemes. Once again Dickens feels the need to defend himself against charges that this character is "unrealistic," linking his creation to actual financial scandals of his time:

> If I might make so bold as to defend that extravagant conception, Mr. Merdle, I would hint that it originated after the Railroad-share epoch, in the times of a certain Irish bank, and of one or two other equally laudable enterprises. (Dickens, Introduction to *Little Dorrit,* 1857)

"Society" with a capital "s", worships Merdle, the most powerful financier of his time, just as the ancient Israelites worshiped the Golden Calf. Most of the characters in *Little Dorrit,* from the Tite Barnacles, to Arthur Clennam and little Dorrit's newly enriched father, entrust their fortunes to Merdle, convinced that he is to be trusted absolutely.

From the first, Dickens' ironic description of Merdle alerts the reader that he is, on the contrary, not to be trusted at all:

> Mr. Merdle was immensely rich; a man of prodigious enterprise, a Midas without the ears, who turned all he touched into gold. He was in everything good, from banking to building. He was in Parliament, of course. He was in the City, necessarily. He was Chairman of this, Trustee of that, President of the other. The weightiest of men had said to projectors, "Now what name have you got? Have you got Merdle?" And the reply being in the negative, had said, "Then I won't look at you."

When Dickens resorts to capital letters like this, his message to the reader is clear: "Look out!"

Yet this Merdle who is worshiped by everyone is as isolated and lonely as a Scrooge or Ralph Nickleby. He has a wife, who is interested only the trappings that wealth brings her: the grand parties, the jewels, and the adulation of "Society." She has no interest in her husband, and the feeling is evidently mutual. She is for him just another possession: "It was not a bosom to repose upon, but it was a capital bosom to hang jewels upon. Mr. Merdle wanted something to hang jewels upon, and he bought it for that purpose."

Merdle is a shadowy, secretive figure who hates appearing even at his own parties. He prefers to spend time alone in a room with his wife's pet parrot. Everyone idolizes him, but nobody truly knows him. This may be just as well, since he, like Madoff, is evidently one grand Ponzi scheme; he takes peoples' money promising lucrative return on investment, but it mysteriously disappears. Those who invest with him will lose everything.

In the end, Merdle has ruined nearly all the book's characters, the good as well as the bad. Arthur Clennam has persuaded his honest partner Daniel Doyce to invest their fledgling factory's money in Merdle's schemes, and loses it all. William Dorrit, who has actually been changed for the worse by receiving an unexpected inheritance that permits him to leave prison and live like a snobbish aristocrat, loses both his money and his mind. Even the powerful Barnacles face ruin. From the high to the low, all will go down. Those who survive the financial wreckage with some shred of dignity intact are only those whose values are diametrically opposed to Merdle's. At the end of the novel, little Dorrit and Arthur, now happily married,

> …went down into a modest life of usefulness and happiness. Went down to give a mother's care, in the fullness of time to Fanny's (her sister's) neglected children no less than their own, and to leave that lady going into Society. Went down to give a tender nurse and friend to Tip (her brother) for some few years, who was never vexed by the great exactions he made of her…

By contrast, when his mercenary schemes are about to be exposed, Merdle, like Sadleir and some desperate millionaires in the Wall Street crash of '29, kills himself. His suicide is as quiet and lonely as his interior life. He is un-mourned by anyone, dying in the total isolation that threatens Scrooge in "the Ghost of Christmas Future" before he repents. The "Society" that once worshiped Merdle only grieves the loss of its investments. Dickens persistently reminds us that if poverty is painful, wealth, especially ill-gotten wealth, can never buy true happiness.

Bolgia 8: the False Counselors—Carker, Tulkinghorn

The example of Merdle shows how some of Dickens' characters might easily fall into more than one circle of Hell. As financial advisor to the British Empire, Merdle is a false prophet, a thief, a false friend, as well as a false counselor. But certain characters, like James Carker in *Dombey and Sons*, are explicitly placed in a situation to give advice, and their abuse of this position can be seen clearly as a form of "false counsel." Carker is Paul Dombey's assistant who at first seems a loyal and trusted worker, though never given complete respect as he is not a member of the family. He is always referred to, not without *double entendre*, as "The Manager." At first, he faithfully carries out Dombey's instructions, both in business and in personal affairs, but as the novel evolves, his darker side emerges. He is always watching and waiting, plotting for his own benefit in the firm. He is described by Dickens as stealthy and cat-like:

> Mr. Carker the Manager, sly of manner, sharp of tooth, soft of foot, watchful of eye, oily of tongue, cruel of heart, nice of habit, sat with a dainty steadfastness at his work, as if he were waiting at a mouse's hole.

At first he seems to act merely as Dombey's agent, loyally carrying out his wishes in keeping Florence from the young man she loves, and away from Dombey himself. In fact, Carker is jealous of anyone who is close to Dombey, including the son Paul he idolizes, who will die young.

On a business level, we see Carker cunningly tracking all the accounts at Dombey's business to make sure he will benefit personally. He is compared not merely to a sneaky cat with sharp teeth and claws, kept well hidden, but to a clever card player. He is, in fact, especially sharp at all games and always wins:

> The face of Mr. Carker the Manager was in good keeping with such a fancy (the player of cards). It was the face of a man who studied his play warily: who made himself master of all the strong and weak points of the game: who registered the cards in his mind as they fell about him, who knew exactly what was on them what they missed, and what they made: who was crafty to find out what the other players held, and who never betrayed his own hand.

In short, Carker is the perfect schemer and fraud. He succeeds in manipulating everyone around him, especially Dombey, all the while wearing his fake smile.

From the first, Carker is described by his smile; he is constantly smiling, even when cruel, as he is to his own younger brother John and his unhappy sister Harriet whom he has abandoned. The ever-present "teeth," that Dickens never fails to mention, reveal his true nature. He manipulates poor young Rob Toodle, persuading him that he is his "patron," and uses him to spy on Florence Dombey:

> "And take care," returned his patron, bending forward to advance his grinning face closer to the boy's, and pat him on the shoulder with the handle of his whip: "take care you talk about affairs of mine to nobody but me."
>
> "To nobody in the world Sir," replied Rob shaking his head.
>
> "Neither there," said Mr. Carker, pointing to the place they had just left, "nor anywhere else. I'll try how true and grateful you can be. I'll prove you!" Making this by his display of teeth and by the action of his head, as much a threat as a promise, he turned from Rob's eyes which were nailed upon him as if he had won the boy by a charm, body and soul, and rode away.

Carker will eventually attempt to steal both Dombey's business and his wife. It is in the latter enterprise, however, that he will eventually fail, and face his true punishment.

As seen in the above circle (Wrath) Edith Skewton Dombey is the only one who is not deceived by Carker, yet she is the one person he sincerely desires to please. Even before she runs away with him, she calls him out for his duplicity towards her husband:

> "It is honest of you, Sir," said Edith, "to confess to your 'limited commendation' and to speak of your disparagement, even of him: being his chief counselor and flatterer."

It is a form of *contrapasso* that Carker will be destroyed both by Edith, who pretends to love then spurns him, and by Dombey himself, who pursues him to a bridge as he runs away, desolate at Edith's rejection.

The sudden glimpse of the man he has betrayed makes Carker lose his footing and fall from the bridge into a train that cuts him into pieces like a whirling mill. Yet as with other Dickens' villains, there may be a flash of consciousness or even of conscience, before he departs this earth. Chilled to the bone, running erratically he knows not where, he sees the sun rise:

> So awful, so transcendent in its beauty, so divinely solemn. As he cast his faded eye upon it, where it rose, tranquil and serene, unmoved by all the wrong and wickedness on which its beams had shone since the beginning of the world, who shall say that some weak sense of virtue upon Earth, and its reward in Heaven, did not manifest itself, even to him? If he remembered his sister or brother with a touch of tenderness and remorse, who shall say it was not then?
>
> He needed some such touch then. Death was on him. He was marked off from the living world and going down to his grave.

Once again, Dickens shows his ability to enter into the mind and soul of his most depraved characters. However, for Carker any possible penitence comes too late, as he is instantly killed. His punishment, to be cut into pieces, would seem to belong to the next of Dante's circles devoted to "the sowers of discord," where the damned literally walk about carrying their own severed body parts. However, Carker does create discord in Dombey's family, helping to keep Dombey from his daughter Florence and his wife Edith, so in a sense, this punishment is fitting.

The powerful lawyer Tulkinghorn in *Bleak House* is another type of false counselor. He is fiercely loyal to Lord Dedlock whom he advises on legal and financial matters, but gradually undermines and ruins Lady Dedlock, his master's adored wife. He correctly suspects that there is some dark secret in her past, and does everything to ferret it out. When he finally discovers the truth—that she has had a child out of wedlock in a former relationship—he ruthlessly blackmails her and forces her to leave her husband, who actually loves her and is willing to forgive her past. Lady Dedlock, seemingly so proud and stately (like Edith Dombey), is in fact extremely vulnerable. She loved the father of her child, who dies an anonymous, lonely death of drugs and alcohol.

She comes to love her daughter Esther, the novel's heroine, once she realizes who she is, and discreetly attempts to make contact with her without revealing her own identity. All this Tulkinghorn, out of misguided loyalty to Lord Dedlock, will destroy. Lady Dedlock is forced to leave her home and become a helpless wanderer through the countryside, where ultimately she becomes ill from exposure and dies. Tulkinghorn, fittingly, will be shot through his own icy heart by the maid Hortense, who resents him for denying her the remuneration she feels is her due for spying on Lady Dedlock.

The lawyers in *Bleak House*, as in so much of Dickens, are on the whole an unsavory lot. From his observations as a clerk in a law office when he was very young, and later as a journalist observing the legal system, Dickens portrays them as parasites, giving false or useless advice, all the while sucking their clients dry or even ruining them. There are a few honest lawyers in Dickens' novels, but they are rare.

Bolgia 9: the Sowers of Discord—Lord Gordon, Gashford, Simon Tappertit, Miss Miggs in "Barnaby Rudge"; the Marquis de St. Evremonde and the Defarges in "A Tale of Two Cities"

To break up a family, as Carker or Tulkinghorn do, is a sin against humanity. To rupture an entire country, setting one social group against the other, is even more terrible. The results can be violent revolution, civil war or even genocide; a whole society can be brought to ruin. For examples of this particular sin, so hurtful to Dante personally, Dickens readers should turn to two novels in particular: *Barnaby Rudge* and *A Tale of Two Cities*. These novels have been seen as "bookends" of Dickens' historical fiction, since one comes at the beginning of his career, the other near the end. However, both show the violence and devastation wrought when social fabric is torn apart by fanaticism.

Barnbaby Rudge is based on the anti-Catholic riots of 1780. Incited by a fanatical Scottish aristocrat Lord George Gordon, the riots began as a reaction against the Catholic Relief Act allowing Catholics for the first time to buy and inherit land in England, among other civil rights.

Initially, Gordon planned for his forces simply to march on Parliament in protest. He expected only 20,000 at the most. However, the frenzied mob grew to 60,000, and over several days terrorized London, burning churches, public buildings and Catholic homes, and even the homes of those who were not sufficiently anti-Catholic. They beat and killed Catholics and their sympathizers, burned Newgate prison and released the prisoners. Dickens suggests that Gordon himself never anticipated such destruction and carnage, although his friend John Forster believed he was too lenient on the man. At the end of the novel, he depicts a penitent Gordon in prison. In reality, Gordon apparently was sorry for what he had wrought, and oddly enough, converted to Judaism at the end of his life. Possibly the virulent Protestant-Catholic conflict made him lose his appetite for all forms of Christianity.

In the novel, Dickens creates fictional conspirators who secretly plot violence, like Gordon's ruthless secretary Gashford (based on Scottish revolutionary and author Robert Watson), Simon Tappertit, apprentice to the locksmith Gabriel Varden, the hangman Dennis, and the duplicitous Sir John Chester. There is also Miss Miggs, a servant in the Varden home, who agitates against the Catholics, all the while resorting to Biblical misquotes and distortions.

Barnaby Rudge proved one of Dickens' most troubled efforts; he had difficulty finishing the novel and apparently in finding a point of focus. Its writing was interrupted by his work on *Oliver Twist, Nicholas Nickleby* and *The Old Curiosity Shop*, not to mention various journalistic projects and the birth of children. Also, he had to contend with real historical situations and characters like Lord Gordon himself. Then there was his own ambivalence about Catholicism, capital punishment, and violent uprisings against injustice. Dickens admits in his Preface to the book that he himself is "one who has no sympathy with the Romish Church," though he "acknowledges as most men do, some esteemed friends among the followers of its creed." (Some of his best friends *were* Catholic.) His *Pictures from Italy* presents a very negative view of the Papacy. On the other hand, so does Dante.

Yet whatever his mixed feelings about Catholicism, Dickens generally opposed prejudice in all its forms: racial, religious and class, and he does so in this novel. The main Catholic characters Emma and Reuben Haredale are portrayed as sympathetic, decent people, in contrast to various hateful Protestant fanatics. Dickens tells us in the same Preface that he intends his story "impartially told" to teach a lesson:

> That what we falsely call a religious cry is easily raised by men who have no religion, and who in their daily practice set at naught the commonest principles of right and wrong, that it is begotten of intolerance and persecution; that it is senseless, besotted, inveterate and unmerciful; all History teaches us.

Though he lacked a strong formal education, Dickens understood well the tragic lessons of human history.

He also demonstrates clearly why Dante's "sowers of discord" are part of the world of fraud. They operate through lies and innuendoes that spread like the plague, precisely through the appeal of mystery to basic human curiosity:

> False priests, false prophets, false doctors, false patriots, false prodigies of any kind, veiling their proceedings in mystery, have always addressed themselves at an immense advantage to the popular credulity, and have been perhaps more indebted to that resource in gaining and keeping for a time the upper hand of Truth and Common sense, than to any item in the whole category of imposture.

He then explains how "a big lie" can grow and create an impassioned movement, whereas the simple facts alone would fail to inspire anybody:

> If all zealous Protestants had been publicly urged to join an association for the avowed purpose of singing a hymn or two occasionally, and hearing some indifferent speeches made, and ultimately of petitioning Parliament not to pass an act for abolishing the penal laws against Catholic priests, the penalty of perpetual imprisonment denounced against those who educated children in that persuasion, and the disqualification of all members of the Romish church to inherit real property (the actual bill before Parliament)...might perhaps have called together a hundred

people. But when vague rumors got abroad that in this Protestant Association a secret power was mustering against the government for undefined and mighty purposes; when the air was filled with whispers of a confederacy among the Popish powers to enslave and degrade England, establish an inquisition in London and turn the pens of Smithfield market into stakes and cauldrons...then the mania spread indeed, and the body still increasing every day, grew forty thousand strong.

In short, prejudice can too easily be inflamed by lies and fear, as we have tragically witnessed through the centuries: from the witchcraft accusations of the Middle Ages, to the distribution of the *Protocols of the Elders of Zion* by Nazis claiming that Jews were bent on destroying Germany, or the myth that the Tutsis in Rwanda had killed their Hutu president, and the devastating consequences of such lies.*** From vague rumors, secret meetings, and falsehoods, the anti-Catholic movement spreads in *Barnaby Rudge* until it creates a full scale human disaster.

The novel opens at the Maypole, the cozy pub at the center of the town's social life, run by a prosperous and ruddy proprietor, John Willett. As in many of Dickens novels, the inn represents the kind of ordinary human "heaven" that stands in opposition to the "hell" of strife and discord. It's a place where people of all beliefs and walks of life are welcomed to drink, eat and share their stories. It is no accident that by the end of the novel the Maypole will be burned to the ground, utterly destroyed by a band of fanatics, its stout, sociable (if somewhat headstrong) proprietor beaten nearly to death.

Another "little bit of heaven" is the clean, orderly and cheerful home of the good locksmith Gabriel Varden:

...there was not a neater, more scrupulously tidy, or more punctiliously ordered house, in Clerkenwell, in London, in all England.

*** Today we see how totally false rumors that President Obama wasn't born in America, isn't a Christian, plans to impose socialism on our country, can be spread through ordinary social networks and mass media, and feed virulent anti-government hatred. So-called "Christian" Congresswoman Michelle Bachmann attempted to unleash a McCarthyite attack on a respected Muslim aide to Hillary Clinton. Fortunately even Senator John McCain was willing to stand up quickly against her lies. Still 35% of Republican voters believe the whopper that President Obama wasn't born in America and is a Marxist and a Muslim.

Dickens' values are immediately on display in these first few chapters: good fellowship and human pleasures, a tolerant society, a family with a happy hearth and home. As the story evolves, all of these will be seriously threatened or destroyed.

From the first, however, there is a serpent, or even several in Varden's little garden of paradise where he lives with his wife and pretty, affectionate daughter Dolly, the object of several suitors in the novel. One of these is Varden's odd assistant Simon Tappertit, a skinny, unattractive fellow who prides himself on his dancing and fine clothes, but who is secretly conspiring with the Gordonites. Then there is Varden's maid Miss Miggs, a religious zealot who continually stirs up trouble through gossip, both within the Varden family and without it. Finally, Mrs. Varden herself, always a bit of a malcontent, allies with the anti-Catholics in spirit if not in action.

Mrs. Varden is mercurial and moody, a fervent Protestant and a difficult wife. She is influenced for the worse by Miss Miggs, who is beguiled by the anti-Protestant crusade, as well as generally misanthropic. Miggs eggs Mrs. Varden on to disputes with her husband, just as she encourages Mrs. Varden's anti-Catholic leanings. From the first, she is a true "sower of discord," both inside and outside the family. After a quarrel with his wife, egged on by Miss Miggs, the generally patient Gabriel Varden wakes from a gentle doze, and murmurs to himself:

> "I wish somebody would marry Miggs. But that's impossible! I wonder whether there's any madman alive, who would marry Miss Miggs!"

Miggs, who is herself in love with Simon Tappertit, jealously plots against Dolly Varden, whom Tappertit desires. She uses her fake sympathy for Mrs. Varden against her husband, always taking the wife's part even when she is at her most irrational. But worst of all, she enters into the Gordonite conspiracy, and encourages Mrs. Varden to do likewise. The personal conspiracies—to separate the Catholic Emma Haredale from Edward, the Protestant son of Sir John Chester, and Dolly from Joe, the son of the Maypole proprietor John Willett—are intertwined with the larger conspiracy of the Protestant fanatics led by Gordon, against all Catholics and their sympathizers.

We first have hints of trouble as Simon Tappertit steals his master's key, and sneaks out of the house in the middle of the night to attend a secret meeting. There are many meetings after this, some of them actually in an upstairs room of the Maypole. Little by little, the adherents to their cause grow in numbers, soon including, among others, Miss Miggs, Mrs. Varden, Barnaby Rudge Jr. and Hugh. It is interesting that as the movement gains momentum, its leader Lord Gordon begins to have doubts himself. After one of his more fiery speeches, he is pondering the event with his secretary Gashford:

> "Did I move them, Gashford?" said Lord George.
>
> "Move them, my lord! Move them! They cried to be led on against the Papists, they vowed a dreadful vengeance on their heads, they roared like men possessed—"
>
> "But not by devils," said his lord.
>
> "By devils, my lord! By angels."
>
> "Yes—oh surely—by angels no doubt," said Lord Gordon, thrusting his hands into his pockets, taking them out again to bite his nails, and looking uncomfortably at the fire. "Of course, by angels—eh Gashford?"

Gordon is already disturbed by the fact that among the mob he has helped create, there were "some plaguey ill-looking characters," but Gashford reassures him that their cause is "godly." This exchange allows us to see how those who create bloodshed all too often see themselves on the "side of the angels," from Christian Crusades of the past, to Islamic "Holy Wars" of today. Gashford reminds Lord Gordon that it was he who first convinced him of the cause and, "stricken by the magic of his eloquence in Scotland, abjured the eloquence of the Romish church, and clung to him as one whose timely hand plucked me from a pit?" In short, it is now too late to turn back from the "holy cause" they have both embraced.

While they are quietly stirring up the masses, some conspirators pose as fair and honorable men. Sir John Chester, the fake aristocrat, has also joined their cause, although he pretends otherwise in conversation with

Mr. Haredale, a former "friend." Here Sir John is reminiscing about the fact that they went to the same school in France, Haredale as a Catholic unable to get an education in England, he as "a promising young Protestant...sent to learn the French tongue from a native of Paris." Haredale, however, is immune to the blandishments of a man who secretly hates him:

> "Add to the singularity, Sir John," said Mr. Haredale, "that some of you Protestants of promise are at this moment leagued in yonder building, to prevent us having the surpassing and unheard of privilege of teaching our children to read and write—here—in this land, where thousands of us enter your service every year, and to preserve the freedom of which, we die in bloody battles abroad, in heaps: and that others of you, to the number of some thousands as I learn, are led to look on all men of my creed as wolves and beasts of prey, by this man Gashford."

For an author who claims he has little "sympathy for the Romish Church," the words Dickens places in the mouth of a Catholic who feels the sting of religious prejudice are extremely powerful. Catholics then (like African-Americans before the days of civil rights, and gays in recent times) were apparently allowed to lay down their lives for a country where they couldn't enjoy its basic civil liberties.

Soon the anti-Catholic movement has moved beyond simple prejudice into open mob rule. When the conflagration comes, it burns completely out of control; the forces of public order, the police and army, are taken by surprise and even, in some cases, sympathize with the conspirators. They temporarily abandon any effort to control the situation, until it actually threatens to bring down the entire capital. Dickens' chapters on the violence that occurs in the course of this uprising provide countless indelible examples of the results of "discord:"

> If Bedlam gates had been flung open wide, there would not have issued forth such maniacs as that night had made. There were men there who danced and trampled on the beds of flowers as though they trampled on human enemies, and wrenched them from their stalks, like savages who twisted human necks. There were men who cast their lighted torches in the air and suffered them to fall on their heads and faces, blis-

tering the skin with deep unseemly burns. There were men who rushed up to the fire, and paddled in it with their hands as if in water;...On the skull of one drunken lad—not twenty, by his looks—who lay upon the ground with a bottle in his mouth, the lead from the roof came down in a shower of liquid fire, white hot; melting his head like wax. When the scattered parties were collected, men—living yet, but singed as with hot irons—were plucked out of the cellars, and carried off upon the shoulders of others, who strove to wake them as they went along, with ribald jokes, and left them, dead, in the passages of hospitals. But of all this howling throng not one learned mercy from, nor sickened at these sights; nor was the fierce, besotted, senseless rage of one man glutted.

And how will the chief conspirators be punished? Lord Gordon himself, who was never proven guilty of actually promoting bloodshed, ends up in prison for five years. While in prison, apparently penitent, he shows kindness to prisoners of all religious beliefs including Catholics, and eventually converts to Judaism. Since he is an historical figure, Dickens can't do much to alter his fate. The hangman Dennis, who has so relished his power over others, will be hung, all the while begging for mercy—a true *contrapasso*. In the fighting, Simon Tappertit will lose the legs he has been so vain of, while Miss Miggs is banished from the Varden household, then thrown out of her nephew's home as well. Detested by everyone, she winds up appropriately working as a prison turnkey, where of course she abuses the prisoners who hate her. As for Sir John Chester, we will find him in an even deeper circle, where he meets his well-deserved punishment. Gashford, the violent secretary to Gordon who is also responsible for kidnapping both Dolly Varden and Emma Haredale, has a curious end. He escapes hanging through a legal technicality and drags out a miserable existence for years, but later takes his own life.

Years later, Dickens wrote a second historical novel, *A Tale of Two Cities*, showing the tragic effects of another type of discord: revolutionary fervor carried to extremes. Although sympathetic to the common people who had suffered for centuries under the yoke of the aristocracy, Dickens could never approve the violence unleashed under the Reign of Terror. We have already looked at Madame Defarge, one of the chief revolutionary conspirators, in the Circle of the Violent. To understand the violence in this novel, it is perhaps best to look at the revolutionaries as a collective body, their sins as collective sins.

Although *A Tale of Two Cities* was written later in Dickens' life (1857), the idea for the novel was gestating within him much earlier. Apparently, the scene of the first trial of Charles Darnay at which he is betrayed by the spy Barsad, had its origins in the '40's, around the time of *Barnaby Rudge*. And of course, the chief influence on the book was his friend Thomas Carlyle's *History of the French Revolution*, first read by Dickens in the 1830's. He became fascinated with the topic and asked Carlyle to recommend other books on the French Revolution, all of which became sources for the novel. However, the plot and theme of *A Tale of Two Cities* are Dickens' own. Unlike Carlyle, he viewed the injustices that spawned the revolution to be as significant as the bloody revolt that followed. As early as the 1840's he wrote:

> "It was a struggle on the part of the people for social recognition and existence…it was a struggle for the overthrow of a system of oppression, which in its contempt of all humanity, decency, and natural rights, and in the systematic degradation of the people, had trained them to be the demons that they showed themselves when they rose up and cast it down forever."[5]

In his talk about "natural rights" and "humanity" Dickens echoes the 18th century philosophers, as well as Romantics like Wordsworth, who himself exalted the French Revolution when young:

> "Bliss was it in that dawn to be alive/ But to be young was very heaven." ("The Prelude")

However, the deterioration of this hopeful revolution into the Reign of Terror was as horrifying to Dickens as it soon became to Wordsworth, who found himself in France in the midst of that violent upheaval. Dickens' famous opening words: "It was the best of times; it was the worst of times," seem to echo Wordsworth, and in many ways sum up the entire novel.

The first third of the novel vividly demonstrates the oppressive nature of the French aristocracy; the haughty disregard for the feelings of the poor is shown in the behavior of the Marquis de St. Evremonde, who carelessly rolls his carriage over a young peasant boy and refuses to stop. He is a rapist of young women, a murderer of political dissidents, and a cruelly arrogant man. In this sense, he is just as much "a creator of discord" as the revolutionaries who follow him. Here is his reaction to a distraught father, after his carriage has run over his son:

> "Killed!" shrieked the man in wild desperation, extending both arms at their length above his head, and staring at him. "Dead!"
>
> The people closed round and looked at the Marquis. There was nothing revealed by the many eyes that looked at him but watchfulness and eagerness; there was no visible menacing or anger. Neither did the people say anything; after the first cry, they had been silent, and they remained so. The voice of the submissive man who had spoken was flat and tame in its extreme submission. Monsieur the Marquis ran his eyes over them, as if they had been mere rats come out of their holes.
>
> He took out his purse.
>
> "It is extraordinary to me," said he, "that you people cannot take care of your own children. One or the other of you is forever in the way. How do I know what injury you have done my horses. See! Give him that."
>
> He threw out a gold coin for the valet to pick up, and all the heads craned forward that all the eyes might look down at it as it fell. The tall man called out again with a most unearthly cry, "Dead."

How "extraordinary" too, that Dickens uses the word "rats" to describe the nobleman's attitude to the poor. This was in fact, the very terminology used by the Hutus as they prepared to massacre the Tutsis in the Rwandan genocide; it was the same term used by Libyan dictator Khaddafi as he prepared to kill his country's protestors—language that proved alarming enough to provoke international intervention. In fact, the dehumanization of "the other" required for mass killing is the psychological attribute Dickens conveys so well. It is the same ability to demonize "all the nobles," even a gentle soul like Charles Darnay who has purposely given up his aristocratic heritage that permits the revolutionaries to become killers. The apparently "submissive" crowd, submissive only because they are forced to be so, will become totally ruthless once their passions are unleashed.

As in *Barnaby Rudge*, the seeds of violence are already being planted in secret conspiracies as the novel opens. Although the people appear to be cowed by the aristocracy, in Part I of the novel we already see foreshadowing of the violence that is to come. In front of Defarge's wineshop, a central meeting place for the conspirators, there is an accidental wine spill, with a huge wine cask lying broken on the ground. The frenzied poor literally drink up the wine from the dirt, covering themselves all over with its red stain:

> Those who had been greedy with the staves of the cask had acquired a tigerish smear about the mouth; and one tall joker and so besmirched his head more out of a long squalid bag of a nightcap than in it, scrawled upon a wall with his finger dipped in muddy wine lees—BLOOD.
>
> The time was to come when that wine too would be spilled on the street-stones, and when the stain of it would be red upon many there.

The use of the term "tigerish," eventually applied to Mme. Defarge and other revolutionaries, indicates how quickly humans in such circumstances can be turned into wild animals. In fact, a few pages later, Dickens tells us:

> In the hunted air of the people there was yet some wild-beast thought of turning at bay. Depressed and slinking though they were, eyes of fire were not wanting among them...the cutlers knives and axes were sharp and bright; the smith's hammers were heavy, and the gunmaker's stock was murderous.

The masses are clearly preparing themselves for a terrible vengeance. The code name "Jacques" is the secret password passed among the revolutionaries. It not only protects their real identities, but creates a bond among them; they are no longer individuals, they will soon be part of a larger cause—and then a mob. The subsuming of the individual into a larger whole was something that Dickens invariably distrusted. Even when he supports the cause itself, such as the just demands of the underpaid workers in *Hard Times*, he criticizes the "group think" that disregards the individual conscience of an honest man like Stephen Blackpool, and actually comes out against the union's actions when they shun Blackpool for not joining the strike.

Women as well as men take a leadership role in the French Revolution in *A Tale of Two Cities* (apparently historically accurate), in sharp contrast to the majority of Dickens' generally docile women characters. By the end of Part II, they are shown knitting with particular ferocity: "The fingers of the knitting women were vicious, with the experience that they could tear." In fact, it is clear that Madame Defarge, once unloosed, will be even more ferocious than her husband Ernest. Whereas he eventually shows a drop of pity for the family of his former master Dr. Manette, she will have none of it.

If Ernest Defarge sounds the initial call to action, the women take it up with bloodthirsty glee:

> "Patriots!" said Defarge, in a determined voice, "are we ready?"
>
> Instantly Madame Defarge's knife was in her girdle; the drum was beating in the streets, as if it and a drummer had flown together by magic; and the Vengeance, uttering terrifying shrieks, and flinging her arms around her head like all the forty Furies at once, was tearing from house to house, rousing the women.
>
> The men were terrible, in the bloody-minded anger with which they looked from widows, caught up what arms they had, and came pouring down into the streets; but the women were a sight to chill the boldest.

Their rage is terrifying, but Dickens shows that it comes from the depth of their suffering; they have silently stood by, watching their husbands and fathers killed and their children die of starvation. Horror marked with sympathy generally marks Dickens' descriptions of the revolution, as it takes fire and spreads.

At first, the targets of the revolution are those who have truly done wrong, like the Monseigneur (who comes to stand for his entire class). But soon relatively innocent servants of that class, like the tax collector Monsieur Gabelle, whom they incorrectly blame for the heavy taxes they bear, will fall under the knife. Irrationality and bloodthirstiness take hold; the guilty and the innocent will all be charged by the mob and killed horribly.

The rest, as we say, is History. Heads roll from the bloody guillotines of the revolutionaries who now control France. Chateaux, churches and administrative offices are burnt to the ground. Charles Darnay, Lucie Manette and their innocent daughter, although initially protected by Defarge, will be threatened with death when Madame Defarge turns against them. As the novel's protagonists, they are eventually spared, but thousands of innocent victims of the Reign of Terror, like the young girl who precedes Sydney Carton to the guillotine, are not.

It is difficult to say this particular novel has a "happy ending." The revolutionary bloodshed continues, even while the principle characters are saved. In the case of Charles Darnay, this will be through the Christ-like self-sacrifice of Sydney Carton, his flawed alter ego, who is redeemed in his noble death by taking Darnay's place at the guillotine.

More significantly the ending of *A Tale of Two Cities* is a caution to humanity against injustice, and the chaos it invariably breeds:

> All the devouring and insatiate Monsters since imagination could record itself are fused into the one realization, Guillotine. And yet there is not in France, with its rich variety of soil and climate, a blade, a leaf, a root, a sprig, a peppercorn which will grow to maturity under conditions more certain than those that have produced this horror. Crush humanity out of its shape once more, under similar hammers, and it will twist itself into the same tortured forms. Sow the same seed of rapacious license and oppression over again, and it will surely yield the same fruit according to its kind.

In other words, as the Bible tells us, and Dickens himself so often repeats, "As ye sow, so shall ye reap."(Galatians: 6:7) The French aristocrats, with their heads literally severed from their bodies, come to resemble Dante's "sowers of discord," who carry their own severed heads around with them for all eternity.

Bolgia 10: The Falsifiers: Impersonators, Alchemists and Counterfeiters—Scadder, Montague Tigg, Sir John Chester and Alfred Jingle

For Dante, this broad category of sinner includes a wide variety of tricksters and con artists. Alchemy, considered a legitimate occupation in the Middle Ages when performed honestly, only became fraudulent when people pretended to turn base metals into gold. This specific practice could hardly be found in Dickens, except insofar as Boffin "the golden dustman" of *Our Mutual Friend* is able to turn a profit off the heaps of "dust" he inherits—in a metaphorical sense, turning dust into gold. In Dickens' time, it was a lucrative practice to buy and sell the huge piles of dirt and rubbish around London, which often contained valuable discarded articles. Of course, Boffin is an honest man, and could never be accused of "alchemy" or consigned to Hell.

However, if not "alchemy" *per se,* similar forms of "falsification" can certainly be found throughout Dickens novels, ranging from the comic or innocent to the deadly serious. From the swindlers in *Martin Chuzzlewit,* to the many impersonators in other novels, the deliberately deceitful abound along with their all too credulous victims.

As noted, American readers, who adored Dickens' other novels, were horrified at the stinging satire of their country in *Martin Chuzzlewit*; in Dickens' portrait, a land filled with con artists of every stripe: lying newspaper editors, phony aristocrats, pretentious philosophers, fake generals, and purveyors of useless land. However, in part, the satire is of young Martin himself; he is in an unfamiliar land, too easily gulled by those around him. He has impetuously run away to America in a rage against his hypocritical patron Pecksniff and his grandfather, who has appeared to disown him. Martin's headstrong nature and inability to heed the good advice of others also contributes to his downfall. When he is brought to a seedy land office by his new American acquaintance General Choke, he is told that the parcel of land called Eden is a paradise, and is convinced to buy it by a sleazy land agent named Scadder:

"You know we didn't wish to sell the lots off right away to any loafer as might bid," said Scadder, "but had concluded to reserve 'em for Aristocrats of Natur'. Yes!"

"And they are here, sir!" cried the General with warmth, "They are here, sir!"

Like all good salesmen, the General mixes flattery with his pitch:

"These gentlemen air friends of mine, or I would not have brought 'em here, sir, being well aware, sir, that the lots at present go entirely too cheap."

The map of Eden on the wall of the office, is of course, a total counterfeit, depicting a beautiful "architectural city" (sure to appeal to young Chuzzlewit) complete with "banks, churches, cathedrals, market-places…" Martin's only disappointment is that "there will be nothing left for me to build." Assured that that is not the case, he soon parts with his small savings, along with his friend Mark Tapley's more considerable one.

Once they arrive in Eden, they realize with horror their tragic mistake. Instead of a rich and prosperous land with fruitful soil, they find a dismal, disease-infested swamp with sick and dying inhabitants.

At the urging of the stout-hearted Tapley, Martin gamely tries to make the best of the situation, but gives in to despair once he knows how fully they have been tricked. Both nearly die of swamp fever, but are eventually spared. In the case of *Martin Chuzzlewit*, we cannot say that the Scadders and General Chokes of America will get their just desserts. Martin and Mark will simply escape with their lives—and go back to England, while the scams they suffer will doubtlessly be perpetrated on other poor victims. The lesson of their saga rests not so much in the punishment of the villains, but in Martin's own moral development as he learns from his follies. In this, *Martin Chuzzlewit*, like its predecessor *The Pickwick Papers*, is a kind of allegory, representing a pilgrimage from ignorance to wisdom through suffering. It also resembles earlier picaresque novels, like those of Smollett and Fielding, much beloved by young Dickens, *Don Quixote*, another childhood favorite, and Voltaire's classic philosophical tale *Candide*.

As for "impersonators," a choice example comes from the same novel in the character of Montague Tigg, co-conspirator with Martin's cousin, the unsavory Chevy Slyme. Like some of Dickens' other villains, Tigg is as comic as is he unscrupulous. He changes his costume to the elaborate outfit of a nobleman and his name to Tigg Montague, in the belief that an elegant appearance will more easily deceive his victims, as of course, it does. Like Merdle, Tigg operates a kind of Ponzi scheme, using his investors' money to pay other investors just enough to keep them lending him more.

Tigg first appears on the scene in the Blue Dragon Inn, where he immediately attempts to ingratiate himself with Pecksniff, implying he is a member of the Chuzzlewit family through his connection with his "adopted brother" Chevy Slyme. Like Alfred Jingle, a deceptive and troublesome acquaintance of the Pickwick club, he is first a "stranger," but very quickly attaches himself to those he can manipulate for financial gain. Also like the humorous Jingle, he is full of high spirits and manic eloquence, a born actor whom Dickens may deprecate, but clearly enjoys immensely. He is dressed in a ragged multi-colored costume, like a clown. After he first tries to pass himself off as Slyme, he attempts to overwhelm his target (Pecksniff) with his grandiose speech:

> "I understand your mistake, and I am not offended. Why? Because it's complimentary. You suppose I would set myself up as Chevy Slyme. Sir, if there is a man on earth whom a gentleman would feel proud and honored to be mistaken for, it is Chevy Slyme. For he is, without exception, the highest-minded, the most independent spirited, most original, spiritual, classical, talented, the most thoroughly Shakespearean, if not Miltonic, at the same time the most disgustingly under-appreciated dog I know. But sir, I have not the vanity to attempt to pass for Slyme. Any other man in the wide world I am equal to; but Slyme is, I frankly confess, a great many cuts above me."

Of course Pecksniff is not exactly bowled over by this pretty speech, but little by little, Tigg insinuates himself into the Chuzzlewit family.

At first, he only tries to borrow "a trifling loan, as a crownpiece" from Pecksniff, but has no idea how tight-fisted this particular mark can be. He doesn't get his loan, but does succeed in playing on Pecksniff's feelings of rejection by Old Martin enough to make his presence in the Chuzzlewit family circle acceptable. From this vantage point, he conspires with Slyme to get a chunk of the Chuzzlewit fortune. When this effort proves unprofitable (Old Martin holds tightly to his money, as we have seen), he reinvents himself as Tigg Montague, impersonating a man of high social standing and great wealth. Tigg now understands the importance of appearance; no longer in his clownish rags, he dresses royally and installs himself in a palatial office complete with servants—none of which have been paid for.

The title of Chapter 27 where the "new and improved" version of Tigg first appears is appropriately "Showing that old friends may not only appear with new faces, but in false colours. That people are prone to bite; and that biters may sometimes be bitten."

Tigg now appears a completely different man:

He had a world of jet-black shining hair upon his head, upon his cheeks, upon his chin, upon his upper lip. His clothes, symmetrically made, were of the newest fashion and the costliest kind. Flowers of gold and blue and blushing red were on his waistcoat; precious chains and jewels sparkled on his breast;...And yet, though changed his name and changed his outward surface, it was Tigg. Though turned and twisted upside down, and inside out, as great men have been sometimes known to be; though no longer Montague Tigg but Tigg Montague; it was still Tigg: the same Satanic, gallant, military Tigg. The brass was burnished, lacquered, newly stamped; yet it was the true Tigg metal notwithstanding.

The contradictory list of adjectives (Satanic, gallant, military) betrays Dickens' ambivalence about his own creation; Tigg is of course evil, but as an ingenious self-made man, he is also rather impressive. As with other Dickens' villains, in Tigg there is a bit of the author himself—a man sometimes noted for his dandified, overly colorful style of dress and certainly for his self-creation of a great man out of lowly beginnings.

Tigg's scam, however, is not quite so playful. He sets himself up as the head of the "Anglo-Bengalee Disinterested Loan and Life Assurance Company" from which operation he will, like Merdle, will quickly part innocent investors from their money. The scheme, as implied in Dickens' sly aside "as great men have been sometimes known to be" is yet another dig at some of the shady financial schemes taking place in England at the time. By opening a series of offices at the same time—with no start-up money at all—Tigg's sheer bravado makes him, for a time at least, a rich and happy man.

Unfortunately, he makes the fatal error of joining with, and then betraying Jonas Chuzzlewitt, not a character to be charmed or trifled with. When Chuzzlewit realizes that he too has been robbed by Tigg, he plots to murder him and abandon his body out on a desolate country road:

> Never more beheld by mortal eye or heard by mortal ear: one man excepted. That man, parting the leaves and branches on the other side, near where the path emerged again, came leaping out soon afterwards:
>
> What he had left within the wood, that he sprang out of it, as if it were a hell!
>
> The body of a murdered man. In one thick solitary spot it lay among the last year's leaves of oak and beech, just as it had fallen headlong down. Sopping and soaking in among the leaves that formed its pillow;...went a dark, dark stain that dyed the whole summer night from earth to heaven.

As he often does, Dickens has quickly shifted from light-hearted satire to a sinister scene of darkness and violence. Tigg may be a funny, even at times appealing character, but his *contrapasso* is death at the hands of a dangerous man he has attempted to defraud. Tigg's murder is foreshadowed in an earlier chapter, when Jonas and Tigg are traveling in a carriage at night, and their horses stumble, casting their carriage to the ground. At this moment, Tigg is knocked unconscious, and Jonas actually tries to direct the hooves of the horses towards his head, but the presence of another person in the carriage temporarily keeps him from fulfilling his sinister aim.

The murder of Tigg by a co-conspirator is strongly reminiscent of Chaucer's *The Pardoner's Tale*, where three thieves seeking gold wind up dead by each other's hands, a cautionary tale against greed. In this case, the caution is not only against greed, but also against fraud. Tigg thinks he has deceived everyone; but he hasn't deceived Jonas, who nurtures a quiet hatred of him, awaiting his moment to strike.

An even more heinous "impersonator" appears in *Barnaby Rudge* in the person of Sir John Chester. Chester is not of noble birth, but he displays a fake family crest. In fact, his title was bestowed after some legal finagling on his part:

> But how Sir John? Nothing so simple or so easy. One touch with a sword of state, and the transformation was effected. John Chester, Esquire, M.P. attended court—went up with an address—headed a deputation. Such elegance of manner, so many graces of deportment, such powers of conversation could never pass unnoticed. "Mr." was too common for such merit.

In reality, Chester's background is dubious, to say the least:

> He had stood in danger of arrest; of bailiffs and of jail—a vulgar jail, to which the common people with small incomes went...He offered—not indeed to pay for his debts, but to let him sit for a close borough when his own son came of age, which if he lived would come to pass in twenty years.

Through the vagaries of the law, Chester is able to enter Parliament, is knighted, and thus "became Sir John."

Throughout the novel, this phony aristocrat disports himself exactly like the real "Monseigneur" in *A Tale of Two Cities*. He lives a life of luxury, complete with a retinue of servants, and sips his "chocolate" daintily, while treating everyone around him with haughty contempt. He is depicted as cold, cruel and selfish, and is repeatedly called by Dickens—with heavy irony—"The Knight."

The person he dominates the most, the rough stableman Hugh, is—unbeknownst to—him his own son, a fact only revealed at the very end of the novel. Hugh was born to a beautiful gypsy, for a time Chester's lover, a woman eventually hung in prison for a minor infraction of the law. She takes the secret of Hugh's birth to her grave, but one of her cell-mates overhears the story and much later reveals it to Gabriel Varden. Chester's acknowledged son Edward is in love with the Catholic Emma Haredale, niece to Reuben Haredale, a man Chester detests. John Chester manipulates both of his sons, conspiring against Edward's love affair and using Hugh as a secret instrument in the anti-Catholic cause.

Hugh, who fears no one else, instinctively obeys Chester like a dog. After he has faithfully performed one of Chester's devious deeds, Hugh returns to him for more humiliation:

> "Where have you been? What harm have you been doing?"
>
> "No harm at all," growled Hugh with humility. "I have only done as you ordered."
>
> "As I what?" returned Sir John.
>
> "Well then," said Hugh uneasily, "as you advised, or said I ought, or said I might, or said that you would do if you was me. Don't be so hard upon me, master."
>
> Something like an expression of triumph in the perfect control he had established over this rough instrument appeared in the knight's face for an instant; but it vanished instantly.

Chester is not only a false nobleman; he is a false human being, pretending to be a man of peace while secretly stoking the fires of anti-Catholicism.

Like Shakespeare's duplicitous Iago, he speaks the truth only when he is alone:

> "Let me see. My relative and I, who are the most Protestant fellows in the world, give our worst wishes to the Roman Catholic cause; and to Saville, who introduces their bill, I have a personal objection besides; but each of us has himself for the first article of his creed, we cannot commit ourselves by joining with a very extravagant madman, such as this Gordon most undoubtedly is. Now really, to foment his disturbances in secret through the medium of such a very apt instrument as my savage friend here, may further our real ends; and to express at all becoming seasons, a disapprobation of his proceedings...will certainly be to gain a

character for honesty and uprightness of purpose, which cannot fail to do us infinite service..."

Hugh, as his "instrument," will eventually be caught and hung. Before this happens, however, Chester learns the truth about him from Gabriel Varden, who has learned it from a fellow prisoner of Hugh's. Varden dashes to Chester's home to tell him that Hugh is in fact his own son, begging him to save Hugh's life. Although he "turns deathly pale" for a moment upon hearing this story, Chester refuses to do anything for Hugh, who will be hung for the very crimes Chester encouraged. In this cruel act, Chester proves himself a "false father" as well as a false knight and a false human being.

Hugh, who dies never knowing his true parentage, curses his absent father as he awaits execution:

"On the head of that man, who in his conscience, owns me for his son, I leave the wish that he may never sicken on his bed of down, but die a violent death as I do now and have the night-wind for his only mourner. To this I say, Amen, amen."

Of course, Hugh's dying curse will prove prophetic.

Although Chester is too clever and devious to be caught by the law, he will meet his *contrapasso* at the hand of his sworn enemy Reuben Haredale, the man he has tried to ruin because they were once in love with the same woman, his son Edward's mother. She married Chester, but died of his cruel mistreatment. Chester has encouraged the world to falsely believe that Haredale was guilty of his brother's death, conspired to separate Emma Haredale, Haredale's beloved niece from his son Edward and is even complicit in a plot to kidnap Emma and Dolly Varden. Despite the many plots against them, Chester's son Edward has finally been able to marry Emma, bitter gall to his father. At the end of the novel, he and Haredale meet accidentally on a dark night—although it is implied that he may have been lying in wait for Haredale. Although Haredale hates Chester with a passion, he initially resists Chester's attempt to goad him into a fight:

"I have acted," cried Mr. Haredale, "with honour and good faith. Do not force me to renew this duel tonight!"

"You have said my 'wretched' son I think?" said Sir John with a smile. "Poor fool! The dupe of such a shallow knave—trapped into marriage by such an uncle and by such a niece—he well deserves your pity. But he is no longer a son of mine: you are welcome to the prize your craft has made, sir."

"Once more," cried his opponent wildly stamping on the ground, "although you tear me from my better angel, I implore you not to come within the reach of my sword tonight. Oh! Why were you here at all! Why have we met!"

Naturally the two were fated to meet. Chester attacks Haredale who just happens to be carrying a sword lent to him by a concerned friend, worried about his walking alone at night on a desolate road. Reluctantly, he is goaded into a duel, where he is repeatedly stabbed by Chester:

> It was directly after receiving one of these (stab wounds) in his arm, that Mr. Haredale, making a keener thrust as he felt the warm blood spurting out, plunged his sword through his opponent's body to the hilt.

Chester, false to the end, actually smiles as he dies:

> ...he gazed at him with scorn and hatred in his look; but seeming to remember, even then, that this expression would distort his features after death, he tried to smile, and faintly moving his right hand as if to hide his bloody linen in his vest, fell back dead—the phantom of last night.

This reflexive action on the part of Chester, hiding his blood as he dies, bizarrrely echoes his fake family crest. Death at the hand of his mortal enemy is a fitting *contrapasso* for this cruel and fraudulent man.

For his part, although he is guilty only of killing in self-defense, the genuinely moral Haredale goes into a monastery, "repairing straight to a religious institution known throughout Europe for the rigour and severity of its discipline," takes monastic vows, and dies a few years later "buried in its gloomy cloisters." Because he is truly penitent, Haredale is not bound for Hell. However, the gravity of taking a human life, especially that of a man he hates, weighs on his conscience, as in Dickens' eyes, it should.

Yet another consummately evil "impersonator" is the genteel murderer Rigaud in *Little Dorrit*. A vicious man with a drooping black moustache "that goes up and goes down," he changes his name to Blandois, reinventing himself as a gentleman of wealth. We have already visited him in the Circle of the Violent, because he killed his wife, and his real life prototype was a serial killer. However, it's worth mentioning him again here, as he deviously attempts to entice Mrs. Clennam in one of his business schemes by impersonating a well-connected businessman. His *contrapasso*, as we have seen, is to be killed when Mr. Clennam's house collapses on him.

As a would-be actor himself, Dickens also has his share of light-hearted impersonators like Alfred Jingle in *The Pickwick Papers*, who begins the novel by wearing another man's borrowed clothes and forcing him into a comedic duel. A chronic trouble-maker for the Pickwick Club, Jingle ends up posing as a decorated army officer called Captain Fitz-Marshall so he can win the hand of a wealthy girl. He is finally exposed and brought to prison, but will ultimately be pardoned by Pickwick himself, and sent of to a new life in exile, where he becomes a hard working individual and is eventually redeemed. Humorous villains like Alfred Jingle are, as we have mentioned, similar to the actors Dickens adored. In fact, his on stage "impersonations" of his villains became a kind of obsession.

However, in the diabolical Sir John Chester, Dickens shows us the truly sinister face of fraud and impersonation. Since he betrays his country as well as both his sons, it is perhaps natural that he is found in the circle closest to Dante's next and deepest circle: the Traitors.

VII

The Traitors

For Dante, the ninth and deepest circle of the *Inferno* is also the most evil. For him, treason betrays "a deep iciness of the heart," so it is fitting that Lucifer himself is found there, trapped in the frozen lake Cocytus. Intriguingly, there is even more ice in Dante's version of the Inferno than the fire we generally associate with Hell.

For Dickens as well, "coldness of heart" is connected with all his darkest villains. The inability to love one's fellow human beings or to feel an ounce of compassion for their sufferings is, for Dickens, the worst of sins. Indeed this view may suggest he is a "Sermon on the Mount Christian" after all, because in this section of the Bible Jesus teaches his followers the essence of their faith: "to love the Lord thy God with all thy heart and all thy might, and love thy neighbor as thyself." Dickens no doubt appreciated the fact that after this sage advice, it is a nitpicking "lawyer" who presses Jesus to define his terms: "And who is my neighbor?" Jesus then follows up with the famous Parable of the Good Samaritan, whose underlying message is that your "neighbor" is any other human being, regardless of geography, race or religion. Of course this would accord perfectly with Dickens' own beliefs.

Some of Dickens' traitors are also frauds and murderers; however, they may be even worse because they have turned against those closest to them, or those they should most naturally love: family and friends, country, guests, patrons and God.

Traitors to Family and Friends

With apologies to those who remain unconvinced that he is the murderer in Dickens' unfinished last novel *The Mystery of Edwin Drood*, let us begin with John Jasper, surely one of Dickens' creepiest characters. Jasper is both traitor to family, as the person he kills is his nephew Edwin Drood, and traitor to guest, since at the beginning of the novel Edwin is being welcomed into his uncle's home for dinner. Jasper is the organist at the town cathedral, itself described as gloomy and sinister:

> That same afternoon, the massive gray square tower of an old Cathedral rises before the sight of the jaded traveller. The bells are going for daily vesper service, and he must needs attend to it, one would say, from his haste to reach the open Cathedral door. The choir are getting on their sullied white robes, in a hurry when he arrives among them, gets on his own robe, and falls into the procession filling in to service. Then, the Sacristan locks the iron barred gates that divide the sanctuary from the chancel, and all of the procession having scuttled into their places, hide their faces; and then the intoned words, 'WHEN THE WICKED MAN' rise among the groin of arches and beams of the roof, awakening muttered thunder.

To make the scene darker still, Jasper has just arrived after awakening from a troubled, nightmare-filled sleep in an opium den, to the sounds of the hymn "When the wicked man..." (How much more foreshadowing does the reader need?) It is interesting that the town where this mystery is set is Cloisterham, a fictionalized version of Portsmouth, the town of Dicken's childhood which is depicted so cheerfully in his first novel *The Pickwick Papers*. The atmosphere pervading this, his final novel, is, however, almost unremittingly dark. Secret crypts, constant references to the bodies of the dead, dim passageways, smoky opium dens, all run throughout this half completed novel, written when Dickens was exhausted, seriously ill and perhaps sensing his own imminent death.

Jasper himself is relatively young, an unlikely uncle to Edwin who is near to his own age. Yet as we experience his character throughout the novel, he feels much older. Is this, as some biographers have suggested, because he is a stand-in for Dickens himself, at the time of this writing in his fifties, and like Jasper, obsessed with a very young woman? Of course, this is mere speculation. What is not speculation is that Jasper himself is dark and like Dickens at this time, apparently depressed:

> Mr. Jasper is a dark man of some six-and-twenty, with thick, lustrous, well-arranged black hair. He looks older than he is as dark men often do…his manner is a little sombre. His room is a little sombre, and may have its influence on forming his manner. It is mostly in shadow.

Also not in dispute is Jasper's obsessive love for his music student, the beautiful young orphan girl Rosa Bud who unfortunately, has been informally promised in marriage to Edwin Drood in their dead parents' wills. This, of course, is the crux of the entire "mystery." Rosa does not love Jasper; in fact she fears him and loathes his attentions. Meanwhile Rosa and Edwin, though warm childhood friends, are not in love with each other, and unbeknownst to Jasper will eventually break off their engagement.

At first Jasper tries to keep this passion to himself, still hoping to win Rosa's love by keeping her as his pupil. He seems to feel some real affection for his nephew Edwin, at least in the beginning, and welcomes him to his home when he first comes to town. He calls him "my dear Ned," treats him to an excellent dinner, and even confides his feelings of depression over his job:

> "Anyhow my dear Ned," Jasper resumes, as he shakes his head with a grave cheerfulness. "I must subdue myself to my vocation; which is much the same thing outwardly. It's too late to find another now. This is a confidence between us….I have reposed it in you, because—"
> Edwin breaks in, "I feel it, I assure you. Because we are fast friends, and because you love and trust me, as I love and trust you. Both hands, Jack."

The two shake hands warmly. At this point Jasper may yet hope that a marriage between the two young people will never actually take place, as their family's arrangements were made a long time before. However, even in this apparently friendly scene, he is already dropping hints of danger. Edwin rattles on amiably, revealing that he probably will marry "Pussy" as he affectionately calls Rosa, even though he's not sure he's in love with her, and carry her off with him as "Mrs. Edwin Drood." Jasper, who has been watching him attentively during his speech, has an expression of "musing benevolence," but then:

> He remains in that attitude after they are spoken, as if in a kind of fascination attendant on his strong interest in that youthful spirit that he loves so well. Then he says with a quiet smile:
> "You won't be warned then?"
> "No, Jack"
> "You can't be warned, then?"
> "No, Jack, not by you. Besides that I don't really consider myself in danger, I don't like your putting yourself in that position."

Of what exactly is his "uncle Jack" warning him? Edwin innocently believes he is only being advised not to enter into a marriage of which he is unsure. He has absolutely no idea of the "danger" he is really in.

Little by little, Jasper begins to put his plot into action. Unlike Bradley Headstone, who must be worked into an emotional frenzy over Lizzie Hexam before being driven to murder, John Jasper acts with cool calculation throughout the novel. First he manages to get Durdles, the old watchman of the crypts drunk, and steals one of his keys. Clearly he plans to secrete something (a body?) in one of the empty crypts. He then takes a watch belonging to his nephew which he later plants by the ocean, in order to lay the blame for Edwin's murder on Neville Landless, who also likes Rosa. He encourages the two men to quarrel, and drops persistent hints to everyone that he thinks young Landless might "do Edwin some harm."

The reader never sees the actual murder take place—hence the tempting "mystery" of the book. After Jasper has accidentally seen Rosa and Edwin kissing—in reality a farewell kiss, as they have both admitted to each other that they are not in love and shouldn't marry after all—Edwin simply disappears. It is this absence of an actual murder scene that leads some readers to maintain that Jasper is not the murderer, or even that Edwin has simply run away. Since he never contacts anyone for years afterwards, even his banker, his family or his friends, such a scenario seems highly unlikely.

Although Dickens didn't live to reveal to readers that Jasper murdered his nephew, he did apparently tell his children and his editor-biographer John Forster who the killer was, and they later insisted it was Jasper. There are also numerous hints dropped by the author: the secret crypt where Edwin's body presumably lies, Jasper's exceptionally long scarf (insisted upon by Dickens to illustrator Luke Fildes), probably used to strangle Edwin that somehow disappears, and Jasper's attempt to place the blame on Neville Landless. Even more revealing, Jasper falls into a deathly faint when he learns from Rosa's advisor and friend Grewgious, that the two were not going to marry after all, revealing that the murder of his nephew was not only evil, but ultimately unnecessary.

Finally, we see Jasper's frenzied attempt to seduce Rosa, despite her instinctive aversion to him. In this, he clearly resembles Bradley Headstone. A year after Edwin's disappearance, he finally confesses his true feelings:

> "Rosa, even when my dear boy was affianced to you, I loved you madly, even when I thought his happiness in having you for his wife was certain, I loved you madly; even when I strove to make him more ardently devoted to you, I loved you madly…in the distasteful work of the day, in the wakeful misery of the night, girded by sordid realities or wandering through Paradises and Hells of visions into which I rushed, carrying your image in my arms, I loved you madly."
>
> If anything could make his words more hideous to her than they are in themselves, it would be the contrast between the violence of his look and delivery, and the composure of his assumed attitude.

Here we see the true face of Fraud and Treachery; Jasper is virtually admitting that he killed Edwin and why. Rosa is horrified, as she now suspects Jasper may be guilty of more than unreciprocated passion. She hurls her anger at him:

> "You were as false throughout, sir, as you are now. You were false to him daily and hourly."

This strong rejection doesn't deter Jasper, who continues his suit with an "easy attitude rendering his working features and his convulsive hands absolutely diabolical." His aggressive harassment frightens Rosa so much she has to go into hiding from him, with the help of Mr. Grewgious, Canon Crisparkle and other devoted friends. According to some biographers, Dickens intended that Jasper would be found out at last, and sent to prison, where he meditates upon his fate before hanging.[1]

Of all forms of "traitor to family," patricide is surely one of the worst. In this sense, Jonas Chuzzlewit's attempted poisoning of his father so that he may inherit more quickly makes him the perfect candidate for *Caina*, Dante's name for this particular section of the Traitor's circle. Indeed, Dickens directly refers to Chuzzlewit as "Cain." Towards the end of the novel, Jonas, afraid that he has been found out, attempts to flee:

> When he looked back across his shoulder, was it to see if his quick footsteps still fell dry upon the dusty pavement, or were already moist and clogged with the red mire that stained the naked feet of Cain!

Of all the sinners in *Martin Chuzzlewit*, most of whom like Pecksniff or Tigg have elements of humor, Jonas Chuzzlewit is the most frightening. He is driven solely by greed, and is without a shred of humanity or even family feeling. Dickens tells his readers that this is because of his false upbringing; his father Anthony has raised him to care for nothing but money:

> But being so born and bred, admired for that which made him hateful, and justified from his cradle in cunning, treachery and avarice; I claim him as the legitimate issue of the father on whom those vices seem to recoil. And I submit that their recoil upon that man, in his unhonoured age, is not a mere piece of poetical justice, but is the extreme exposition of a direct truth.

Lest we miss the point, Dickens once again reminds us: "As we sow, so shall we reap."

The fact that Jonas has been raised to avarice by his father is certainly not meant by Dickens to excuse his evil deeds. Anthony Chuzzlewit himself is not quite as greedy as his son. He is beloved by his faithful servant Chuffey, whom he has apparently treated well. Chuffey feels the kind of fidelity towards his master that Jonas, his own son, totally lacks. Moreover, when Jonas attempts to poison his father, we later learn that the old man actually realizes his son's plot in time, but out of despair at having raised a murderer, takes the poison himself.

Jonas sees his father as nothing more than "a piece of property":

> ...he had gradually come to look, with impatience, on his parent as a certain amount of personal estate, which had no right whatever to be going at large, but ought to be secured in that particular iron safe which is commonly called a coffin, and banked in the grave.

This chilling metaphor conveys the singularly cold-blooded attitude Jonas has towards his father. For him, it is only one short step from seeing him in monetary terms (something that might be said of other badly raised children) to actually murdering him. This does not mean, however, that he is totally unaffected by the crime. Immediately after, as the dead body lies upstairs in their home awaiting the undertaker, Jonas does have haunted feelings, although they are more of fear than remorse:

> The weight of that which was stretched out stiff and stark, in the awful chamber above-stairs, so crushed and bore down Jonas, that he bent beneath the load. During the whole long seven days and nights, he was oppressed and haunted by a dreadful sense of its presence in the house. Did the door move, he looked towards it with a livid face and starting eye, as if he fully believed the ghostly fingers clutched the handle. Did the fire flicker in a draught of air, he glanced over his shoulder, as almost dreading to behold some shrouded figure fanning and flapping at it with fearful dress.

Eventually, after a biblical "seven days and nights," Jonas becomes calm and resumes the coolly indifferent demeanor he usually wears. However, the presence of the honest servant Mr. Chuffey, the only person who sincerely mourns Anthony Chuzzlewit, serves as a continual reproach and even a threat. Chuffey's loud outcries of sorrow after the funeral suggest to Jonas that he may suspect what really happened. Chuffey has just been reproached for his excessive grief by the family doctor, on the grounds that he isn't even a family member (of course, none of the family members care at all):

> "This is bad, selfish, very wrong Mr. Chuffey. You should take example from others, my good sir. You forget that you were not connected by ties of blood with our deceased friend; and that he had a very near and dear relation, Mr. Chuffey."
>
> "Aye, his own son!" cried the old man. "His own, own, only son."
>
> "He's not right in his head, you know," said Jonas, turning pale. "You're not to mind anything he says. I shouldn't wonder if he was to talk some precious nonsense."

At one point Jonas seriously considers doing away with Chuffey as well, but instead decides to simply dub him "crazy," and keep him upstairs, carefully attended by Mrs. Gamp who becomes more of a jailer than a nurse.

In addition to attempting to murder his father, Jonas murders Tigg, as we have seen. He is also cruelly abusive to his wife Mercy (Merry) Pecksniff, who after teasing and flirting with him in the early days of their courtship, soon learns that she is under his total domination and held in check by terror, like other abused women. In short, Jonas is one of Dickens' "thoroughly bad" characters. These are the people for whom there is no hope; only some real-life version of Hell.

If Jonas shows signs of fear after killing his father, his mind truly begins to unravel after he has murdered Tigg. He listens for strange sounds about the house, constantly awaiting the discovery of Tigg's body:

> He tried—he had never left off trying—not to forget it was there, for that was impossible, but to forget to weary himself by drawing vivid pictures of it in his fancy; by going softly about it among the leaves, approaching it nearer and nearer through a gap in the boughs, and startling the very flies that were sprinkled over it, like heaps of dried currants... And the more his thoughts were set upon the discovery, the stronger was the fascination which attracted them to the thing itself: lying alone in the wood...If he had been condemned to bear the body in his arms, and lay it down for recognition at the feet of every one he met, it could not

have been more constantly with him, or a cause of more monotonous and dismal occupation than it was in this state of his mind.

Still he was not sorry. It was no contrition or remorse for what he had done that moved him; it was nothing but alarm for his own security.

As we have seen with Barnaby Rudge Sr., Bill Sikes and Fagin, their mental suffering is mainly fear for themselves, not repentance for their sins. The "Hell" they experience is the torment created by their own minds. It's ironic that at the last moment Jonas will be cleared of his father's murder by old Chuffey, who knows the truth, that the poison planned by Jonas was in fact self-administered by his father. However, Jonas' relief at being cleared of patricide, of which he was guilty by intention, is short-lived when he is immediately proven guilty of the murder of Tigg by witnesses who have been shadowing him.

Jonas will wind up killing himself once his crimes have been revealed, and he is about to be taken to prison. The fact that he takes the same poison he originally meant for his father is certainly a form of *contrapasso*.

Yet another villainous "traitor to family" is Edward Leeford, a.k.a. "Monks," half-brother to Oliver in in *Oliver Twist*. In a sense, Monks is Oliver's true antagonist throughout the novel, even though his role is only revealed late in the story. Monks is aware of Oliver's parentage (they have the same father who had Oliver out of wedlock with Oliver's mother), but schemes to keep it a secret so that he can keep the family inheritance. It is Monks who plots with Fagin to snatch Oliver and turn him into a criminal, because their father's will—which makes Oliver his inheritor—has a clause that disinherits him if he commits any criminal act.

The theme of the "illegitimate child" who is in fact a particularly decent character, is an intriguing one that runs through a number of Dickens' novels. These include Oliver, the virtuous Esther Summerson in *Bleak House* and Arthur Clennam in *Little Dorrit*. Dickens' approach to these characters suggests that his sense of morality, although profound, is clearly not the conventional morality of his time which looked down on "bastards." The harsh treatment of Esther by the aunt who raises her is more typical of the attitude of the time; Dickens is an exception. We might recall that Dickens himself may have had a child out of wedlock with Ellen Ternan. In Dickens' novels, it appears to be more "sinful" to produce a monstrous offspring from a miserable legal marriage, like Monks, than a true "love child," like little Oliver or Esther Summerson.

Monks is described as a sinister-looking man, with a red mark on his neck (the mark of Cain?) and a strange habit of gnawing at his hands. It is through Nancy's precise descriptions of the man she has seen conspiring with Fagin that Monks, a.k.a. Leeford, will ultimately be identified. Here she is speaking to Mr. Brownlow, Oliver's protector, and Rose Maylie who will turn out to be Oliver's aunt on his mother's side:

> "He is tall," said the girl, "and a strongly made man, but not stout; he has a lurking walk; and as he walks, constantly looks over his shoulder, first on one side, and then on the other. Don't forget that, for his eyes are sunk into his head so much deeper than any other man's, that you might almost tell him by that alone. His face is dark like his hair and eyes; and though he can't be more than six or eight and twenty, withered and haggard. His lips are often discoloured and disfigured with the marks of teeth; for he has desperate fits and sometimes even bites his hands and covers them with wounds...Upon his throat: so high that you can see a part of it below his neckerchief when he turns his face: there is—"
>
> "A broad red mark, like a burn or a scald?" cried the gentleman.

At this moment, Mr. Brownlow realizes that Monks and the man he knows as Leeford are one and the same, the son of his old friend who died many years before. He begins to piece together the truth that Oliver is also the man's son, and that it is he who is rightfully entitled to the inheritance claimed by Monks.

Monks has done everything to hide the truth, including disposing of a small locket with a portrait of Oliver's mother. However, when finally faced with a possible charge of complicity in the murder of Nancy Sikes, Monks reluctantly agrees to tell the truth about the will, even though there is no longer any physical evidence linking Oliver to his father.

In a Christian spirit of love for his old friend and hopes for redemption for Monks, Mr. Brownlow agrees to forgive the villain and even give him half the inheritance. Oliver, now happily safe and surrounded by loving family and friends, agrees. However, Monks' own fundamentally evil character takes a hand in setting his final destiny:

> Monks, still bearing that assumed name, retired with his portion to a distant part of the New World; where, having quickly squandered it, he once more fell into his old courses and, after undergoing a long confinement for some fresh act of fraud and knavery, sunk under an attack of his old disorder, and died in prison.

"The New World," whether in America, the West Indies, South Africa or Australia, gives many of Dickens' villains and flawed characters their second chance. For some, like little Emily, it will mean a kind of redemption; for others like Monks, it will be just another chance to fall into sin and perdition. Indeed, one might say that it represents a part of Dickens' world that best resembles Dante's Purgatory because it offers hope and a second chance to sinners.

Oliver Twist is less complex than his later novels. In it, the virtuous characters are generally rewarded with wealth and happiness while the evil are punished with prison or death. As his work develops, Dickens becomes somewhat more nuanced. Of course, we sometimes see the good suffer even in Dickens' early works—characters like the poor little Dick in *Oliver Twist*, little Nell and Smike—but in the later works we may also see the "bad" like Mrs. Clennam's crafty servant Flintwinch in *Little Dorrit* occasionally get away with their crimes. In short, Dickens' sense of realism occasionally overtakes his religious conviction that the evil are inevitably punished. As for the "good" who suffer, like Nell, Dickens makes it clear that their reward must be in the next life, not in this mortal vale of tears.

Since this particular section of the Circle of Traitors includes Traitors to Friends, it is a fitting place to finally discuss the duplicitous Silas Wegg, one of the many villains in Dickens' last completed novel *Our Mutual Friend*. One might be tempted to place Wegg in the Circle of Avarice, as he is certainly driven by greed, but his devious, persistent plotting against Mr. Boffin, the friend and patron who has always treated him kindly, would best place him among the traitors.

Silas Wegg is among the avaricious poor that can also be found in Dickens' novels. (Dickens was enough of a realist to understand that not all victims of poverty were saints.) He lives off of selling fruit and halfpenny ballads in the streets, or digging out whatever he can find from the city dust heaps. He also has one wooden leg, and at first seems somewhat pathetic. In fact, he attracts sympathy from his friend Mr. Boffin, who hires Wegg to tutor him, since Boffin, who has inherited wealth from his former master, is illiterate and wants to improve himself. For his part, Wegg is trying to get enough money to buy back his original leg (to "complete himself"). In this case, as with Monks in *Oliver Twist*, a physical deformity is symbolic of a moral deformity as well. Wegg pretends to be Boffin's friend, but secretly plots with Mr. Venus, a taxidermist, to blackmail Boffin and get all his money.

From their first arrangements to pay for lessons, we see that Wegg considers the uneducated Boffin to be an easy mark. They are negotiating a fee for Wegg to teach Boffin how to read, and Wegg quickly gets Boffin to double his offer:

> "What do you think of the terms, Wegg?" Mr. Boffin then asked, with unconcealed anxiety.
>
> Silas, who had stimulated this anxiety by his hard reserve of manner, and who had begun to understand this man very well, replied with an air; as if he were saying something extraordinarily generous and great:
>
> "Mr. Boffin, I never bargain."
>
> "So I should have thought of you!" said Boffin admiringly.
>
> "No sir. I never did 'aggle and I never will 'aggle. Consequently I meet you at once, free and fair with Done, for double the money!"
>
> Mr. Boffin seemed a little unprepared for this conclusion, but assented with the remark, "You know better than I do Wegg," and again shook hands with him upon it.

At this point, Boffin's self-consciousness about his illiteracy seems to make him a natural victim for a man Dickens terms "that ligneous sharper." Boffin appears even more hapless when he humbly presents the book he hopes to learn to read as "The Decline and Fall of the Rooshian Empire." Wegg condescendingly sets him straight that it is in fact, *The Decline and Fall of the Roman Empire,* but in terms of real knowledge of history, he isn't much more advanced than Boffin. He can read the book aloud by rote to Boffin, but has little idea of what the words really mean.

Despite his own minimal education, Wegg's ambitions know no bounds. He has always coveted the Harmon mansion that sits across from his little stall, because he once did some odd jobs for old Mr. Harmon. As the novel develops, he gradually begins to refer to this mansion as "our house." Meanwhile his greed and resentment of Boffin intensify when Boffin inherits the entire Harmon fortune (old man Harmon disinherited his son John out of sheer nastiness) and sets himself up in the luxurious home as a gentleman. To make matters even worse, Boffin hires John Rokesmith—in reality John Harmon—the novel's main character as his secretary, a position that Wegg feels rightfully belongs to him. He confides his bitter resentments to the man he believes to be his partner in crime, Mr. Venus the taxidermist.

Without unravelling the entire complex plot of the novel, we can reveal that by scavenging the dust piles, Wegg thinks he has found a newer copy of the will that would disinherit both Boffin and John Harmon. Through blackmail, he plans to reduce them both to penury, while he finally sets himself up in the mansion lording it over those he now bitterly resents.

The tables are eventually turned on him by characters that turn out to be less gullible than they first seem, and his plots will be foiled. Even after Wegg has been exposed as a total villain, the generous Boffin actually offers "to set him up in another stall" with a few pounds, which he then tries to wheedle into more money. However, Wegg will wind up being lifted up by his collar and tossed into a passing scavenger's cart, where he falls "with a prodigious splash." In a very fitting *contrapasso,* a man who has done his dirty work as a scavenger will end up as just another piece of garbage. And of course, the multi-volume work he has been slowly teaching Boffin, *The Decline and Fall of the Roman Empire,* provides a ready parallel to his own outsized ambitions.

Traitors to Country—Barsad and Cly in A Tale of Two Cities

In a sense, the "sowers of discord" can also be considered traitors, since they wreak such havoc on their countries, yet few Dickens characters deliberately set out to betray their nations. Perhaps because loyalty to England and its empire was axiomatic for Dickens himself, outright treason may have seemed almost unthinkable to him. One character who is literally a traitor is Barsad the spy in *A Tale of Two Cities.* Barsad is actually English, but poses as a Frenchman, and works as a kind of double agent; at the beginning of the novel, he spies for the French revolutionaries; later he spies for the British against the French revolutionary government. Although he is a relatively minor character, Barsad plays a pivotal role in the novel's plot, sometimes in collaboration with another spy, Roger Cly.

Like most spies, Barsad is also a fraud—in this case an impersonator. Towards the end of the novel we discover that his real name is Solomon Pross, and that he is actually English and the long-lost brother of Miss Pross, believed by her to be dead.

Early in the novel, during the first treason trial of Charles Darnay, Barsad "bears false witness" against Darnay, accusing him of carrying messages to the French government against the British. With his familiar heavy irony, Dickens introduces Barsad into the legal proceedings:

> Mr. Solicitor-General then, following his leader's lead, examined the patriot (Barsad): John Barsad, gentleman by name. The story of his pure soul was exactly what Mr. Attorney-General had described it to be—perhaps if it had a fault, a little too exactly. Having released his noble bosom from its burden, he would have modestly withdrawn himself, but that the wigged gentleman with the papers before him, sitting not far from Mr. Lorry, begged to ask him a few questions...Had he ever been a spy himself? No, he scorned the base insinuation. What did he live upon? His property. Where was his property? He didn't precisely remember where it was.

Needless to say, Barsad is about as much of a "patriot" as Chester is "a knight" or Rev. Stiggins "a shepherd."

The case against Darnay rests primarily on the testimony of Barsad, an obviously unreliable witness and his co-conspirator "the virtuous servant" Roger Cly. Cly is another shady character, as Darnay's lawyer exposes with Cly's shabby protestations:

> He loved his country, and couldn't bear it and had given information. He had never been convicted of stealing a silver tea-pot; he had been maligned respecting a mustard-pot, but it turned out to be only a plated one.

At first, it looks as though Darnay will be convicted on the testimony of these two villains, showing the unreliability of a legal system Dickens so often satirizes.

However, in this case Darnay will be exonerated through a demonstration of his uncanny resemblance to his lawyer Sydney Carton, confounding the testimony against him. Darnay's honest lawyers Stryver and Carton (showing that even the legal profession has its exceptions) expose Barsad to the jury for what he really is:

> ...showing them how the patriot Barsad, was a hired spy and traitor, an unblushing trafficker in blood, and one of the greatest scoundrels upon earth since the accursed Judas—which he certainly did look rather like. How the virtuous servant Cly, was his friend and partner, and was worthy to be; how the watchful eyes of those forgers and false swearers had rested upon the prisoner as a victim, because some family affairs in France, he being of French extraction, did require his making some passages across the channel—

Unfortunately, unlike other Dickens' novels where the villain once properly unmasked is punished, this is only the beginning of Barsad's treachery.

When Barsad is suspected by the Defarges to be a spy commissioned for their quarter who will supposedly work for the revolutionaries, we get a fitting description of the man from M. Defarge:

> "...dark; generally, rather handsome visage, eyes dark, face thin, long and sallow; nose aquiline, but not straight, having a peculiar inclination towards the left cheek; expression, therefore, sinister."

Here Dickens uses the word "sinister" in both its Latin meaning (left) and in the usual English sense of the word. When Barsad appears in the wine shop, he avidly questions Madame Defarge, but does not tell her who he is. For her part, she inspects him cautiously. He tries to draw out her Republican sympathies, but she is far too wily to show her cards to a stranger:

> "Ah, the unfortunate, miserable people! So oppressed—as you say."
> "As you say," madame retorted, correcting him and deftly knitting an extra something into his name that boded him no good.

Once again, we find a woman far too clever to be taken in by someone who is obviously there to pry out information:

> The spy, who was there to pick up any crumbs he could find or make, did not allow his baffled state to express himself in his sinister face; but stood with an air of gossiping gallantry...

Neither Madame Defarge nor her husband allow themselves to be drawn into revealing their true political opinions to someone they neither know nor trust. They give Barsad nothing, but unfortunately, he deliberately imparts the fatal fact that Lucie Manette is about to marry Charles Darnay, a member of the aristocratic family Madame Defarge bitterly hates. This encounter, apparently so casual, inspires the train of events that will place Lucie and Darnay in mortal danger.

Barsad appears to work with the revolutionaries, although they never really trust him, becoming a turnkey in the prison they establish for doomed aristocrats. It is here, at the end of the novel, that he involuntarily plays a key role for good. Sydney Carton has discovered that he has been a double agent working for the British, a fact he will expose unless Barsad helps him free Charles Darnay from prison where he awaits the guillotine. Carton sits Barsad down and talks to him as if they were playing a game of cards:

> "In short," said Sydney, "this is a desperate time, when desperate games are played for desperate stakes."

He then proceeds to play his card, what he has learned about Barsad:

"Mr. Barsad...Sheep of the prisons, emissary of the Republican committees, now turnkey, now prisoner, always spy and secret informer, so much the more valuable here for being English than an Englishman is less open to suspicion of subornation in those characters than a Frenchman, represents himself to his employers under a false name. That's a very good card, Mr. Barsad, now in the employ of the republican French government, formerly in the employ of the aristocratic English government, the enemy of France and freedom. That's an excellent card. Inference clear as day in this region of suspicion, that Mr. Barsad, still in the pay of the English government, is the spy of Pitt, the treacherous foe of the Republic crouching in its bosom..."

Barsad at first attempts denial and stubbornly refuses to help Carton. But he finally understands that Carton's threat to denounce him "to the nearest Section Committee" of the revolution will most certainly place his own head under the guillotine, and he reluctantly agrees to cooperate in order to save himself. In fact, he realizes that even more facts might eventually come out about him than even Carton knows:

> Thrown out of his honourable employment in England, through too much hard swearing there—not because he was not wanted there; our English reasons for vaunting our superiority to secrecy and spies are a very modern date—he knew that he had crossed the Channel and had accepted service in France: first as a tempter and an eavesdropper among his own countrymen there: gradually as a tempter and an eavesdropper among the natives.

Evidently his initial visit to Defarge's wine shop was at the behest of the English. Will this unmitigated traitor and scoundrel, repeatedly called by Dickens "the spy" be "redeemed" by helping Carton free Charles Darnay, completely against his own will? It seems not.

In his prophetic last comments of the novel, Dickens predicts Barsad's ultimate fate. He imagines what Carton would have told us, had he lived to see into the future:

> "I see Barsad and Cly, Defarge, The Vengeance, the Juryman, the Judge, long ranks of the new oppressors who have risen on the destruction of the old, perishing by the retributive instrument (the guillotine)

before it shall cease out of its present use. I see a beautiful city and a brilliant people rising out of the abyss, and in their struggles to be truly free,
in their triumphs and defeats, through long years to come, I see the evil
of this time and of the previous time of which this is the natural birth,
gradually making expiation for itself and wearing out."

In gazing beyond the boundaries of his own novel, Dickens informs
us that Barsad and others like him will eventually be punished, and true
justice restored. It is an oddly hopeful note, since as of the writing of the
novel France had been thrown into political turmoil again and again,
and the relatively peaceful democracy it enjoys today was only a distant
reality. Following the democratic revolution of 1848, Louis Bonaparte
installed himself as head of the country through a *coup d'etat*, abolishing
most elements of democracy, a situation that still existed in 1859. The
uprising of 1870, and the violent suppression of the Paris Commune, an
attempt by the working classes to improve their lot, was, of course, yet to
come, but the social unrest that precipitated it was already present. Similarly in England at this time, social upheaval threatened the country—a
factor, according to some, in inspiring Dickens to write this cautionary novel. In any case, Dickens' ultimate vision of a free, peaceful, and
democratic country seems more based on his idealism and inherent need
to see righteousness prevail, than on historical reality.

*Traitors to Patrons and to God—Satan (Lucifer), Uriah Heep, and
Daniel Quilp*

In this, the deepest part of the 9th Circle named *Judecca*, Dante places Judas Iscariot, as well as Brutus and Cassius, betrayers of Julius Caesar
(considered divine by the Romans and thus a father figure to Dante's
Italy.) Finally at the bottom of the Inferno, he encounters Satan himself,
a huge and terrifying figure frozen up to the neck in ice.

In Dickens' novels, it is difficult to find one character that quite approaches Dante's fearful image of Satan, with his three faces of different
colors, his six eyes dripping bloody tears, and his three mouths perpetually crushing other smaller sinners to death. Such a colossal figure of

supreme evil seems almost beyond Dickens' imagination. This apparent failure of the imagination may also flow from Dickens' inherent belief "that good is always stronger than evil."

Dickens does, however, have a few characters that are cosmically evil, not guilty of one or even two sins, but of many. Such characters seem to take a particular delight in the suffering of others. In this, they resemble Shakespeare's Iago, "that demi-devil," whose true motive for destroying Othello remains somewhat obscure, and indeed such characters are often referred to as "devils" by Dickens. Rigaud-Blandois whom we have mentioned several times before, is one such evil character—uncannily frightening to all who encounter him. However, the single character who most clearly embodies pure, unmotivated evil is Daniel Quilp, the demonic dwarf in *The Old Curiosity Shop*. Unlike Satan, he is small, except for his gigantic head, and at times even humorous, but Quilp is almost supernaturally villainous like an evil dwarf from a fairy tale, a form the novel is sometimes compared to.

As for "traitors to patrons," the most ruthless example in Dickens would easily be "that heap of infamy," Uriah Heep in *David Copperfield*.

Heep is one of Dickens' many characters whose appearance instantly betrays his true personality. From their earliest encounter, when both are fifteen years old, David is repelled by him. David recalls his first impressions of Heep:

> Though his face was towards me, I thought for some time, the writing being between us, that he could not see me; but looking that way more attentively, it made me uncomfortable to observe that, every now and then, his sleepless eyes would come below the writing, like two red suns, and stealthily stare at me for I dare say a whole minute at a time, during which his pen went, or pretended to go, as cleverly as ever.

Dickens' ability to size up a character in a single long sentence is uncanny. We see Heep's shiftiness, and perhaps even some association with Satan, who in Dante has terrifying eyes, and according to some mythical accounts, never sleeps. Moreover, Heep evokes the physical repulsion that characterizes Dickens' most evil characters. He is pale, with pale red hair, virtually no eyebrows or lashes, and "skeletal," a truly sinister apparition. At the end of the chapter, David offers Heep his hand as courtesy demands:

> But oh, what a clammy hand his was! As ghostly to the touch as to the sight! I rubbed mine afterwards to warm it, AND TO RUB HIS OFF.

Heep's true nature is amplified rather than diminished by his fawning obsequiousness and his incessant protestations that he is "umble." He tries to gain sympathy by tales of his difficult past:

> "I am well aware that I am the umblest person going," said Uriah Heep, modestly; "let the other be what he may. My mother is likewise a very umble person. We live in a numble abode (sic), Master Copperfield, but have much to be thankful for. My father's former calling was umble. He was a sexton."
>
> "What is he now?" I asked.
>
> "He is a partaker of glory at present, Master Copperfield."

Heep's character manages to incorporate a number of the sins we have encountered before in other circles: fake religiosity, hypocrisy, false counsel, greed and even lust—as we will see later in his designs on Agnes, the innocent daughter of his patron Mr. Wickfield. At times in the novel, he is literally alluded to as "a devil."

His persistent addressing of David as "Master Davey" has a double meaning. In England at this time "master" was the term used for a young man, which is what David is when he first encounters him. As he continues to call him "master" until the end of the novel, when David is an adult, it becomes a subtle form of disrespect. At the same time, it is Heep's hypocritical way of feigning respect for David, who he claims is "above him" in station, in other words, his "master." When they first meet, Heep is a lowly clerk for Mister Wickfield, David a guest in his home and the adopted son of Wickfield's client Betsey Trotwood. They are not as far apart in class as Heep maintains; his humility is both exaggerated and false.

In the course of the novel, Heep, like a malignant tumor, or as Dickens at one point calls him "an incubus," thrives on his patron, little by little rising to the status of a partner in the law firm. All this is done, however, by slowly destroying Wickfield financially, emotionally and physically, preying on his noticeable weakness for alcohol. David tries to be sociable when they first meet, even encouraging Heep's ambition to succeed. In this, he inadvertently predicts what will occur, little realizing the evil methods Heep will use to get ahead:

> "Perhaps you'll be a partner in Mr. Wickfield's business, one of these days," I said to make myself agreeable; "and it will be Wickfield and Heep, or Heep late Wickfield."
> "Oh no, Master Copperfield," returned Uriah, shaking his head, "I am much too umble for that."

As Heep gradually worms his way into Wickfield's home and business, David is preoccupied with other matters: his marriage to Dora, his tragic friendship with Steerforth and the Peggotty family, his own work and ambition. Meanwhile Mr. Micawber, David's friend and former landlord gets a job in the Wickfield home, where he unhappily finds himself collaborating with Heep. In fact he takes over Heep's position as clerk, while Heep rises to the status of a partner in the firm. At this point Micawber becomes strangely secretive, refusing to express himself even to his loyal wife. He is so unlike his usual cheerful, loquacious self, Mrs. Micawber becomes worried about what is happening to her husband and confides to David her worries over his changed character.

When David sees Agnes Wickfield after a long absence, she too confides her concerns about Heep, who is now a partner in the firm, just as David predicted. She tells David:

> "I am afraid I may be cruelly prejudiced—I do not like to let papa go away alone, with him."
> "Does he exercise the same influence over Wickfield still, Agnes?"
> Agnes shook her head. "There is such a change at home," that you would scarcely know the dear old house. They (Heep and his mother) live with us now."

The effects of Heep and his mother on the Wickfield household, bit by bit taking control of everything, parallels David's own early experience with the Murdstones and their malignant influence on his helpless young mother. With Heep's encouragement, Mr. Wickfield has gradually become a pathetic alcoholic, weak and utterly dependent. David remarks sorrowfully, "If I had seen an Ape taking command of a man, I should hardly have thought it a more degrading spectacle."

At the same time, Heep is trying to get close to Agnes, whom he actually hopes to marry once Wickfield is completely in his power, although she understandably despises him.

By the end of the novel, thanks to Micawber who like other fundamentally decent characters that temporarily enable villains (Mr. Venus, Pancks) has finally rebelled, Uriah Heep's schemes and illegal practices are revealed to all. Micawber is a kind-hearted man although his chronic indebtedness made him vulnerable to Heep. When he has finally had enough, he righteously denounces Heep:

> "If there is a scoundrel on this earth," said Mr. Micawber, suddenly breaking out again with the utmost vehemence, "with whom I have already talked too much—that scoundrel's name is HEEP!"

Once Heep feels himself being cornered by his victims: Micawber, David, Agnes, and Betsey Trotwood, he erupts in threats against them all:

> "Miss Wickfield, if you have any love for your father, you had better not join that gang. I'll ruin him, if you do. Now come, I have got some of you under the harrow. Think twice before it goes over you. Think twice you, Micawber, if you don't want to be crushed."

Even David is shocked at Heep's viciousness once he is exposed:

> Though I had long known his servility was false, and all his pretenses knavish and hollow, I had no adequate conception of the extent of his hypocrisy, until I now saw him with his mask off. The suddenness with which he dropped it, when he perceived that it was useless to him; the malice, insolence, the hatred he revealed…took even me by surprise, who had known him so long and disliked him so heartily.

David has now looked upon the naked face of evil, and is appalled by what he sees.

Threats, however, can't help Heep now that Micawber possesses the documents that will expose his illegal dealings. With his usual gift for understatement, Micawber dubs him "probably the most consummate Villain that has ever existed." If he had only added, "in Dickens' novels," he would not be far wrong. Heep is revealed as a forger and cheat, having falsely put Mr. Wickfield's name on various documents in order to steal his money. He has attempted to deceive Mr. Wickfield about the real state of his finances, letting him think he is bankrupt, in order to put the poor man totally in his power. Once he has him, he plans to rob him of everything he has, including his house, down to the last stick of furniture, his business, and his beloved daughter.

Heep eventually lands in prison for fraud, after being forced to turn over to Mr. Wickfield everything he has stolen. First, however, he is soundly beaten with a ruler by Micawber who is now beside himself with rage. These fictional beatings seem to be a way for Dickens to vent his own outrage at some of his villains, without doing them serious physical harm. This, however, does not extend to his murderers, who will themselves be killed.

Uriah Heep has shown himself to be a traitor to his patron Mr. Wickfield. He is also similar to the Devil himself, in his cunning ability to ferret out and prey on the weaknesses of others. Perhaps the only crime Heep is not guilty of is murder, so may be fitting that his penalty isn't death, but rather prison, humiliation and poverty, the very things he has spent a lifetime trying to avoid.

At last we come to our ultimate villain, the diabolical dwarf Daniel Quilp in *The Old Curiosity Shop*. Is Quilp Dickens' version of Satan? Perhaps not quite, but like other incarnations of the devil, Quilp seems not entirely human, with his hideous appearance and grotesque behavior. He is described as he first appears to Nell as:

> ...an elderly man of remarkably hard features and forbidding aspect, and so low in stature as to be quite a dwarf, though his head and face were large enough for the body of a giant. His black eyes were restless,

sly and cunning; his mouth and chin bristly with the stubble of a coarse hard beard; and his complexion was of the kind that never looks clean or wholesome. But what added most to the grotesque expression of his face was a ghastly smile which, appearing to be the result of habit and to have no connection with any mirthful or complacent feeling, constantly revealed the few discoloured fangs that were yet scattered in his mouth, and gave him the aspect of a panting dog...His hands, which were of a rough coarse grain, were very dirty; his fingernails were crooked, long and yellow.

This description of Quilp evokes another association with the Devil, sometimes known as "the Beast." He looks slightly animalistic; he even threatens his wife that he will "bite her" if she crosses him. He crunches eggs whole with their shells on, "devoured gigantic prawns with their heads and shells on, chewed tobacco at the same time, and with extraordinary greediness, drank boiling tea without winking..." Like Uriah Heep with Mr. Wickfield, he holds Nell's grandfather in his power by playing on an old man's weakness, in this case gambling. He has the bills that Nell's grandfather owes him, and when they can't be paid, seizes his business and home. He also has designs on his granddaughter, even though she is just a child and Quilp is already married.

Quilp's actual occupation remains somewhat vague. He is a landlord to Nell's grandfather among others; but this isn't his only job. The murky nature of his business involvements reinforces the almost supernatural sense we have about him as someone not quite real:

Mr. Quilp could scarcely be said to be of any particular trade or calling, though his pursuits were diversified and his occupations numerous. He collected the rents of whole colonies of filthy streets and alleys by the waterside, advanced money to seamen and petty officers...had a share in the ventures of divers mates of East Indiamen, smoked his smuggled cigars under the very nose of the Custom House, and made appointments on the 'Change with men in glazed hats and round jackets pretty well every day.

Like the devil himself, he is everywhere and nowhere.

Despite his repulsive appearance and behavior, Quilp exerts a strange fascination over some women, particularly his own wife, who is completely in his thrall. She tells her friends that if something happens to her, he will have no difficulty finding another wife. At the same time, he terrorizes her, enjoying her submission and fear. He actually tells Nell that he only plans for the wife to live for a few more years; after that he proposes to marry Nell who by then will be "old enough for him." (She is only fourteen.) Needless to say, this proposition petrifies Nell:

> So far from being sustained and stimulated by this delightful prospect, the child shrank from him in great agitation and trembled violently. Mr. Quilp, because frightening anybody afforded him a constitutional delight, or because it was pleasant to contemplate the death of Mrs. Quilp number one...only laughed and feigned to take no heed of her alarm.

Once Quilp discovers Nell's grandfather's gambling addiction, he not only refuses to loan him any more money, but calls in his debts, taking over his only means of support, the Old Curiosity Shop. At this point the old man falls seriously ill with shock and seems at the point of death. However, he does recover, and finally determines to take Nell and flee in the night, taking with them what little money he has hidden away.

Quilp pursues them relentlessly, furious that they have eluded his grasp. He uses every possible connection to Nell in order to ferret out information of their whereabouts, and many times comes close to catching up with them. Their long, miserable flight from Quilp is made even more desperate by Nell's grandfather's gambling away their money, although they meet various kindly "helpers" along the way who try to save them. This journey through the countryside, compared at one point in the novel to *A Pilgrim's Progress,* is the substance of the book. However, Quilp periodically appears to them, either in reality or in Nell's nightmares, terrorizing her and forcing her and her grandfather to continue their wanderings.

They find temporary asylum under the protection of the kindly manager of a waxworks theater, Mrs. Jarley, who offers them work and a place to stay. However, one night, as she is returning to Mrs. Jarley's traveling-carriage where she is to sleep, Nell catches a glimpse of Quilp lurking under a low archway:

> There was an empty niche from which some old statue had fallen or been carried away hundreds of years ago…when there suddenly emerged from the black shade of the arch, a man. The instant he appeared, she recognized him—Who could have failed to recognize in that instant the ugly misshapen Quilp!

How he has come to be there, we never know; he is like the demons that haunt children in their nightmares, relentless and omnipotent. Luckily, he doesn't see her at that moment, and Nell is able to escape— for the time being. Nell, however, has been properly frightened out of her wits.

Dickens frequently revisits Quilp back in London, as he manipulates others into a conspiracy against Nell and her grandfather. In this, his sole object is revenge, because he already knows they have no money. At the same time, he is conspiring against his own co-conspirators, for various reasons. First, he manipulates Nell's wastrel brother Fred (no doubt modeled after Dickens' own brother Frederick, a man perpetually in debt). Quilp hates Frederick because he falsely believes his wife is attracted to him. He encourages Fred's greedy belief that the old man is really very rich, and is only pretending to be poor to swindle Fred out of his rightful inheritance. Like Satan, Quilp immediately intuits and preys on Fred's weaknesses. Fred, both out of greed and resentment over his grandfather's rejection, has his own plan: he wants to catch Nell and marry her off to his friend Dick Swiveller, splitting their supposed "fortune."

As for Dick Swiveller himself, Quilp ensnares him in the plot as well, by making him an assistant to his crooked lawyer Samuel Brass and his sister Sally. Swiveller himself is not a bad person, only weak. He has already been seduced into the plot to get Nell by Fred, who has also played on his frailties:

It is sufficient to know that vanity, interest, poverty, and every spend-thrift consideration urged him to look upon the proposal (to aid Fred) with favor, and that where all other inducements were wanting, the habitual carelessness of his disposition stepped in and still weighed down the scale on the same side.

Quilp is aware of this weakness as well, and uses it against Swiveller, whom he hates because of an inadvertent fight he once had with one of Quilp's boy assistants. He knows full well that Nell is destitute, but like Fred, encourages Dick in his fruitless suit. For his part, Quilp is delighted at the thought of ruining both his supposed partners in crime:

> "Ha ha ha! He shall marry Nell. He shall have her, and I'll be the first man, when the knot's tied hard and fast, to tell 'em what they've gained and what I've helped 'em to. Here will be a clearing of old scores, here will be a time to remind 'em what a capital friend I was, and how I helped them to the heiress. Ha ha ha!"

Quilp, sometimes dubbed "the dwarf," sometimes "a goblin" takes a grotesque pleasure in the suffering of others. He maliciously turns Nell's grandfather against her kind protector and friend Kit Nubbles by claiming that Kit had informed Nell about his gambling. He conspires with the Brasses to put Kit in prison by setting him up for a false theft. Here, however, is where he goes too far. When Kit is eventually exonerated, the police go after Quilp for defrauding the law.

Now Quilp becomes "the pursued." He is ensconced in his cozy retreat where he has just finished a pleasant steak supper and is about to light up a cigar, when his wife brings him a letter from Sally Brass, alerting him that Sampson Brass has confessed their plot to the police who are on their way to arrest him. He hears a knocking at his door and runs out into the pitch black night onto a broken pier, where he loses his footing and falls into the rushing water below. Like Satan, his "fall" brings him to his certain death. He fights against the current in vain:

> One loud cry now—but the resistless water bore him down before he could give it utterance, and, driving him under it, carried him away a corpse.

It toyed and sported with its ghastly freight, now bruising it against the slimy piles, now hiding it in mud or in rank grass, now dragging it heavily over rough stones and gravel…until tired of the ugly plaything, it flung it upon a swamp—a dismal place where pirates had swung in chains through many a wintry night—and left it there to bleach.

And there it lay, alone. The sky was red with flame, and the water that bore it had been tinged with the sullen light as it flowed along.

Unlike Fagin, Bill Sikes or even Jonas, Quilp hasn't a moment's concern for any of his victims, or even a single regret. In fact his very last thoughts are of how he'd like to have Sampson Brass there with him so he could take an awful revenge on his betrayer. In death, Quilp has now become for Dickens an "it," a thing, even less human than he was when alive. The "red" sky suggests a descent into the Hell this "demi-devil" so richly deserves. If he is not quite as awe-inspiring as Dante's Lucifer, Quilp comes frighteningly close.

Having reached the end of his own Inferno and faced down Lucifer himself, Dante looks up at the sky and suddenly "sees the stars." It is a message of hope, before he begins the steep ascent up the ledges of Purgatory and finally into the bliss of Paradise. In many ways, the ending of the allegorical *Old Curiosity Shop* featuring Nell's peaceful death with bands of angels accompanying her to heaven (its final illustration), the good characters rewarded, its evil punished, and the imperfect "purged" of their sins, perfectly echoes Dante.

VIII

Purgatory

As we have seen, Dickens' novels, like Dante's *Commedia,* contain three
types of characters: his villains, his "angels" and many that are neither
saint nor sinner, simply flawed human beings struggling to become better. These characters might find themselves in Purgatory, a place that
permits redemption, but only after a period of suffering and sincere repentance.[1] It should be noted that while medieval Catholics believed in
a literal Purgatory, Protestants like Dickens did not. Catholics believe
that Purgatory comes after death, when the soul needs further purification before ascent to heaven.[2] For Dickens' characters, we have treated
the punishments of the sinner mainly as they occur in this life—although the notion of an afterlife is certainly implied. While there is
no physical place called Purgatory in Dickens, the spiritual concept
remains very similar to that made concrete by Dante, who imagined
Purgatory as a mountain with seven ledges. Also, one Dante scholar
has noted that even Dante's notion of Purgatory is not exactly that of
the Catholic Church; it is predominantly a spiritual and not a formal
process:

> But with all his profound reverence for the Church, Dante maintains
> throughout that the soul's destiny lies in the soul itself, not in any ec-
> clesiastical pronouncement on it.[3]

Dante described the mountain of Purgatory as being formed when
Satan crashed to earth, creating the deep pit of the Inferno and forcing
the earth upwards; so the size of this mountain is related inversely to the
descent into Hell. Because of this, the journey upward is equally long

and difficult. The sins illustrated in Dante's *Purgatorio* correspond to the medieval idea of "the seven capital vices" (popularly known as the seven deadly sins). However, they are all sins of weakness or incontinence, not of malice. They are understood to be forms of excess, extreme versions of something that is not in itself bad.[4] Desire for love, for example, is a good thing, except when carried to extremes. Enjoyment of good food and drink isn't evil—except when carried to excess. However, the sins of malice are different. They require an evil intention, and are not so easily forgiven. There are no murderers, frauds or traitors in Purgatory; instead there are the slothful, the lustful and the envious. There are no "Avaricious," only the less malevolent "Covetous." Since the ledges of Purgatory ascend towards Heaven, the worst of the sins lie at the bottom; the least serious at the top. Finally, although there are punishments in Dante's Purgatory, these are generally lighter than those in Hell, and considered "purgative" or cleansing, rather than punitive.[5] All of the inhabitants of Purgatory are, with lesser or greater speed, ultimately bound for heaven.

For Dickens, many characters and even some of his major protagonists might easily be found in Purgatory. Each is flawed in some important way, and through a process of remorse and suffering, either mental, physical or both, must be "cleansed" in order to achieve true happiness or for Dickens "heaven on earth." These include Pip the hero of *Great Expectations, Martin Chuzzlewit,* Bella Wilfer and Eugene Wrayburn in *Our Mutual Friend,* little Emily in *David Copperfield,* Lady Dedlock in *Bleak House,* and Paul Dombey in *Dombey and Sons.* Of course, there is always Ebenezer Scrooge, whose lonely miserable life and nightmare glimpses of his past, present and future become his "purgation."

The Proud—Estella, Martin Chuzzlewit (old and young), Pip, Lady Dedlock, Dombey

Since pride (*superbia*) was considered the worst of the venial sins depicted in Dante, it comes first in Purgatory, closest the Inferno and furthest from Paradise. As the Bible says, "pride goeth before a fall," and Dickens' characters that embody this particular sin inevitably pay dearly. Although we have already placed Estella of *Great Expectations* in the circle of the *Inferno* known as Limbo, she is quite possibly the most arrogant character in all of Dickens and perhaps also deserves some mention here. In a sense, Estella's ultimate fate depends on which ending of the novel one chooses, the published one where she repents and is united with Pip in true love, or the original, more realistic one where she is left saddened and chastened. If we go with the published ending, Estella is redeemed by love and ultimately will make her way into Paradise after an appropriate period of suffering and cleansing. Thus a passage through Purgatory may befit her.

Pip first encounters Estella as a poor young boy when he is asked to "play" with her at Miss Havisham's. From the first, she treats him with total contempt, calling him "boy," making fun of his poverty, coarse clothes and manners:

> "What coarse hands he has! And what thick boots!"

Pip reflects on her comment:

> I had never thought of being ashamed of my hands before; but I began to consider them a very indifferent pair. Her contempt for me was so strong, that it became infectious, and I caught it.

Estella's contempt for Pip is based simply on the fact that she is rich while he is poor, and quickly becomes the catalyst for his own change of character, as we will see later in this chapter. Of course she is unaware of the fact that her own parentage is even more lowly than Pip's; her mother was a murderess, spared through the offices of the lawyer Jaggers, and her birth father, as we learn at the end of the novel, is none other than "Pip's convict" Abel Magwitch. Estella will be amply punished—first of course by a loveless home with Miss Havisham, then by marriage to an abusive husband. Whether or not she is emotionally capable of true redemption through love depends on which version of the novel one chooses to believe. In any case, Estella's cold pride will either leave her trapped in Limbo for eternity, or passing through Purgatory en route to Paradise.

Then there are the Chuzzlewits. Dickens considered selfishness to be the dominant vice of the Chuzzlewits (Introduction to *Martin Chuzzlewit*), but their particular kind of selfishness is closely linked with pride. Dickens ironically alludes to the family's pride in the very first chapter:

> If it should ever be urged by grudging or malicious persons, that a Chuzzlewit, in any period of the family history, displayed an overweening amount of family pride, surely the weakness will be considered not only pardonable but laudable, when the immense superiority of the house to the rest of mankind, in respect to this its ancient origin, is taken into account.

For old Martin, it is pride that keeps him aloof and manipulative, never trusting anyone in his family to love him, always requiring proofs of loyalty from all. It is pride that keeps him distant from Mary, his young ward who truly cares for him, as well as his grandson Martin, who very nearly dies because of the old man's harsh test of his loyalty.

As for young Martin, his pride forces him to leave England without asking for his grandfather's help, and pride makes him hold himself—for a time at least—above his companion Mark Tapley, a man who is lower in class background, but a far better person morally. By the end of the book, he is forced to concede that without the loyal and steadfast Mark, he would not have survived in the "wilds" of America. Martin's humbling comes, as we have seen, in the form of exile, poverty and a serious illness that very nearly kills him. When he finally returns to England, he is clearly penitent and subdued. He throws himself at the feet of his grandfather, and expresses to both him and Mary his profound repentance for his selfishness and pride:

> "But that I might have trusted to your love, if I had thrown myself manfully upon it; that I might have won you over with ease, if I had been more yielding and more considerate; that I should have best remembered myself in forgetting myself, and recollecting you; reflection, solitude and misery have taught me. I came resolved to say this and ask your forgiveness: not so much in hope for the future, as in regret for the past: for all that I would ask of you is, that you would aid me to live. Help me to get honest work to do, and I would do it...Try if I be self-

willed, obdurate and haughty as I was; or I have been disciplined in a rough school."

As in the Catholic notion of Purgatory, Martin has been forced to sincerely repent, suffer, and make amends to those he has injured before he can be forgiven.

Of course, his grandfather ultimately forgives him, but old Martin has his own penance to make. Once the family secrets have finally been revealed, the murder of his brother Anthony, the perfidy of Pecksniff, and the unnecessary suffering of his grandson, the old man realizes his role in the family tragedies that have occurred:

> In every single circumstance, whether it were cruel, cowardly or false, he saw the same pregnant seed. Self, grasping, eager, over-reaching, self; with its long train of suspicions, lusts, deceits, and all the growing consequences, was the root of the vile tree.

Certainly, the Dickens character whose false pride is most profoundly tested would be Pip, the self-deluded hero of *Great Expectations*. Pip, an orphan raised in humble circumstances by his kindly brother-in-law Joe Gargery and shrewish older sister Mrs. Joe, is granted an unexpected inheritance that ultimately proves more curse than blessing. As a young boy, Pip seems reasonably content with his life; he is apprenticed to Joe who is a blacksmith and hopes Pip will inherit his trade. While Pip suffers from unfair beatings by his sister, he is warmly treated by Joe and by Biddy, a young country girl slightly older than himself, who loves him and teaches him to read and write.

Unfortunately two accidents occur in his life, both linked in the plot. The first is his encounter on the moors with an escaped convict named Abel Magwitch, whom he helps by giving him some meat pie and drink when he is starving. The second is his invitation to the home of a rich, demented old woman Miss Havisham who lives in grimly gothic splendor with her young ward Estella. Miss Havisham supposedly wants Pip as a "companion" to herself; in fact she brings him in to be a victim of her adopted daughter Estella's beauty. Pip is entranced with Estella, and even with Miss Havisham, imagining her to be his benefactress when he unexpectedly inherits a fortune. Thus begin Pip's "great expectations" of a life filled with wealth, luxury, and eventual marriage to the haughty Estella. He hears of the inheritance from the lawyer Jaggers who refuses to reveal his benefactor.

Pip has already begun to change after his first visit to Miss Havisham's, when he is still a young boy. As we have seen, Estella makes him immediately ashamed of his lower class origins, something he had never cause to regret before, as he had known nothing else. One day Estella brings him some food:

> She put the mug down on the stones of the yard, and gave me the bread and meat without looking at me, as insolently as if I were a dog in disgrace. I was so humiliated, hurt, spurned, offended, angry sorry.... that tears started to my eyes.

From this point on, Pip begins to look at himself, Joe, Biddy and his life at the forge with different eyes, now aspiring to the life of a "gentleman."

Years later, when he is about to leave his family for his new-found inheritance, we already see how the youth who has hitherto been affectionate, modest and fairly content, has changed. His sister is lying on the bed in the comatose state induced by a beating from an unknown assailant (in fact, Orlick, a bitter worker fired from the forge). Joe is sitting gazing into the fire. Biddy is doing needlework at the fireplace. Pip muses,

> The more I looked into the glowing coals, the more incapable I felt of looking at Joe; the more the silence lasted, the more unable I felt to speak...I took it upon myself to impress Biddy (and through Biddy, Joe) with the grave obligation I felt my friends under to know nothing and to say nothing about the maker of my fortune. It would all come out in good time, I observed, and in the meanwhile, nothing was to be said save that I had come into great expectations from a mysterious patron... and then they congratulated me again, and went on to express so much wonder at the notion of my being a gentleman that I didn't half like it...
> I never would have believed it without experience, but as Jo and Biddy became more at their cheerful ease again, I became quite gloomy.

Dissatisfied with my fortune, of course I could not be; but it is possible that I may have been, without quite knowing it, dissatisfied with myself.

In this small scene lies the essence of the entire novel. Joe loves Pip like a father; Biddy loves him as more than a sister, but in their honest affection, both try to conceal their sadness at his leaving, expressing only joy at his good fortune. For his part, Pip is already beginning to look upon them and his class origins with resentment and false pride.

When he finally leaves them for good, Pip has a significant discussion of different kinds of "pride" with Biddy. He condescendingly offers to "lift Joe up" by giving him money once he has acquired his fortune, but she quietly demurs, suggesting that Joe may be just as happy as he is:

> "Have you never considered that he may be proud?"
>
> "Proud?" I repeated with disdainful emphasis.
>
> "Oh, there are many kinds of pride," Biddy said, looking full at me and shaking her head. "Pride is not all of one kind…He may be too proud to let anyone take him out of a place that he is competent to fill, and fills with respect."

After this comment, Pip unfairly accuses Biddy of being "envious" and showing "the bad side of human nature." In this, he begins to sound uncannily like the false moralizer Pecksniff, who invariably accuses others of the faults he himself possesses. The contemptuous pride Pip increasingly shows towards Joe and Biddy is the very kind that "goeth before a fall."

In the course of the novel, Pip will essentially cast aside both Joe and Biddy, the two people who most faithfully love him. He looks down on his former life of manual labor. He rarely returns home, and when Joe comes to visit him in his new "gentleman's" world in London, Pip is visibly ashamed of his clumsy manners and unfashionable dress. In many respects, this novel may represent some of Dickens' own guilt at some of those he left behind in his ascent to fame and fortune.

Pip throws himself into the pampered life of a young gentleman of means and actively pursues Estella, whom he feels has now become his class equal and therefore a candidate for marriage. At first Estella, who has plagued Pip since they first met, seems to respond favorably. But soon, Pip receives his first "purgation."

Pip discovers that his benefactor is not Miss Havisham as he always believed, but the criminal Abel Magwitch whose money (although honestly earned as a sheep herder in Australia) he can no longer accept. He also understands that Miss Havisham has deliberately toyed with his emotions for years. He confronts her and Estella, and learns the bitter truth from both of them:

> "I know I have no hope that I shall call you mine, Estella. I am ignorant what may become of me very soon, how poor I may be, or where I may go. Still I love you, I have loved you since I first saw you in this house."
>
> Looking at me perfectly unmoved with her fingers busy (knitting) she shook her head again.
>
> "It would have been cruel of Miss Havisham, horribly cruel to practice on the susceptibility of a poor boy, and to torture me through all these years with a vain hope, and an idle pursuit, if she had reflected on the gravity of what she did. But I think she did not. I think that in the endurance of her own trial, she forgot mine, Estella."
>
> I saw Miss Havisham put her hand to her heart and hold it there, as she sat looking by turns to Estella and at me.

For an instant, it seems that Miss Havisham actually does possess "a heart," which is more than can be said for Estella, who delivers Pip yet another blow:

> "It seems," said Estella very calmly, "that there are sentiments, fancies—I don't know how to call them—which I am not able to comprehend. When you say you love me, I know what you mean as a form of words, but nothing more. You address nothing in my breast, you touch nothing there. I don't care for what you say at all. I have tried to warn you of this now, have I not?
>
> I said in a miserable manner, "Yes."

Then Pip learns an even more terrible truth; Estella is about to marry Bentley Drummle, a violent, rich man whom Pip has always detested.

Pip is utterly devastated. His expectations for a life of fortune and even more importantly, Estella's love have all been shattered.

At this moment, however, he cannot afford to give into despair. He is called upon to help his benefactor Magwitch, who is in danger of being captured and sent back to prison. It is here that we actually see the beginning of Pip's redemption. Painfully humbled, he no longer views Magwitch with the contempt he first showed him, but with a dawning appreciation of the old man's true generosity. He also comes to know Magwitch's life story from his own mouth. He was "a ragged little creeter" left on his own, constantly thrown into jail as if he were a hardened criminal, "tramping, begging, thieving, working sometimes when I could..." In short, Magwitch was once just another of Dickens' many sympathetic abandoned children.

While Magwitch is threatened with capture, Pip endures yet another blow, this time a physical assault by an old enemy Orlick. Orlick, always jealous of Pip, tries to kill him and throw his body into a kiln so nobody will ever recognize him. Here we see Pip's transformation, as he fights Orlick for both his life and his reputation:

> My mind with inconceivable rapidity, followed out all the consequences of such a death. Estella's father (Magwitch) would think I had deserted him would die accusing me...Joe and Biddy would never know how sorry I had been that night, none would ever know what I had suffered, how true I had meant to be, what an agony I had passed through. The death close before me was terrible, but far more terrible than death was the dread of being misremembered after death.

With the aid of friends, ironically one of whom he once looked down on, ("Trabb's boy") Pip escapes, but even more suffering is in store for him. Magwitch is captured and dies, Pip's fortune is gone, and he even becomes seriously ill, eventually nursed back to health by the ever faithful Joe and Biddy.

One might expect he would ultimately receive his "heavenly reward"—Estella—and he does in the revised version of the novel. But the original version has a far more somber ending; Pip encounters Estella one last time when he revisits Miss Havisham's where she has also happens to be by pure chance—or fate. Her brutal husband Drummle was killed in a fall from a horse, but Estella is now remarried to a kindly doctor who helped her through her ordeal. She like Pip is chastened, but their encounter is one of tender friendship, not love. In this original ending, Pip lives out his life working diligently in a legal firm with his old friend Herbert, reconciled with Joe and Biddy who are now married to each other, and serving as a fond uncle to their daughter who is named Pip after him.

Of course in the final published ending, Pip and Estella leave together:

> I took her hand in mine and we went out of the ruined place…and in the broad expanse of tranquil light they showed me, I saw no shadow of another parting from her.

Love has somehow conquered all—even the "heartless" Estella. In either case, it is clear that Pip himself has been tempered through trial by fire. Joe's forge, as well as the kiln where Orlick threatens to throw him after he kills him can be seen as metaphors for the purgation and redemption of a sympathetic, but deeply flawed hero.

Other characters, like Lady Dedlock in *Bleak House* and Paul Dombey in *Dombey and Sons* are also guilty of the sin of pride, and ultimately redeemed by suffering. Lady Dedlock's haughty attitude towards the world, based on her marriage to a rich and powerful lord, is eventually softened by reencountering her abandoned illegitimate child Esther, the heroine of the novel. Esther has now become a lovely woman, although she is at first unaware of her relationship to Lady Dedlock. As the dark secret of her former love affair and love child is revealed, Lady Dedlock is threatened with loss of her position as a grand lady by the malevolent lawyer Tulkinghorn. She wanders off into the countryside, becomes chilled and exhausted, and dies of a fever in Esther's arms, loving and penitent.

As mentioned above, Dickens explicitly considered the dominant sin in the novel *Dombey and Sons* to be that of pride. At the very end of the novel Paul Dombey finally recognizes his pride and coldness towards his daughter Florence, after losing everything: his young son and heir, his second wife and his fortune. Through the connivance of Carker, he has lost his business, the only thing he once valued, but eventually reconciles with the faithful daughter who has always loved him.

However, neither Lady Dedlock nor Paul Dombey experiences the depth of Pip's purgation and gradual evolution towards humility through loss. This is the heart and soul of *Great Expectations*, considered by many to be one of Dickens' greatest and most perfect novels.

The Envious—Sydney Carton, Tattycoram

Sydney Carton, the anti-hero of *A Tale of Two Cities* has long intrigued Dickens' readers. Some have seen him as another version of Dickens himself, as the hero he closely resembles, Charles Darnay, bears Dickens' initials, while the original name Dickens planned for Carton, Dick Carton is their mirror opposite.[6] He is also frustrated in his love for Lucy Manette, as Dickens was apparently frustrated in his love for Ellen Ternan. Carton's uncanny physical similarity allows him to replace Darnay at the guillotine, saving the husband of the woman he loves.

We might, at this point, place Carton on the Purgatorial ledge of Lust, but he really belongs in the domain of Envy. He envies Darnay at the beginning of the novel—sensing the attraction between him and Lucie Manette. In fact, he envies the entire character and life of a man he deems to be better than himself. While Darnay is upright, honest and respectable, Carton, for reasons we never quite learn, is a lazy, alcoholic cynic, lonely and self-degrading. Because of this, of course, he is arguably the most interesting and sympathetic character in the novel.

After he "saves" Charles for the first time, as his lawyer in a false treason suit, the two men go for a drink. Charles is deeply grateful, but Sydney, sullen and increasingly drunk, rejects Darnay's overtures of friendship. Afterwards, he returns to his home and regards himself in the mirror. The uncanny resemblance between himself and Darnay is the trick he used to exonerate his client. His accuser can't quite tell one man from the other. But the face he sees in the mirror gives Sydney no pleasure:

"Do you particularly like the man?" He muttered at his own image; "why should you particularly like a man who resembles you? There is nothing in you to like; you know that. Ah, confound you! What a change you have made in yourself! A good reason for taking to a man that he shows you what you have fallen away from, and what you might have been! Change places with him, and would you have been looked at by those blue eyes as he was, and commiserated by that agitated face as he was? Come on, and have it out in plain words! You hate the fellow."

In this brilliant passage, Dickens conveys the ambiguity of Carton's emotions. "You hate the fellow" could apply just as well to his own image, since Carton does in fact despise himself, as to Charles Darnay. At the same time, we witness Carton's jealousy of Darnay, not merely for being the apple of those "blue eyes," but for being a better man than himself.

However, in the course of the novel, Carton gradually changes for the better. Most importantly, the scene in which he declares his love to Lucie, and receives from her in return a compassionate and caring friendship, begins to effect his transformation. He determines to be Lucie's loyal friend—to death if necessary. Even after she marries Darnay, he seems able to greet his rival with a new sense of cordiality. He becomes a true friend and protector to the whole family.

Finally, when Darnay is arrested again, this time by the revolutionaries, Carton makes the ultimate sacrifice, dying in place of Darnay and uttering the famous words:

"It is a far, far better thing I do than I have ever done. It is a far, far better rest I go to than I have ever known."

For Sydney Carton, purification goes far beyond that of other characters in Purgatory; it is a Christ-like self-sacrifice for those he loves: Lucie, Charles and their children.

Another character eaten up by envy as well as wrath (one step up in Purgatory) is Harriet, known as Tattycoram, the adopted child-servant of the Meagles family in *Little Dorrit*. We first encounter her when Arthur Clennam meets the family after a trip abroad. They have been exposed to malaria, and therefore must be kept in quarantine before their return to England can be approved. This is a symbolic encounter, as they each suffer from some form of spiritual malady that must eventually be cured, and the fates of all the characters will become intertwined in the course of the novel. We never quite know how the kind and wealthy Meagles family brought Tattycoram into their family. Her position is ambiguous; she is described as a "servant," but they clearly view her as part of the family. However, her bitter envy of their real daughter, the spoiled and beautiful "Pet" Meagles, is evident from the first. She confides her feelings immediately to the mysterious Miss Wade, who takes an odd kind of pleasure in her resentment:

> "I am younger than she by two or three years, and yet it's me that looks after her as if I was old, and it's she that is always petted and called "Baby!" I detest the name, I hate her. They make a fool of her, they spoil her. She thinks of nothing but herself, she thinks no more of me than if I were a stock or a stone!"

It's true that Tattycoram's position in the family somewhat resembles that of a house slave, and indeed in one *Masterpiece Theater* production she was convincingly represented as African. However, Dickens suggests that her jealousy and wrath are excessive, even as he clearly demonstrates the patronizing way she is treated by the Meagles family. As in other cases, Dickens is somewhat ambivalent about his own character—sympathizing with her feelings of slight, while condemning her extreme reaction.

As we have seen, Tattycoram will eventually run away with Miss Wade, who at first acts as her friend, but then fills her life with nothing but misery. Life with Miss Wade, in fact, will be her purgation. At the end of the novel, Miss Wade comes into possession of certain documents essential to the happiness of the major characters little Dorrit and Arthur Clennam. Even more filled with resentment than Tattycoram, she refuses to give them up. However, in her newfound penitence, Tattycoram steals the crucial documents and brings them to Mr. Meagles, who is Arthur's friend, while Arthur lies gravely ill in debtor's prison after losing all his money in the Merdle scandal. Tattycoram bursts into the cell where Mr. Meagles is visiting him:

> "Eh? Good gracious!" said Mr. Meagles, "this is not Miss Dorrit! Why, Mother look! Tattycoram!"
>
> No other. And in Tattycoram's arms was an iron box some two feet square...This, Tattycoram put on the ground at her old master's feet; this Tattycoram fell on her knees by, and beat her hands upon it, crying half in exultation and half in despair, half in laughter and half in tears, "Pardon, dear Master, take me back dear Mistress, here it is!"

A modern reader might feel slightly queasy at this servile self-abasement before her "Master and Mistress," but Dickens evidently does not. He believes that the Meagles genuinely love the orphan girl, who has been wallowing in anger and misery in the hands of Miss Wade:

> "Oh! I have been so wretched," cried Tattycoram," weeping much more, after that than before, "always so unhappy and so repentant! I was afraid of her (Miss Wade) from the first time I ever saw her. I knew she had got a power over me, through understanding what was bad in me so well."

The Meagles welcome her back warmly into the fold, but not without a last lecture on the virtues of "Duty," using little Dorrit, who has just entered the scene, as their prime example. Little Dorrit has patiently tolerated a difficult existence as "a child of the prison," lovingly devoted to her selfish father, wastrel brother and vain sister. She is clearly Dickens' model of perfection. Needless to say, Tattycoram is redeemed by her suffering, repentance, and her help in bringing back the documents that will restore Arthur's fortune and free him from debtor's prison.

The Wrathful—Neville Landless

From a psychological standpoint, anger and envious resentment are often so intertwined that characters like Tattycoram and Neville Landless in *The Mystery of Edwin Drood* might easily migrate between this purgatorial "ledge" and the one immediately adjacent. Like Tattycoram, Neville Landless and his sister Helena are penniless orphans who have been brought to England by their bombastic guardian Reverend Honeythunder. They are also depicted as "dark" and foreign, hailing from Ceylon and therefore treated with suspicion by the English, not unlike the plight of many immigrants in America today. Neville and Edwin Drood take an instant dislike to each other, partly because Neville is attracted to Rosa, who is affianced to Edwin, partly because of he is envious of Drood's air of monied ease. For his part, Edwin dislikes Neville's rude manners and his careless treatment of Rosa:

> Neville Landless is already enough impressed by little Rosebud, to feel indignant that Edwin Drood (far below her) should hold his prize so lightly. Edwin Drood is already enough impressed by Helena, to feel indignant that Helena's brother (far below her) should dispose of him so coolly, and put him out of the way so entirely.
>
> After hurling mutual insults they had both become savage; Mr. Neville out in the open; Edwin Drood under the transparent cover of a popular tune, and a stop now and then to admire picturesque effects in the moonlight before him.

At one point, his temper leads Neville to a physical fight with Edwin, but he is eventually calmed down by the Minor Canon Crisparkle who has become his spiritual mentor and protector. The compassionate Crisparkle understands that his hot temper is the result of mistreatment by a cruel stepfather in Ceylon, and that he is at heart a good person.

Nevertheless, Neville's fight with Edwin places him under suspicion of murder when Edwin abruptly disappears. According to Neville, he and Edwin had reconciled and simply taken a walk by the river the night before. However, Jasper does everything to cast suspicion on him, constantly dropping dark hints about Neville's "murderous temper." While there have been some bizarrely revisionist interpretations of the novel (like that of the recent self-described "deconstructionist" version by *Masterpiece Theater*), none of them hold Landless to be the murderer. It is made obvious in the existent portion of the novel that he has been falsely accused, and is in fact eventually released for lack of evidence.

Since we lack the last half of the novel, we will never know if Neville is finally united with Rosa, who seems attracted to him as well. Given

Dickens' penchant for happy endings to his love interests, as well as his sense of irony, it is surely possible. However, we do experience Neville's terrifying ordeal when he is falsely accused of murder, and see him join in the efforts to keep Rosa away from Jasper. His spiritual work with Canon Crisparkle helps cure him of his fiery temper. All this may be enough to suggest his ultimate pardon for the sin of anger.

The Slothful—Mr. Micawber (David Copperfield), Dick Swiveller (The Old Curiosity Shop)

Wilkins Micawber in *David Copperfield* is one of Dickens' most beloved characters. Loosely based on Dickens' regularly indebted father and immortalized on film by the impeccable W.C. Fields, he, like all the characters we find in Purgatory, has serious weaknesses, but is capable of salvation.

Micawber, young David's landlord and friend when he is first cast out into the world on his own, is always warm and fatherly towards him. Unfortunately, he seems incapable of finding or maintaining employment for very long, while his growing family sinks into poverty and like John Dickens, eventually into debtor's prison. In this, we may say that Micawber is definitely guilty of sloth. While invariably charming and optimistic that "something will turn up," somehow it never does. It is never quite clear what his occupation is. He seemed to have had some connection with the navy like Dickens' own father. David muses on his friend's situation early in their acquaintance:

> I cannot satisfy myself whether she (Mrs. Micawber) told me that Mr. Micawber had been an officer in the Marines, or whether I had imagined it. I only know that I believe to this hour that he was in the Marines once upon a time, without knowing why. He was a sort of town traveller for a number of miscellaneous houses, now, but made little of it, I am afraid.

Like other "slothful" characters, Micawber also has an over-fondness for alcohol and is frequently found preparing elaborate rum punches for his friends and family. He is also given to grandiosity and flowery speech, both in person and in letters. At times, he is prone to self-pity, but doesn't show quite as much compassion towards his struggling family.

Eventually, Micawber finds stable employment, unfortunately as we have seen as a clerk for Uriah Heep who takes advantage of his financial desperation. For a time Micawber collaborates in Heep's schemes against Mr. Wickfield, and in so doing becomes alienated from everyone, even his beloved wife. This, in fact, is his real penance. Micawber is a sociable, family-oriented man; emotional isolation is for him the cruelest form of punishment. When Heep's devious schemes become too much for him, he finally rebels and exposes his employer, thereby saving Wickfield, Agnes, David and himself.

Micawber then receives a stipend from Betsey Trotwood, who has been able to recover her own money thanks to his exposure of Heep. He and his family will immigrate to a "purgatory" in the New World for his fresh start. It will not be without some last minute glitches, of course, as a frantic letter from him to David and his Aunt Betsey reveals:

> "My dear Madam, and Copperfield,
> The fair land of promise lately looming on the horizon is again enveloped in impenetrable mists, and forever withdrawn from the eyes of a drifting wretch whose Doom is sealed!
> Another writ has been issued (in His Majesty's High Court of King's Bench at Westminster), in another cause of Heep v. Micawber, and the defendant in that cause is the prey of the sheriff having legal jurisdiction in this bailiwick…"

However, the irrepressible Micawber quickly adds a P.S. showing that all has finally been arranged satisfactorily:

> "P.S. I reopen this to say that our common friend, Mr. Thomas Traddles (who has not yet left us, and is looking extremely well) has paid the debt and costs, in the noble name of Miss Trotwood, and that myself and family are at the height of earthly bliss."

It is now off to the New World for Micawber, who finally takes up a life of legitimate labor for himself and his ever-growing family. We might simply mention here that "redemption through work" is not only a favorite theme for Dickens, but for Protestantism in general.

Dick Swiveller, the indolent friend of little Nell's brother Frederick in *The Old Curiosity Shop*, is another character whose weakness temporarily allies him with far more evil characters—in this case, Frederick, Daniel Quilp and his unscrupulous lawyers Samuel and Sally Brass. First, he allows himself to be drawn into Frederick's plot to engage him to Nell in an effort to get his hands on his grandfather's presumed fortune. Swiveller is good natured, but he is careless, even about his personal appearance:

> His attire was not, as he himself hinted, remarkable for the nicest arrangement, but it was in a state of disorder which strongly induced the idea that he had gone to bed in it. It consisted of a brown body-coat with a great many brass buttons up the front and only one behind, a bright neckerchief, a plaid waistcoat, soiled white trousers, and a very limp hat, worn with the wrong side foremost, to hide a hole in the brim.

Swiveller's sloppy appearance is not so much a sign of poverty, to which Dickens was invariably sympathetic, as it is of a general negligence about his life—to which he was not. Dickens was apparently fanatical about neatness, both in his personal appearance and in his household. He was also, as we know, a man of incessant labors.

Like Micawber, Swiveller is in debt and in no great hurry to find any means of employment. He has been halfheartedly courting a young lady named Sophie Wackles, but again, without any firm intentions. He is a man who allows himself to be idly led by others, first by Frederick then by Quilp:

> It would be tedious to pursue the conversation (with Fred) through all its artful windings, or to develop the gradual approaches by which the heart of Richard Swiveller was to be gained. It is sufficient to know that vanity, interest, poverty, and every spendthrift consideration urged him to look upon the proposal with favour, and that where all other inducements were wanting, the habitual carelessness of his disposition stepped in and still weighed down the scale on the same side.

Then Quilp gets him a job in the law offices of Sally and Sampson Brass, where he is required to take part in various illegal schemes and plots against Nell and her family. When the Brasses—at Quilp's instigation—use him to set up Nell's devoted young friend Kit Nubbles for a theft he didn't commit, Dick, like Micawber, finally rebels. He is saved by his fundamental sense of decency, along with his growing fondness for a tiny maltreated servant girl in the Brass household whom he calls "the Marchioness." This also allows him to save Kit and everyone else from Quilp, since he, also like Micawber, has the secret information that can put Quilp in prison.

At the end of the novel, as we have seen, Quilp is dead and the Brasses exposed to the law for fraud. After a lengthy illness (one of Dickens' favorite form of purgation) Dick recovers and is aided financially by those he has freed from Quilp's clutches. He helps the little Marchioness to get the education she never had, and once she is nineteen, marries her. His very name, Swiveller, suggests that he has at last managed to turn his life around.

The Covetous: Bella Wilfer

The redundantly beautiful Bella in *Our Mutual Friend* is initially portrayed as a spoiled malcontent. Like other poor but beautiful women in literature—most notably the legendary *Madame Bovary*—she feels she was cut out for a life far superior to the modest one she inhabits. She unhappily covets the riches of others, until the Boffins, who have inherited wealth and a luxurious lifestyle, take her under their wing. Bella's greatest strength is her honesty. From the beginning of the novel she is completely forthright about her greed. She has just discovered that the rich young man (John Harmon) she was to marry has drowned, and although she never knew or cared for him, feels disappointed:

> "It was ridiculous enough to know I shouldn't like him—how could
> I like him—left to him in a will like a dozen of spoons, with everything
> cut and dried beforehand, like orange chips?...Those ridiculous points
> would have been smoothed away, for I love money, and want money—

want it dreadfully. I hate to be poor, and we are degradingly poor, offensively poor, miserably poor, beastly poor."

Of course the Wilfers are not nearly as impoverished as other characters in the novel, who manage to bear up against their poverty with dignity. Not Bella. She incessantly quarrels with her sister and mother and whines for better clothes and a better life, until they decide to let her move out of the family and in with the newly rich Boffins, who treat her like a daughter and lavish all the luxuries on her she could ever hope for.

The irony of the situation is profound; the Boffins are in fact living off the inheritance of John Harmon, the man Bella was "left to," supposedly drowned but in reality very much alive and living as a tenant in her parents' home, then secretary to Boffin under the name of John Rokesmith. He has, in fact, nearly drowned, but has been mistaken for another man who really did drown after trying to rob and kill him. Confused and disoriented at first, he determines to continue the pretense, in order to find out what kind of young woman he has been promised to. Unfortunately, his first impressions of Bella are far from favorable. Nevertheless, he is drawn to her and despite himself, falls in love.

Bella's transformation comes not through her own suffering; rather it is a gradual evolution to a moral position through exposure to the sufferings of others. She befriends those much poorer than herself, in particular Lizzie Hexam and Betty Higden, and learns to admire their nobility of spirit in times of deepest suffering.

At the same time, she critically observes the apparent change of character in her patron Mr. Boffin, who seems to have become altered for the worse by new-found wealth. He begins to treat his secretary Rokesmith with contempt, while Bella has gradually begun to care for him. Boffin's behavior becomes an object lesson for Bella, as she confides one day to her father:

> "But Mr. Boffin is being spoilt by prosperity, and is changing every day."
>
> "My dear Bella, I hope and trust not."
>
> "I have hoped and trusted not too, Pa; but every day he changes for the worse. Not to me—but to others about him. Before my eyes

he grows suspicious, capricious, hard, tyrannical, unjust…And yet, Pa, think how terrible this fascination of money is! I see this, and hate this, and dread this, and don't know but that money might make a much worse change in me."

Like Estella (whose name has a similar ring, echoing that of Nelly Ternan?), Bella often claims to be heartless. She confides to Sophronia Lammle, "I don't mind telling you Sophronia, that I have no heart, as people call it; and that I think that sort of thing is nonsense." However, Bella has been raised by a loving father whom she obviously adores, and a mother who, while annoying, is a far cry from the crazed Miss Havisham. It is obvious that Bella's claims about her own bad character have been exaggerated.

When put to the ultimate test by Mr. Boffin, who seems to turn against Rokesmith for daring to court Bella, her better nature rises to the fore. Boffin, having ordered Rokesmith out of the house, pretends that Bella has now "been righted."

> But Bella, so far from appearing to feel it, that she shrank from his (Boffin's) hand and from the chair, and stretching out her arms, cried, "Oh! Mr. Rokesmith, if before you go, if you could but make me poor again and take me home! I was bad enough there, but have been so much worse here. Don't give me money, Mr. Boffin, I won't have money. Keep it away from me, and only let me speak to good little Pa, and lay my head upon his shoulder, and tell him all my griefs. Nobody else can understand me, nobody else can love me, nobody else knows how unworthy I am and yet can love me like a little child."

There is a double dramatic irony in this key scene. Rokesmith is actually John Harmon, the true inheritor of Boffin's fortune, but is pretending to be poor—in part to test Bella. Boffin is pretending to be a hardhearted miser, in order to test both of them. Bella, however, is deeply in earnest. She renounces the life of wealth and comfort which she feels is corrupting her, and returns to her parents. Eventually, of course, she will marry Rokesmith-Harmon, whom she has come to love, although she isn't entirely aware of this at first. When they do marry, it is initially without money, yet they are content. Everything that Bella once "coveted" has turned to ashes; her true happiness will ultimately lie in the simple family love Dickens always idealizes.

The Gluttonous: Flora Finching in Little Dorrit, Mr. Wickfield

In Dante's Purgatory, the category of the "gluttonous" includes the excesses of both food and alcohol. For an example of this "sin" we have Flora Finching in *Little Dorrit*. Her addiction to food and alcohol, however, seems to harm nobody so much as herself. When Arthur Clennam, the love of her youth, comes to visit her after a long absence abroad, he hopes to find the lithe young beauty he once adored. However, he discovers a silly widow, who flirts with him outrageously and inappropriately. For him, Flora has changed "from a lily to a peony." She talks incessantly and incoherently, sentimentally referring to the fond old days of their past. This rather cruel depiction of Flora is virtually identical to Dickens' own reencounter later in life with Maria Beadnell, the young woman who once rejected him for a wealthier suitor. Indeed, his satiric portrayal of Flora might be seen as a kind of revenge for this early disappointment in love.

When he first comes to dinner with Flora and her father after his long absence in China, Arthur is thoroughly disillusioned:

> Once upon a time Clennam had sat at that table taking no heed of anything but Flora; now the principal heed he took of Flora was to observe, against his will, that she was very fond of porter, that she combined a good deal of sherry with sentiment, and that if she were a little overgrown, it was upon substantial grounds.

Flora is not mean-spirited. However, her initial desire to help little Dorrit comes less out of altruism than her sense that Arthur is interested in the poor girl. She fully hopes to win Arthur back when she hires little Dorrit as a seamstress. For a time, her main concern is to keep Arthur as close to herself as possible, although like others in the novel, she cannot help but grow sincerely fond of the sweet-natured Amy Dorrit.

By the end of the novel, when Arthur winds up seriously ill in debtor's prison, Flora loyally visits him, no longer as a hopeful lover, but in the capacity of an old and concerned friend. Having been tried by the permanent companionship of her demented Aunt F. and by the bad temper of her own father Christopher Casby, Flora now seems greatly chastened. When she realizes that Arthur actually loves little Dorrit, she takes the news in good spirit, conceding Arthur gracefully to little Dorrit, though not without her customary verbiage. She confesses her feelings to little Dorritt:

"Over and above which," said Flora, "I earnestly beg you as the dearest thing that ever was if you'll still excuse the familiarity from one who moves in very different circles to let Arthur understand that I don't know after all whether it wasn't all nonsense between us though pleasant at a time and trying too and certainly Mr. F. did work a change and the spell being broken nothing could be expected to take place without weaving it afresh which various circumstances have combined to prevent...but jealousy is not my character nor ill-will though many faults."

As for little Dorrit, "without having been able to follow Mrs. Finching through this labyrinth, little Dorrit understood its purpose, and cordially accepted the trust."

Flora, who proclaims that she "must now retire into privacy and look upon the ashes of departed joys no more," actually attends the small private wedding of Arthur and little Dorritt, where she will serve as a kind of informal bridesmaid, holding one of little Dorrit's arms during the ceremony, while Maggie, a homeless girl befriended by the bride, holds the other.

Despite her weakness for food and drink, Flora is no alcoholic. This condition, as portrayed in a number of Dickens' characters, is far more harmful. Three characters whose alcoholism proves destructive to them and those around them are Agnes Wickfield's father in *David Copperfield*, Stephen Blackpool's wife in *Hard Times* and the hapless father of Jenny Wren, the doll's dressmaker in *Our Mutual Friend,* whom she refers to as "a bad boy." Of these, Mr. Wickfield is the most fully developed character, so we can observe his transformation more closely.

From the first time David meets him, when he is welcomed into the Wickfield home as a young student and employee, he immediately notices Wickfield's appetite for alcohol. Mr. Wickfield has never recovered from the death of his beloved wife, and although he appreciates and loves his devoted daughter Agnes, he can't quite keep away from the bottle.

> When we had dined, we went upstairs again, where everything went exactly as on the previous day. Agnes set the glasses and decanters in the same corner, and Mr. Wickfield sat down to drink, and drank a good deal.

Later the same evening, Mr. Wickfield drinks still more:

> He had drank wine that evening (or I fancied it) until his eyes were bloodshot. Not that I could see them now, for they were cast down, and shaded by his hand, but I had noticed them a little while before...
> "A dull old house, and a monotonous life, but I must have her (Agnes) near me, I must keep her near me. If the thought that I may die and leave my darling, or that my darling may die, and leave me, like a specter, to distress my happiness hours and only to be drowned in—"

At this point Wickfield breaks off, but his meaning is clear.

Although the Wickfield home represents a peaceful retreat for David when compared with life with the Murdstones, Mr. Wickfield's depression and addiction are evident from the first. His anxieties are only assuaged by drink and the constant attentions of his daughter Agnes, yet another of the saintly child care-takers that abound in Dickens.

Ultimately this fatal weakness proves the undoing of his happy home. Uriah Heep, fully aware of the old man's weakness, takes full advantage of it as we have seen. At the end of the novel, when Heep has been exposed and some of the Wickfield fortune restored, Mr. Wickfield finally tells his life story to David, with a sense of penitence.

> "My part in them (the past events)," said Mr. Wickfield shaking his white head, "has much matter for regret—for deep regret and deep contrition, Trotwood, as you well know. But I would not cancel it, if it were in my power...I should cancel with it," he pursued, "such patience and devotion, such fidelity, such a child's love, as I must not forget—No!—even to forget myself."

In other words, to deny what he has done would be to deny also the loving sacrifice Agnes has made for him. He then proceeds to explain the guilt over his young wife's death that led him to drink. She married him and was cast off by her own family, then "pined away and died." With some psychological insight, the old man concedes that his selfish love for his dead wife was "a diseased love," but at this point we may assume all that is over. In his final dinner with Agnes and David, the old man abstains from alcohol entirely. David will marry "his sister" Agnes, once he finally realizes that he loves her as a woman, and the whole family will live in tranquil happiness, raising beloved children and grandchildren.

The Lustful—Little Em'ly, Eugene Wrayburn

The contrast between the lust of the seduced, in this case the innocent "little Em'ly" in *David Copperfield* and a would-be seducer like Eugene Wrayburn in *Our Mutual Friend* might make us pause before placing them together on the same "ledge" of Purgatory. Nevertheless, both characters allow their uncontrolled passions to wreak havoc on themselves and others, and both ultimately "repent" their weaknesses after being put through extreme suffering.

Emily lives a simple life in a cast-off boat on the Yarmouth beach with her adoptive father the retired seaman Daniel Peggotty, brother to David's beloved old nurse Peggotty. She is engaged to a rough but kindly young man named Ham who adores her. She is content with her life, that is, until David casually brings his handsome friend Steerforth for a visit. She is immediately drawn to Steerforth, who later secretly courts her without telling David. Emily's fearful clinging to Ham and to her family just after she meets Steerforth suggests her own foreboding that she will be swept away by her immediate attraction to the dashing young man.

> "Oh pray, Aunt, try to help me! Ham, dear, try to help me! Mr. David, for the sake of old times, do please, try to help me! I want to be a better girl than I am. I want to feel a hundred times more thankful than I do. I want to feel more what a blessed thing it is to be the wife of a good man, and to lead a peaceful life. Oh me, oh me! Oh my heart, my heart!"

Rarely has an author created such a poignant description of the struggle between the demands of morality and those of passion, and it is evident that Dickens sympathizes deeply with Emily. Emily, of course cannot resist; she runs off with Steerforth. Yet she will not wind up in Hell. She is "saved" by her innocent hope that Steerforth will marry her: "He will bring me back a lady." When he fails to do so and in fact abandons her, suggesting she marry his devious companion Littmer instead, Emily exiles herself as a form of self-punishment. She runs off to London, but does not become a prostitute as her family has feared. Eventually they learn that she has found "honest work" with a family.

It is true that Emily's decision to run away with Steerforth proves catastrophic, not merely to her loving family, but to her loyal fiancé Ham, who later drowns trying to save Steerforth. Eventually her own trials, penitence and the all-forgiving love of her adoptive father Daniel Peggotty will lead her to safe shores in Australia, among the "redeemed." Emily will never quite attain Dickens' version of "Heaven," since she never marries, but life with her uncle in Australia represents a kind of Purgatory existence for her.

A more guilty character is Eugene Wrayburn, who like Steerforth, allows his "lust" to propel him towards a lower class woman he never intends to marry. In this case, Lizzie Hexam proves a stronger personality than Emily, and staunchly resists Wrayburn's persistent advances. At the same time, she has even more serious problems at hand, since she is being simultaneously pursued by the psychopathic Bradley Headstone (see *Chapter III*).

Wrayburn is portrayed from the first as slothful as well, someone drifting purposelessly through his privileged life. He has been assigned the job of solicitor by his wealthy family, but has no interest in this kind of work. He confides this to his good friend Mortimer Lightwood, himself a solicitor, but one who actually chooses to apply himself:

"And I," said Eugene, putting his legs up on the opposite seat, "have been 'called' seven years, and have had no business at all, and never shall have any. And if I had, I shouldn't know how to do it..." "I hate," said Eugene, putting his legs up on the opposite seat, "I hate my profession."

For a workaholic like Dickens, Wrayburn's aimlessness already makes him a fairly unappealing character. He is also lazy in his social life, spending far too much time dining at the rich and superficial Veneerings whom he despises, all the while sneering secretly at them and their friends.

At first, he seems to slide into a fascination with Lizzie Hexam for lack of anything better to do with himself. Understandably resistant to an arranged marriage by his father, who has planned his entire life, Eugene glimpses Lizzie while accompanying his friend Mortimer Lightwood on a legal case—the apparent drowning of John Harmon. He is immediately drawn to the beautiful young woman. He and Lightwood are secretly watching the home of Gaffer Hexam, who has been falsely accused of the murder. Eugene watches Lizzie through the window, as she waits for her father to return home:

> It was a little window of four pieces of glass and was not curtained; he chose it because the larger window near it was. It showed him the room, and the bills upon the wall respecting the drowned people starting out and receding by turns. But he glanced slightly at them, though he looked long and steadily at her. A deep rich piece of colour, with the brown flush of her cheek and the shining lustre of her hair, though sad and solitary, weeping by the rising and the falling of the fire.

After this early encounter, Eugene casually seeks out Lizzie's company, sometimes at the home of her friend the small crippled "doll's dressmaker" Jenny Wren. Like another of Dickens' intelligent, diminutive female characters, the sharp-tongued Miss Mowcher in *David Copperfield*, Jenny has an unerring knack for truth-telling and eliciting truth from others. Eugene claims to be only passing by to keep up with the case of the drowned man, but then says what he really thinks:

> "Generally, I confess myself a man to be doubted," returned Eugene coolly, "For all that."
>
> "Why are you?" asked the sharp Miss Wren.
>
> "Because my dear," said the airy Eugene, "I am a bad idle dog."
>
> "Then why don't you reform and be a good dog?" inquired Miss Wren.

"Because, my dear," returned Eugene, "there's nobody who makes it worth my while."

He then renews his proposal to become a tutor to Lizzie who, although she has taught herself to read and write, has had no formal education. Of course, Eugene has ulterior motives, as is instantly perceived by Lizzie's brother Charlie, who is pressing her to marry his teacher Bradley Headstone instead. He is also warned not to seduce Lizzie by his friend Mortimer Lightwood, since nothing good can come of it for either of them. But Eugene ignores all warnings, and continues to seek her out.

As the attraction between the two deepens, with apparently no prospects of honest marriage because of the gap in their social stations, Lizzie finally decides to flee—both from Headstone who frightens her, and from Eugene whom she is starting to love. The dangerous outcome of Eugene's relentless pursuit of Lizzie is of course the attempted murder by Bradley Headstone, who has been stalking him. As mentioned before, this scene like many in this novel symbolically involves water. Like John Harmon, who nearly drowns, but is reborn under another name, and Rogue Riderhood, who nearly drowns, but is brought back to life as ill-tempered as before, Eugene is pushed into the water by Headstone, yet rescued by Lizzie physically and morally. Accidentally passing by in her boat, Lizzie finds the strength to drag him out of the water and bring him home. She also has the strength of character to nurse him faithfully back to health, selflessly disregarding her own complex feelings.

Hovering between life and death with Lizzie now ever at his side, Eugene becomes a transformed man. Once he has regained consciousness, he begs his friend Mortimer to arrange for a marriage between him and Lizzie. This is his first truly unselfish act, as he doesn't believe he will live, but hopes to leave Lizzie some security after his death. Lightwood cheerfully undertakes a mission he heartily approves:

"Observe my dear Eugene; while I am away you will know that I have discharged my trust with Lizzie by finding her here, in my present place at your bedside, to leave you no more. A final word before I go. This is the right course of a true man, Eugene. And I solemnly believe, with all my soul, that if Providence should mercifully restore you to us, you will be blessed with a noble wife in the preserver of your life, whom you will dearly love."

"Amen. I am sure of that. But I shall not come through it, Mortimer."

In the end, of course, he does come through it, and although he continues to have serious doubts about the worthiness of his own character, Eugene determines to live and be a good husband to Lizzie. He even momentarily contemplates giving up the inheritance that has subsidized his idle existence and bring Lizzie away with him to the "colonies." When Mortimer agrees this might actually be a good idea, he indignantly protests that it is, on the contrary, "Wrong!" He will take up an occupation but has no intention of running away or hiding his wife from the" Society" that looks down their marriage. Instead, he will fight for her good name and character before the Veneerings and all his snobbish friends:

> "When I hide her, or strike for her, faintheartedly, in a hole or a corner, do you, whom I love next best upon earth, tell me what I shall most righteously deserve to be told: that she would have done well to have turned me over with her foot that night when I lay bleeding to death, and to have spat in my dastard face."

It is now evident how much of his own story Dickens has poured into this character, at first glance so different from himself. At the time this novel was written, Dickens himself was apparently "hiding" the woman he loved from Society, and although separated from his wife, unable to bring on the public shame of divorce and remarriage.[7] Some have rightly noted that in each of Lizzie's two relentless suitors, the obsessive Headstone, who has dragged himself up from poverty, and the careless entitled Eugene Wrayburn, who covets Lizzie sexually but hesitates to marry her, there are significant pieces of the author himself.

We now see how the moral struggles of Dickens' characters are in many ways his own. Like Dante, in the act of artistic creation, he seems able to understand his own battle between good and evil through a deepened understanding of his characters. While the happy endings Dickens prescribed for his characters sadly eluded him in real life, by creating them, he invariably gives himself as well as his readers hope for redemption.

And a Brief Word About the "Angels"

Although this book's primary focus has been on the *Inferno* and the problem of sin, it is impossible to leave Dickens without at least some mention of his "angels," who would all certainly be found Dante's *Paradiso*. Many literary critics have objected to Dickens' angelic women as his most unrealistic characters; and of course as perfect beings, they are. However, they play an important symbolic role, just as the idealized Beatrice has a crucial role in Dante's *Inferno*. For both authors they represent a Christian ideal that is unattainable in the real world, but which is the eternal object of human aspiration. We have already mentioned that for Catholics as well as many Protestants, the goal of the religious life is the attempt to emulate Jesus, who was "perfect" and sacrificed himself for sinful humanity. Once again, it is intriguing that Dickens had a dream of his sister-in-law Mary dressed in blue, like the Virgin Mary. It is also interesting to note that Dickens began to attend church regularly after the death of Mary, and indeed to become more serious about religion after this tragic experience, for some reason one of the most traumatic of his life. [1]

One of the major themes for all Dickens' angels is sacrifice; all instinctively sacrifice their own comfort and feelings for the well being of others. As we have noted, some feminists have rightly objected to the fact that the majority of these sacrificial lambs are women, giving up their own happiness for unworthy male figures. These of course include Nell, Agnes, Florence Dombey and little Dorrit. However, Dickens does create a few male "angels"—generally, it might be noted from the working class—who suppress their own desires and needs out of a pure, devoted love for others. Humble Joe Gargery understands that Pip is moving into a world that cannot include him. Nevertheless, he generously supports Pip's aspirations without ever a word of reproach or personal hurt. At the end of *Great Expectations*, he faithfully nurses Pip back to health, after having been ignored by Pip through most of the novel. Pip has just regained consciousness, and Joe tries to cheer him with fond memories of the past. "Which dear old Pip, old Chap," said Joe, "you and me was ever friends. And when you're well enough to go out for a ride—what larks!" Pip reflects:

> After which, Joe withdrew to the window, and stood with his back towards me, wiping his eyes. And as my extreme weakness prevented me from getting up and going to him, I lay there penitently whispering, "O God bless him! O God bless this gentle Christian man."

In *David Copperfield* Daniel Peggotty is willing to leave his home and old life behind in order to seek out and save his beloved niece Little Em'ly. Once again, there is no pride or selfishness in any of his actions, only the simplicity and generosity of true and perfect love.

Finally there is Sydney Carton, certainly no saint as depicted in the novel, but willing to sacrifice—his own life, for the woman and family he loves. Self-sacrifice is an important part of the concept of "The Imitation of Christ" mentioned in our Introduction.

As for Dickens' angelic women, there are distinctions to be made among them, just as in Dante, who presents degrees of perfection even in his *Paradiso*. Dante's purer souls come closest to God as they move upwards in Paradise. The most perfect, saintly (and least realistic) of Dickens' angels is Nell in *The Old Curiosity Shop*. She unwaveringly follows her grandfather into a life of poverty, begging and misery, never once reproaching him or seeking a drop of comfort for herself. It is arguable that Nell's selflessness is to the point that she has no real "self." She does not quite withdraw from the world, as proposed in Kempis's *Imitation of Christ*. However, if Nell is "in" this world, she is never quite "of" it. It is significant that at the end of her life, she is living in a church and will die there, to be buried in its gloomy churchyard. This seems to be more of Nell's true "home" than the Old Curiosity Shop, or any of the other places she temporarily resides in the course of her short, sad pilgrimage through life. Unlike other of Dickens' angelic women, Nell cannot be rewarded in this life, as there is nothing mortal she desires. As we have noted, from the beginning of the novel she is clearly destined to die.

Closest to Nell in her endlessly generous and forgiving spirit is little Dorrit. She also stands by her selfish father, even when he seems unappreciative of her devotion, especially towards the end of the novel. She continues to live in debtor's prison with him, although she has the chance to escape through marriage to the prison warden's son. In a sense, the prison is like a monastic retreat; she is happier there tending to her father's every need than when they suddenly become rich and she is asked to live like a woman of privilege. Unlike her spoiled sister Fanny, she hates adorning herself in new clothes and jewels, and prefers to wear the plain garb she wore when poor. Little Dorrit's sensibility is very close to the kind of enclosed monasticism Thomas à Kempis prescribed. However, unlike Nell, she seems a real woman with feelings of her own. She is in love with Arthur Clennam and is pained by his temporary infatuation with another woman (Pet Meagles), although she will never do or say anything to advance her own interests.

Similarly, Agnes in *David Copperfield*, while endlessly patient and generous to David who often refers to her as his "guardian angel," does subtly attempt to let him know that she loves him until, of course, he marries the unworthy child-bride Dora. After this, like Amy and Nell, Agnes will renounce her own feelings and think only of David's. It helps that on her deathbed, Dora cedes David to Agnes, something she conceals from David until he is able to declare his love at the very end of the novel.

Advancing further along the scale of complex and realistic womanhood is Esther Summerson in *Bleak House*. Esther is also generous, kind and self-abnegating. She devotes herself as a housekeeper to her uncle John Jarndyce and her cousins, and also tends the poor and the sick. She contracts disfiguring smallpox when she selflessly takes in and nurses the abandoned Jo. But she is also capable of her own thoughts and actions.

Some of the novel is from her point of view, and we can see her revulsion towards a silly unwanted suitor, the law clerk Mr. Guppy, as well as her growing attraction to Dr. Woodcourt. She agrees to marry her patron John Jarndyce out of loyalty and gratitude, but it is clear she is conflicted. When she is disfigured by smallpox, she feels herself unworthy of any man's love, and devotes herself to helping others, yet she never entirely renounces the hopes and dreams of a full-blooded woman.

Finally, there is Lizzie Hexam. Although she is also a devoted daughter and sister, she is a strong working class girl, capable of standing up for herself when necessary. As we have seen, she runs away from a man she loves when she realizes he won't marry her. Eventually, she physically and morally saves his life. She is also capable of standing up to her brother, who is bent on her marrying the revolting Bradley Headstone—mainly to advance his own prospects. In short, Lizzie may be an "angel," but she is no "insipid goodie."

Dickens supposedly based his perfect women characters in part on his sister-in-law Mary, but they also exist as a necessary part of his Christian theology. There must be angels in the world for salvation, and for a sense of what Paradise might ultimately be. Dickens clearly believed, not only in Hell and Purgatory, but in the possibility of a true Heaven, both in this world and the next.

X

Afterthoughts on Dickens and "Moral Fiction"

When Dickens died suddenly at the relatively young age of fifty-seven, he was deeply mourned and virtually canonized by millions of his readers in England and elsewhere, who were largely unaware of his personal failings. While certainly aware that canonization was not in order, when I abruptly arrived at the end of *The Mystery of Edwin Drood*, I experienced a similar shock of loss and grief. This was not merely because I knew it to be the last novel by Dickens I would ever read. It was because in the incomplete novel itself, I would never find that inevitable sense of justice accomplished that appeases us in all his other works. I would never know for certain whether John Jasper winds up in prison, repentant or unrepentant. Some readers would never even know that he is the actual murderer.

Dickens can be surprisingly dark, and all his novels, even the lightly comic *Pickwick Papers* (when Pickwick lands in debtor's prison) have their moments of despair. Yet in each of his novels there is a ray of humanity and hope. It may be the redemption of the larger society—as he promises for the distant future in *A Tale of Two Cities*—or only an individual character like Sissy Jupe in the relatively bleak *Hard Times*, but Dickens refuses to leave his readers in state of utter hopelessness. As biographer Fred Kaplan says of *Bleak House,* "he untwists the chains and unravels the plots to promote the possibilities of personal if not societal redemption. No matter how gloomy the contemporary reality, he maintained a residual hope for social reform." [1] Here, of course, is where fiction offers the satisfactions that can rarely be found in life, where the "good" too often suffer while villains thrive.

It can be easy for the more cynical modern reader to dismiss Dickens' happy endings as unrealistically sentimental. However, I would argue that as human beings, whether Christian or Jew, Moslem, Buddhist or secular humanist, most of us have an innate craving for justice and a need for hope. Whether we believe in capital punishment, harsh or lenient punishment, or even whether or not we believe in Heaven and Hell, most of us feel outraged when, for example, a murderer goes free on a legal technicality, a corporate raider makes millions while despoiling his own company, its workers and stockholders, or an innocent child is sold into prostitution. If we cannot find justice in the real world, we at least hope to find some of it in fiction. As Pip notes in *Great Expectations*, even very young children have this innate sense of justice:

> In the little world in which children have their existence whosoever brings them up, there is nothing so finely perceived and so finely felt as injustice.

For children, such injustice may be felt mainly in relationship to their own lives; but as they mature, they may begin to develop an equal awareness of injustice towards others. This is certainly true in the case of Pip. Even when he is being grossly unfair to those who love him the most, he suffers for it and feels miserable.

In his provocative book *On Moral Fiction* written in 1977, author John Gardner argues that great fiction always needs a moral core, a sense of right and wrong, of justice and injustice. Gardner criticizes some of his own literary contemporaries as superficial and trivial, either obsessed with form over content, or overly cynical and despairing. He asserts, "Art (fiction) is essentially serious and beneficial, a game played against chaos and death, against entropy," adding, "Art rediscovers generation by generation what is necessary to humanness."[2] When he speaks of "moral fiction," Gardner certainly does not mean that a novel must always have a happy ending. Nor does he feel that the author should bludgeon us with his or her version of political or religious correctness. In fact, he deplores propagandistic literature from any quarter. He does suggest, however, that no matter how degraded the situation depicted, the "moral" author provides a sense that there could and indeed should be something better. (Oddly, although he particularly singles out Dante as a model of the moral author, Gardner largely ignores Dickens.)

In this sense, one might consider a popular television series like *The Wire* a work of moral fiction. The African-American children presented are trapped in a life of crime, neglect and violence and, like Dickens' street urchins, thoroughly abandoned by society. Too often their individual fates seem hopeless. Yet there are examples of redemption: the boy that is helped by a boxing instructor—himself a reformed criminal, the policeman turned caring math teacher who actually reaches some of his most troubled and troublesome students, even if he is frustrated by a mindless and heartless bureaucracy. There is humanity in some of the police officers, as well as in some of the seemingly most hardened criminals, like the sometimes compassionate killer Omar (many people's favorite character). After eluding the most ingenious and powerful drug dealers for several seasons, Omar is shot, almost accidentally by a young boy standing behind him in a convenience store. Can this be seen as a form of *contrapasso*? Perhaps so.

Today it is sometimes more in popular rather than in literary fiction, works like *The Wire* or the novels of John Grisham, that questions of morality and social justice are raised. In fact, this may be one reason why they are so popular. Grisham, an author generally ignored by the literary establishment, not only tells a suspenseful tale, but grapples with real injustices in our judicial system, especially towards people of color. It is no accident that he is Chairman of the Board of the Mississippi Innocence Project, like Dickens, carrying his moral concerns into social activism. In a recent novel, *The Confession,* Grisham realistically portrays a corrupt criminal justice system in Texas that forces a false confession to rape-murder out of a young black football player, and condemns him to death. Despite the lack of evidence and perjured testimonies that have already been recanted, he is deliberately put to death by political forces committed to capital punishment. This tragic ending is all too realistic.

On the other hand, after his death, the player's crusading lawyer brings the irrefutable evidence of his innocence to the public, and in true Dickensian fashion, ruins the careers of those corrupt police officers, lawyers and politicians who conspired to kill him. The reader feels the same satisfaction at this outcome as we do when Beadle Bumble, the child abuser, is soundly beaten by his own wife and ridiculed by all or when Pecksniff is beaten by old Martin and reduced to penury.

This is not to suggest that there are no serious literary authors with a moral and social conscience writing today. The entry of women writers and particularly writers of color into the world of literature has clearly expanded our sense of the moral. Superb writers like Toni Morrison, Louise Erdrich, Amy Tan and Sandra Cisneros allow contemporary readers into lives and experiences Dickens could never have imagined. Yet Erdrich's most recent novel *The Round House* raises the same issues of justice and injustice as we find in Dickens. She shows that for those who live under the deformed laws applied to the American Indian reservation, a legal solution for rape may be impossible, while other forms of justice remain open.

Moral, socially conscious white male novelists like Russell Banks, Phillip Roth and David Eggars also provide unique lenses into both individual consciousness and the flaws of our society. These contemporary writers are technically brilliant and fundamentally humane. Each demonstrates a faith in the human spirit that Gardner evidently found lacking in the works of some of his own contemporaries like Donald Barthelme or William Gaddis.

Gardner's call for "morality" in fiction rests on a conviction that certain wrongs are universally understood in all times and places: killing, stealing, lying, hypocrisy, mistreatment of women and children, even while practiced everywhere and in all times. According to Gardner, who singles out Dante for particular praise, great literature should rest on certain underlying ideals, no matter how harsh the reality depicted.

Gardner also condemns the tendency of much contemporary literary criticism, whether structuralist, post-structurist, post-modernist, or deconstructionist, to neglect discussions of message and values. Indeed, the trend in current literary studies to elevate criticism and style over the literary works themselves, their authors' aims and content, can be disturbing. Just recently, Kathleen Turner (not the actress), winner of the Massachusetts Teacher of the Year Award and obviously an enthusiastic and gifted young teacher of French, was interviewed about her French studies at Harvard in the *Boston Globe*. When she was asked, "You probably read most of the canon in college, right?" her answer was, "It was spotty. The undergraduate program at Harvard University was focused more on literary theory and women's studies. I read some of the classics, a little of Moliere, but it was not heavy on the canon. I didn't love the program to be honest." (*Ideas* section, *Sunday Globe*, May 27, 2012)

It's hardly surprising that she couldn't "love" a program that apparently didn't include Stendhal (she never read *Le Rouge et le Noir*) and perhaps not even Voltaire, Rousseau, Rabelais, Flaubert, Balzac, Hugo, Baudelaire, Sartre or Camus, but somehow found it more important to read "literary studies" or feminist criticism. She acknowledged that it was "difficult" to read Proust in French, but evidently got little help from her professors in doing so. Unfortunately, the term "canon" has itself come to be somewhat pejorative, implying that "the canon" is simply what young impressionable students were once forced to read by dreary white male traditionalists. The fact that the word actually derives from the Greek term for "rod" doesn't help. ("Spare the canon, and...spoil the undergraduate.")

When I attended Harvard as an undergraduate and a graduate student in the 60's and early 70's, we naturally studied the great classic writers, and they deeply affected my life and my values. I was moved and inspired by Voltaire and Diderot, Balzac, Victor Hugo, Sartre, their moral concerns and their critiques of society. Some young Civil Rights activists were directly inspired by Malraux and the French existentialists. Although Gardner didn't think much of Sartre's version of "morality," Sartre argues in *"Qu'est-ce que la litterature?"* (What is Literature) that all literature inevitably takes a moral and political stance, whether it claims to or not.

The social criticism of 18th century writers like Diderot and Voltaire, and 19th century writers like Balzac and Hugo were extremely important to me. When years later I taught *Candide* to my community college students (in translation) they were easily able to draw parallels between the social evils mocked by Voltaire and those in our time. Similarly they were able to benefit from ethical discussions of the Bible, Shakespeare, the *Odyssey* and Euripides, as well as contemporary writers like Chinua Achebe, Sandra Cisneros and Alice Walker. Mercifully, they had never heard of deconstructionism and I rarely tried to enlighten them.

As a feminist and civil rights activist, I applauded the entry of feminist criticism, writers of color and women writers into the field of literature, in my day dominated by white male authors, critics and teachers. In fact, I taught one of the first Women's Literature classes at M.I.T. and later taught both Women Writers and African-American Literature at the community college. Thanks to the Civil Rights and Women's Movements, I finally came to understand the serious bias in my own education; as an undergraduate, I went through an entire course in American Literature taught by an eminent Harvard professor without reading a single woman writer or writer of color. I went through my degree in French History and Literature without having a single woman professor or reading a woman author. However, it seems that the wheel may have turned too far in the opposite direction. Although feminist criticism can certainly illuminate the works of all authors, including Dickens, to interpret him solely through a feminist lens would seriously distort the man and his work. Never to read great male writers like Dante, Proust, Dickens, Balzac or Voltaire is a tragic loss. And to make literary criticism equal or even superior to the creative works and the authors themselves is a downright travesty.

Some contemporary critics go so far as to claim that the reader is not only *as* important as a work's author, but more important, demeaning the creativity and intentions of the author. It's certainly true that contemporary literary criticism can give insights into literature that were missed by previous generations, but the intentions of the author, while subject to interpretation, actually do matter. This "reader-centered" trend is directly rebutted by fiction writer Jane Smiley in her short biography of Dickens, *Charles Dickens: A Life:*

> My purpose here is to avoid the dreary illusion of superiority that comes when critics and biographers purport to know a subject better than (or more truthfully than or more insightfully than) the subject knows himself. Writers and artists are often portrayed as carriers of their own works, rather like carriers of a disease who communicate them to the world at large unconsciously, giving themselves away without design or intention. My own experience as a writer and a reader is quite different. Writing is an act of *artistic and moral agency* (italics mine) where choices are made that the author understands, full of implications and revelations that the author also understands.[3]

In 1977, Gardner already perceived the unhealthy trend to elevate the literary critic over the author, and with it an emphasis on form over content. It is in part to redress this balance that he published what some might consider a diatribe, but was, in fact, a call to consciousness and a reminder of what is most important about literature.

One might argue that Gardner's premise is too narrow and might unfairly be used against great writers that have no obvious moral or political aim. Certainly the explicit social criticism one finds in Dickens and Dante cannot be found in authors like Proust or Virginia Woolf. Yet both Woolf and Proust, each in their own way, appeal to the profound "truth" of human experience and human dignity, just as Dickens does. Both also implicitly critique the superficiality and falsity of life in "society," as contrasted with the authenticity of the inner life. Proust himself once claimed that when he wrote his master work, he became a better and deeper human being, unlike the superficial man of society he appeared in his real life. Although his works are seemingly autobiographical, the "*moi*" expressed in them is very different from the "*moi*" he appeared to be in the "real world." ("*Contre Sainte Beuve*"). It was in his art that he claimed to find a sense of the divine. In listening to a piece by the composer Vinteuil, Swann (his alter ego in *Á la Recherche du Temps Perdu*) reflects "It is not possible that a piece of sculpture, a piece of music which gives us an emotion which we feel to be more exalted, more pure, more true, does not correspond to some definite spiritual reality." Of his writing, Proust directly states that "a book is the product of a different self from the one we manifest in our habits, in society, in our vices."[4]

Anton Chekhov, who rarely preached politics or religion, and in fact explicitly opposed "lengthy torrents of a politico-socio-economic nature,"[5] affirms in his exquisite short story *The Lady with a Pet Dog* "that when you came to think of it, everything in the world is beautiful really, everything but our own thoughts and actions, when we lose sight of the higher aims of life, and our dignity as human beings." These words are expressed through the thoughts of Gurov, a middle-aged philanderer who has been unexpectedly transformed by authentic love. Gurov is realistically depicted as a serial adulterer, at first out for nothing more than a casual fling, but Chekhov understands that there is more in him—and by inference in all of us—than appears on the surface. It is this quality of human uplift and possibility that John Gardner finds wanting in too many talented and technically skillful contemporary writers, but which we find in writers like Homer, Shakespeare, Dante, Tolstoy, Chekhov and of course, Dickens.

Like Shakespeare, Dickens was literary as well as popular, able to reach a vast audience among all social classes. This popularity at one time led some literary critics to depreciate him. However, he used his public platform, not merely to express his own personal struggles, doubts and fears, nor to earn money and fame—both of course partial motives—but to raise our moral indignation against injustice. As he himself affirmed, and this book has repeatedly emphasized, his morality like Dante's derives principally from the Bible and Christian ethics. But it could also come from any tradition that affirms the ultimate dignity of human life. In the end, his entire value system which we have elaborated in detail in our long journey through his *Inferno*, might be summed up in the marvellously succinct advice of Aunt Betsey Trotwood, in *David Copperfield*, when David (whom she calls "Trot") first leaves her home to obtain an education:

"Never," said my aunt, "be mean in anything; never be false; never be cruel. Avoid those three vices, Trot, and I can always be hopeful of you."

I promised, as well as I could, that I would never abuse her kindness or forget her admonition.

Since David is the character closest to Dickens' heart and life, David's effort to abide by his aunt's advice "as well as I could," might be read as Dickens' admission that he himself could never be perfect. However, the fact that he tried, not merely on the personal and fictional, but on the societal level—in opposing poverty, exploitation, slavery, racism, religious prejudice, war, abuse and cruelty—is what makes him unique. Of course there are talented authors today who decry specific social evils, yet there are none quite like Dickens and Dante that attempt to address the entire spectrum of human injustice. Dickens' passionate outrage against injustice was with him when young, and unlike some who become more conservative as they age, remained with him throughout his life. Biographer Michael Slater sums it up well:

> He wanted to make the world a better place, to champion the poor and oppressed, to instruct readers in social justice matters, and as he later put it when writing *The Chimes*, his most fiercely polemical story, 'to shame the cruel and canting.' One of his dearest women friends, who first met him nine years after this time (in 1836) remembered how his face used to blaze with indignation at any injustice or cruelty. [6]

Did Dickens occasionally disappoint and fall on the morally wrong side of an issue? Of course; he was human, and as he well knew himself, deeply flawed. Apparently, according to a recent essay by the late Christopher Hitchens, Dickens once made some hateful comments about the Indian people who were justly rebelling against the British Empire.[7] However, it is relevant that this was *not* in one of his novels or public articles, but rather in private a letter to a friend (Angela Burdett Coutts). Also, his son was at the time fighting in India against the "Indian Mutiny" which might have temporarily prejudiced his judgement. Hitchens goes so far as to claim, based on the scantiest of evidence, that Dickens was a great writer, but a bad human being. The subtitle of this appallingly biased article is "Why Charles Dickens was one of the Best of Writers and the Worst of Men." Somehow Hitchens manages to ignore Dickens' long term devotion to building homes for prostitutes, his forthright attacks on slavery in the face of his horrified Southern American hosts, the profound sympathy for the slaves and the American Indians expressed in *American Notes*, his prompting of his friend Longfellow to write the very first American anti-slavery poems, his passionate crusading editorials against child labor, prison conditions and poorhouses, not to mention his endless financial generosity to family, friends, struggling artists, "fallen women," and even casual acquaintances.

Hitchens blithely tosses out the one-liner, "We are aware that the great prose-poet of childhood was acutely conscious of having failed his own offspring." This remark (which might at times be said of almost any parent) conveniently ignores the fact that Dickens took a lively interest in his children and their well-being, spending a remarkable amount of time with them when young, involving them in games and plays, seeking for them the quality education he never had, helping them advance professionally when older—all despite his own punishing work schedule. Claire Tomalin, who more than any other biographer reveals the sorry details of Dickens' adulterous affair, has this to say about Dickens at the age of forty-five:

> He was a kind man, with little malice; justifiably proud of his achievements, boyish in his enthusiasms, always eager to help others...Dickens loved children; he played with them and gave them absurd nicknames.[8]

He also supported his indebted father, chronically unemployed brother, and his adult children when they proved unable to support themselves. Was he "the best of humans" or the best of fathers? Certainly not, but he was far from the worst. He no doubt demanded too much of his children, as he did of himself, and surely being a child of the "great man" could be very difficult.

As we now know, he eventually abandoned his wife, publicly justifying himself in a letter by falsely accusing her of never caring for her children. He took most of his adult children to live with him. He was obviously not "the best of husbands." His callous treatment of his wife when he left her is impossible to defend. But he was certainly aware of his own bad behavior and suffered for it. According to biographer Charles Johnson,

> The separation from Catherine and the bitterness with which he was still assailed subjected him to almost unbearable anguish. The continuing newspaper castigations of his "violated letter" (publicly accusing his wife) made him wince with a pain all the more severe because his conscience must have whispered that it was not entirely undeserved.[9]

As with most great authors, Dickens' creative work represents the better part of himself. The justly revered Dante, at least according to Gardner, also "married a woman he did not love and in time seems to have come to hate; and he also contracted in this period (the writing of the *Inferno*) tragic guilt. He could be something of a monster, a man who frequently returned evil for good, a vindictive neurotic who often failed to notice the pettiness, cruelty, and injustice of his own acts. But at times he did notice, and suffered greatly."[10] At the same time, Dante, like Dickens is still often seen as a moral compass in contemporary fiction. In the novel *The Crazed* by contemporary Chinese novelist Ha Jin, an old professor lies in bed after a stroke, his mind ranging over issues from the insanities of China during the Cultural Revolution, to political corruption, to the role of literature. At one point, his mind which at times does seem "crazed," wanders unaccountably to Dante's *Divine Comedy*, which he has always read and loved, despite being a non-believer. His student, who attends him in his hospital room, recalls a past conversation with his teacher about Dante, when the man was still thinking clearly:

> Mr. Yang resumed, "This is my favorite poem. It saved my life."
> "How?" My interest revived.
> "When the Cultural Revolution broke out, I came under attack as a Demon-Monster because I had translated some foreign poems and once argued that Goethe was a great poet. Sometimes the Revolutionary Rebels on campus planted on my head a dunce hat with my family name written on it. Sometimes they tied a bucket filled with water around my neck to bend my body and keep my head low. Sometimes they made

me kneel on a washboard. Even when my knees began bleeding, they wouldn't allow me to get up. But during the torture I would recite to myself lines from *The Divine Comedy*. They could hurt me physically, but they could not subdue my soul…While reciting *The Divine Comedy* in my heart, I felt that my suffering was meant to help me enter purgatory. I had hope. Suffering can refine the soul. Beyond purgatory, there's paradise."

Like Dante, Tolstoy is particularly singled out by Gardner as a consummately moral writer. He was a man whose attempts to live an authentic Christian life of simplicity and non-violence inspired Gandhi's philosophy of non-violent resistance and in turn, Martin Luther King. However Tolstoy treated his wife badly, and made horribly misogynistic comments in his personal diaries, while at the same time managing to create Anna Karenina, one of the most sympathetic female characters in all of literature.

Robert Frost, among the most celebrated and revered American poets, was well known to be selfish, stubborn and irascible. His family life was far from happy; he had two children who committed suicide. Yet as a writer, he can still enlighten us on good and evil ("Fire and Ice"), the barriers we build between each other ("Mending Wall") and the humanity we show to strangers ("Death of a Hired Man"). Frost understood that his poetry expressed his deepest and best self. He once said he never wrote a poem unless it was with "the divine touch." [11]

When we expect our great writers to be saints, as too many did of Dickens, we are invariably disillusioned. This disillusionment can lead to the opposite extreme, such as Hitchens' cynical caricature of Dickens.

Once again, it is in their works that the truly great writers express their higher aspirations, in turn, inspiring their readers to be better people and the world to be a better world. It is this quality and not just their common Christianity that links Dickens and Dante across the centuries. Is there a contemporary Dickens that takes on child prostitution, the suffering of the poor, greedy financiers, racism, war, religious hatred and political hypocrisy? In nonfiction, of course we may find indignant, excellently written books on each of these topics. But in the world of fiction they are rare indeed.

This is significant, because literature, including film and drama, have a unique capacity to appeal to our emotions as well as our intellect, and in so doing, literally transform the way we view the world. This can be, as playwright Berthold Brecht once pointed out, in a negative as well as a positive sense.[12] It is well known, for example, that the film *Birth of a Nation* (based upon the novel *The Klansman*) actively recruited many people to the Klan, and the technically fine but racist film *Gunga Din* inspired many enthusiasts for the cause of British colonialism. On the other hand, no essays affected popular opinion against slavery as powerfully as Harriet Beecher Stowe's *Uncle Tom's Cabin*. Similarly, no tract on the condition of poor children in 19th century England had the impact of *Oliver Twist* or *Bleak House*. We can never identify with a statistic as we do with Oliver, Jo or little Dorrit. In fact Dickens' vast audience was moved by his works of fiction to oppose child labor, eventually helping to change the laws themselves.

As we look at society today, with its trafficking in women and children, its boundless greed, its bloody wars of religion, tribe and country, its grinding poverty and hunger, its dissemination of hate in the name of "God," it becomes impossible to ignore the continued relevance of writers like Dante and Dickens. Tragically, the adjective "Dickensian," so frequently used to describe urban misery and blight, has never become obsolete. And it's hardly surprising that the popular and critically acclaimed television series *Mad Men* began its recent season with morally flawed hero Don Draper lying on a beach reading Dante's *Inferno*, moved on to an episode entitled *A Tale of Two Cities*, and concluded the season with an implicit comparison between Draper and Sydney Carton. When we have nearly given up on Draper altogether, he finally commits an act of self sacrifice for a better man, doing "a far far better thing" than he has done in the entire series.

When Dickens finally dropped his pen for good, and that vast sympathetic mind was felled by a stroke, as his contemporaries noted, the world lost more than one great writer; it lost a unique moral conscience and passionate advocate for all humanity. Edgar Johnson, in the conclusion to his monumental two volume treatment of Dickens' life and works, said it best in 1952:

> More than eighty years have passed since Charles Dickens died. His passionate heart has long crumbled into dust. But the world he created shines with undying life, and the hearts of men still vibrate to his indignant anger, his love, his tears, his glorious laughter, and his triumphant faith in the dignity of man.[13]

Notes

Introduction

1. G.K. Chesterton, *Charles Dickens: A Critical Study*, Conclusion
2. Dorothy Sayers, *The Divine Comedy 2: Purgatory*, Introduction, 14
3. Charles Dickens, *Pictures from Italy*, 185
4. Gary Colledge, *Dickens, Christianity and "The Life of Our Lord,"* 20
5. *Ibid.*, 136
6. Dennis Walder, *Dickens and Religion*, 147
7. George Orwell, "Charles Dickens," *A Collection of Essays*, 100
8. *Ibid.*, 101
9. Fred Kaplan, *Dickens*, 473
10. Dickens' letter to Cornelius Felton (1843) from Pilgrim Edition of *Letters*: 3:455-6
11. Colledge, 70
12. Phillip Collins (1965, 54) cited in Walder, 65

Chapter I: Dickens' Characters

1. T.S. Eliot, quoted by Steve J. Gwertz, 28 April, 2009, David Brass Rare Books, *www.davidbrassrarebooks.com*
2. Frank Thomas Marzials, *The Life of Charles Dickens*, e-book, Project Guttenberg, 2004
3. Juliette John, *Dickens' Villains*, Oxford University Press, 2001, 149
4. John Forster, *The Life of Charles Dickens* 1928, cited in Walder, 11
5. Kate Millett, *Sexual Politics*. Equinox Books, New York, 1970, 70

6. *The Imitation of Christ* is a major 15th century Catholic work thought to be written by Thomas à Kempis. It recommends living a life like Christ's, of simplicity, poverty and self-sacrifice, as well as some degree of withdrawal from the world.
7. Jane Smiley, *Thirteen Ways of Looking at the Novel*, 117
8. Juliette John.
9. Claire Tomalin, *Charles Dickens: A Life*, 322
10. John Forster, *The Life of Charles Dickens* (1874) Chapman and Hall, 214
11. Smiley, 118

Chapter II: Dante's System of Hell

1. My English quotes of Dante's *Inferno* are taken from John Sinclair's translation: *Dante: The Divine Comedy 1. Inferno*, Oxford University Press, Oxford, 1961 and Mark Musa's *Dante: The Divine Comedy Vol. 1: Inferno*, Penguin, New York, 1971. Commentary by the translators is indicated where needed.
2. Mark Musa, Introduction, citing Dante's *Convivio Bk. II*, 35
3. W.H. Reade, *The Moral System of Dante's Inferno*, 345
4. John Forster, *The Life of Charles Dickens V.1* (1874) "...even now famous and caressed and happy, I often forget in my dreams that I have a dear wife and children; even that I am a man; and wander desolately back to that time of my life." 33
5. Mark Musa, *Inferno*, notes on *Canto VII*, 144
6. John Sinclair, *Inferno*, notes on *Canto IX*, 128
7. *Ibid.*, notes on *Canto XII*, 164
8. Musa, notes on *Canto XIII*, 195
9. Sinclair, notes on *Canto XV*, 202
10. *Ibid.*, notes on *Canto XXI*, 279
11. *Ibid.*, notes on *Canto XXXII*, 414

Chapter III: The First Circles

1. John Derry, *A Short History of 19th Century England*, 69
2. Michael Slater, *Charles Dickens*, 245
3. Peter Ackroyd, *Dickens*, 89
4. *Ibid.*, 90
5. Claire Tomalin, *The Invisible Woman: The Story of Nelly Ternan and Charles Dickens*, 64

Chapter IV: Venturing Deeper into Hell

1. Valerie Kennedy, "Challenging Figures: Three of Dickens' Marginal Women," *The Victorian Web*

Chapter V: Circles of Malice

1. Dr. Patricia Brennan, "Oliver Twist: Textbook of Child Abuse," *Archives of Disease in Childhood, www.guardian.co.uk/society/nov.302001*
2. Edgar Allan Poe, "Barnaby Rudge," *Saturday Evening Post*, 1841, reproduced in Philip Collins, *Dickens: The Critical Heritage*, Barnes and Noble, New York, 1971, 105-111

Chapter VI: Fraud

1. Michael Slater (ed.) Introduction to *Nicholas Nickleby*, Penguin Classics, London, 1986, 26
2. "Dickens could not now take risks either with his own reputation or with Nelly's and her family's." Claire Tomalin, *The Invisible Woman*, A. Knopf, New York: 1990, 187
3. Charles Dickens, Preface to *Martin Chuzzlewit* (1849 edition)
4. Edgar Johnson, *Charles Dickens: His Tragedy and His Triumph*, 888
5. Dickens, cited in Ackroyd, 858

Chapter VII: Traitors

1. Apparently Dickens told John Forster, his daughter Katey and his illustrator Luke Fildes that Jasper was the murderer. Fildes needed to be told why Jasper's silk scarf needed to be so long in the illustrations, so Dickens confided his "secret." Edgar Johnson, *Charles Dickens*, V. 1119

Chapter VIII: Purgatory

1. Dorothy Sayers, Introduction to Dante *The Divine Comedy 2: Purgatory*, 54-68
2. *Ibid.*
3. *Ibid.*, 66
4. John D. Sinclair (trans.) notes on *The Divine Comedy 2: Purgatorio*, 54
5. H.W. Reade, *The Moral System of Dante's Inferno.* 434-5
6. Robert Douglas-Fairhurst, *Becoming Dickens: The Invention of a Novelist*, Prologue, 11
7. Claire Tomalin, *The Invisible Woman*, 351

Chapter IX: "A word on the Angels"

1. He had the words "young, beautiful and good" inscribed on Mary's tombstone, and used these same words to describe Rose Maylie, Nell and Florence Dombey. Ackroyd, 227

Chapter X: Afterthoughts

1. Fred Kaplan, *Dickens*, 303
2. John Gardner, *On Moral Fiction*, 6
3. Jane Smiley, *Charles Dickens: A Life* (Introduction)
4. George Painter, *Proust*, v. 2, 6

5. *Anton Chekhov's Short Stories,* A Norton Critical Edition (ed. by Ralph Matlaw), New York, 1979, letter to A.P Chekhov, May 10 1886, 269

6. Michael Slater, *Charles Dickens,* 93

7. Christopher Hitchens, "The Dark Side of Dickens" *The Atlantic Monthly,* May 2010

8. Claire Tomalin, *The Invisible Woman,* 81

9. Edgar Johnson, *Charles Dickens,* V. 2, 941

10. Gardner, 31

11. *Robert Frost: A Lover's Quarrel with the World,* 1988, Robert Chapman, Producer Dr. Peter Hamer, Director; Annenberg CPB project, New York, New York

12. John Willett (ed. and transl.) *Brecht on the Theater: The Development of an Aesthetic*

13. Johnson, V. 2, 1158

Bibliography

Dickens Sources

Ackroyd, Peter. *Dickens.* New York: Harper Collins, 1990

Bertman, Stephen. "Dante's Role in the Genesis of a Christmas Carol." *Dickens Quarterly v. 24., no. 3,* Sept. 2007

Butler, Patrick. "A Novel Insight into Child Abuse." *Society Guardian,* Friday, 30 Nov., 2001, quoting Dr. Patrician Brennan in the British Medical Journal

Chekhov, Anton. *Anton Chekhov's Short Stories,* ed. By Ralph Matlaw. A Norton Critical Edition. New York: Norton, 1979

Chesterton, G.K. *Charles Dickens.* New York: Dodd, Mead and Co., 1906

Colledge, Gary. *Dickens, Christianity and "The Life of Our Lord."* New York: Continuum Press, 2009

Collins, Philip. *Dickens.* New York: Barnes and Noble, 1971

Dickens and Crime. London: McMillan, 1962, republished by St. Martin's Press, 1994

Dickens: The Critical Heritage. New York: Barnes and Noble, 1971

Colon, Susan. "Dickens's *Hard Times* and Dante's *Inferno.*" *The Explicator.* 65.1. Fall, 2006:31-33

Derry, John. *A Short History of 19th Century England.* New York: New American Library, 1963

Doulas-Fairhurst, Robert. *Becoming Dickens: The Invention of a Novelist.* Cambridge, MA: Belknap Press of Harvard University, 2011

Forster, John. *The Life of Charles Dickens.* London: Chapman and Hall, 1873-4

Gardner, John. *On Moral Fiction.* New York: Basic Books, 1978

Hitchens, Christopher, "The Dark Side of Dickens," *The Atlantic*, 2010

House, Madeline et al (ed.) *The Pilgrim Edition of Letters of Charles Dickens v.3*. Oxford: Clarendon Press, 1974

Jin, Ha. *The Crazed*. New York: Pantheon Books, 2002

Johnson, Edgar. *Charles Dickens: His Tragedy and His Triumph (2 v.)*, New York: Simon and Schuster, 1952

John, Juliet. *Dickens' Villains: Melodrama, Character and Popular Culture*. New York: Oxford University Press, 2001

Kaplan, Fred. *Dickens*. Baltimore: Johns Hopkins University Press, 1988

Kennedy, Valerie. "Challenging Figures: Three of Charles Dickens's Marginal Women" *The Victorian Web*.

www.victorianweb.org/authors/dickens/turkey/turklit

Lucas, John. *The Melancholy Man*. London: Methuen and Co., 1970

Marzials, Frank Thomas. *The Life of Charles Dickens*. E-book, Guttenberg, 2004

Millett, Kate. *Sexual Politics*. New York: Equinox Books: New York, 1970

Newlin, George. *Everyone in Dickens*. Westport, Conn.: Greenwood Press, 1995

Nisbet, Ada. *Dickens and Ellen Ternan*. Berkeley: University of California Press, 1952

Orwell, George. "Charles Dickens." *A Collection of Essays*. San Diego: Harcourt, Brace and Jovanovich, 1981

Painter, George. *Marcel Proust: A Biography. V.2*. Vintage: New York, 1978

Poe, Edgar Allen. "Barnaby Rudge." *Saturday Evening Post* 1841, reproduced in Philip Collins, *Dickens: The Critical Heritage*.

Robert Frost: A Lover's Quarrel with the World. (film), Robert Chapman Producer, Dr. Peter Hamer, Director; Annenberg CPB Project, New York, 1988

Slater, Michael. *Charles Dickens*. New Haven: Yale University Press, 2009

Smiley, Jane. *Thirteen Ways of Looking at the Novel*. New York: Alfred Knopf, 2005

    Charles Dickens: A Life (Penguin Lives). New York: Penguin Press, 2002

Tomalin, Claire. *Charles Dickens: A Life*. New York: Penguin Press, 2011

    The Invisible Woman: The Story of Nelly Ternan and Charles Dickens.New York: Barnes and Noble, 1971

Walder, Dennis. *Dickens and Religion*. London and New York: Routledge, 1981

Willett, John. *Brecht on the Theater: The Development of an Aesthetic*. New York: Macmillan, 1964

Dante Sources

Alighieri, Dante. *The Divine Comedy.v.1 and 2: Inferno and Purgatorio*. Italian Text with translation and commentary by John D. Sinclair. New York: Oxford University Press, 1961

    The Divine Comedy: v.1: Inferno. translation with commentary by Mark Musa., *v.2: Purgatory*. Translation with commentary by Dorothy Leigh Sayers, v. 3 *Paradise*, translation with commentary by Mark Musa. New York: Penguin Classics, 1984

    Inferno. Translation by Henry Wadsworth Longfellow. ed. By Matthew Pearl, introduction by Lino Pertile. New York: Modern Library, 2003

    Vita Nuova. Italian text with facing translation by Dino S. Cervigni and Edward Vasta. Notre Dame, Indiana: University of Notre Dame Press, 2002

Reade, W.H. *The Moral System of Dante's Inferno*. Oxford: Clarendon Press, 1909

Singleton, Charles. *The Divine Comedy: v.I. Inferno*, commentary. Princeton, N.J.: Princeton University Press, 1989

Dickens' Works (in order of original publication)

The Pickwick Papers (Edited and with an Introduction by James Kingsley). Oxford: Oxford University Press, 1984

Oliver Twist (With Introduction and notes by Andrew Lang). London: Chapman and Hall, 1897

Nicholas Nickleby (Edited with an Introduction and notes by Michael Slater). London: Penguin Classics, 1986

The Old Curiosity Shop (Edited by Angus Easson, with an Introduction by Malcolm Andrews). London: Penguin Books, 1985

Barnaby Rudge (With an Introduction by John T. Winterich). New York: Heritage Press, 1941

American Notes for General Circulation (Edited with an Introduction and notes by Patricia Ingham). London: Penguin Classics, 2000

A Christmas Carol; New York: Dover Publications, 1991

Martin Chuzzlewit (Edited with an Introduction by P.N. Furbank). London: Penguin Classics, 1986

Pictures from Italy (Edited with an Introduction and notes by Kate Flint). London: Penguin Classics, 1998

Dombey and Sons (Edited with an Introduction and notes by Andrew Sanders). London: Penguin Classics, 2002

David Copperfield; (With an Afterward by Edgar Johnson). New York: New American Library (Signet Books), 1962

Bleak House (Edited by Norman Page with an Introduction by J. Hillis Miller). London: Penguin Classics, 1985

Little Dorrit (Edited with an Introduction by Harvey Peter Sucksmith). London: Oxford University Press (World Classics), 1988

Hard Times (Edited with an Introduction by David Craig). London: Penguin English Library, 1984

A Tale of Two Cities (Edited with an Introduction and notes by Richard Maxwell). London: Penguin Classics, 2000

Great Expectations (With an Afterward by Angus Wilson). New York: New American Library (Signet), 1980

A Tale of Two Cities; London: Penguin Classics, 2003

Our Mutual Friend; New York: The Modern Library, 1992

The Mystery of Edwin Drood (Introduction by Peter Ackroyd). New York: Afred A. Knopf (Everyman's Library), 2004

Acknowledgements

Deep thanks to all those who had faith in this unusual enterprise and encouraged me when I might have given up: David Impastato for his Catholic literary perspective and enthusiasm for the project; Carolyn Eisenberg, Anna Reid Jhirad, Diane (Didi) Stewart, Jean Hodgin and Susan Herman. Thanks to my son Dylan Jhirad for his wonderful cover design and reassurance that being "counterintuitive" isn't necessarily a bad thing. Thanks to Professor Vincent Pollina of Tufts University, for his inspiring course on Dante's *Inferno*, to Debra Benvie and the Dickens Fellowship-North of Boston Branch that keeps alive the love of Dickens, and my book group—Kathy, Avis, Donna, Marion and Minette, for their perceptive insights into *Great Expectations*. Thanks too to my church, the Unitarian-Universalist Church of Medford, for sustaining "the spirit of toleration" that once drew Dickens to Unitarianism, and offering me their pulpit to preach on Dickens. Others who provided words of advice or encouragement: Matthew Pearl, Diana Archibald, Chris Hebert and Steve Wasserman.

Special thanks to my extraordinary editor Marcus Alonso, for his always intelligent critiques, and saving me from the Purgatory of the publishing world.

Last, but certainly not least, thanks to my husband Michael Glenn, my emotional rock and astute literary critic, to my son Dylan Jhirad, daughter Catherine Glenn, and stepsons Jason and Ezra, for their constant love and support.

About the Author

Susan B. Jhirad has a Ph.D. in Romance Languages and Literature from Harvard University and is Professor Emerita from North Shore Community College, where she taught literature and writing for thirty years. She is a lifelong activist in such causes as civil rights, peace, women's liberation and worker's rights. In recent years she has followed Dickens' example, joining a local Unitarian-Universalist church, because of their "spirit of toleration" and social engagement. She is the author of numerous articles published in *The Women's Review of Books, The Boston Globe, Cineaste, Ms.* and *The Radical Teacher,* among others. She has a chapter in the upcoming book published by Bloomsbury Press, *Class and the College Classroom.* She lives in Massachusetts with her husband, Michael Glenn.

CPSIA information can be obtained at www.ICGtesting.com
Printed in the USA
LVOW13s1552071113

360406LV00003B/655/P